# Brando
# for Breakfast

# Brando

Anna Kashfi Brando
and E.P. Stein

# for Breakfast

Crown Publishers, Inc.  New York

**Library of Congress Cataloging in Publication Data**

Brando, Anna Kashfi.
Brando for breakfast.

1.  Brando, Marlon.  2.  Moving-picture actors and
actresses—United States—Biography.  I.  Stein, E. P.,
joint author.  II.  Title.
PN2287.B683B74     791.43′028′0924   [B]      79-11048
ISBN 0-517-53686-2

BOOK DESIGN BY RHEA BRAUNSTEIN

That which in the beginning may be just like poison, but at the end is like nectar, and which awakens one to self-realization, is said to be happiness in the mode of goodness.

*Bhagavad Gita*

# Preface

Few books can have had so hazardous a genesis as this one. It was nearly aborted when the pain of resurrecting buried traumas culminated in an overdose of sedatives and mistreatment by an incompetent physician. For four days I lay in a coma while a prognosis of imminent death summoned the draft of my burial arrangements and a priest to administer last rites.

My case was deemed sufficiently unusual as to warrant chronicling in a medical journal. Dehydration of body tissues had progressed, I was later told, beyond the threshold of recovery. Yet I survived. And that survival led, inevitably, to introspection, to reevaluation, to resolution.

Marlon Brando had dominated my concerns for more than two decades. Lying in a hospital bed, I had my first opportunity, enforced, to assess the consequences of those years. They were years of bitterness, of rancor, of temper tantrums; they were years of thorns and vinegar.

I had nothing left of Marlon after twenty years. His image had become splintered and dispersed in my mind, as if seen through a fractured prism. I had almost nothing left of our son, Christian Devi, who flickered occasionally into focus before me but who lived with and emulated his father. And I had little left of myself.

It seemed as if I had never come to the United States, never had an acting career, never met Marlon Brando, never was pregnant, gave birth, or nurtured a child. To reassure myself of the reality of these events, I forced myself to relive them — to replay them in the mind's projection room. I have recorded that replay in the form of this book.

There exists substantial temptation to improve on thoughts and judgments formed earlier, reshaping and ennobling them with hindsight. I have tried to avoid such self-serving distortions. Although I am no detached observer, I have also tried to extricate myself from the swirl of emotionality, to look back dispassionately, to gain a measure of perspective. Yet the book remains intensely subjective. Given a personality so protean as that of Marlon Brando, no two biographies of him could have more than cousinly relation. The same events through other eyes would no doubt paint a different portrait. Truth can have as many faces as an Indian goddess. What follows are the memoirs of one of those faces.

ANNA KASHFI BRANDO

# Brando
# for Breakfast

# One

**M**arlon Brando has been described as a whirlpool of sensuality that sucks in and exhausts every passing creature. I have tumbled and twisted at the center of that vortex, loved it, loathed it, endured it, and finally struggled for years to escape its grasp.

Marlon's appeal is difficult to particularize. As a conversationalist he ranks with Mortimer Snerd—stumbling, mumbling, inarticulate, sometimes incoherent. Yet he attracts chroniclers, intellectuals, and a legion of emulators. As a creative artist he is a jackdaw with ideas, scattering them with weedy profligacy to disrupt the more cultivated soil of other minds. Yet his ideas have devastated his co-workers, ridiculed his motion pictures, and brought a major studio to the door of bankruptcy. As a seducer he is clumsy. As a lover he is inconsiderate. Yet an endless line of sexual partners—men, women, and a few indeterminates—await his pleasure.

In short, Marlon Brando is modern gothic: grotesque, contradictory, impossible.

At the end of the *Ramayana*, the Brahmin sage Valmiki is asked by Rama if there is anything in the world he believes to be real. Valmiki answers that "there are three things which are real: God, human folly, and laughter. Since the first two pass our comprehension, we must do what we can with the third." In looking back at the Brando years—our love affair, marriage, our son Devi, divorce, the innumerable court battles—I think only laughter encouraged me to survive—laughter in the sense of the human comedy, in the sense of savoring absurdities. Since the events of those years passed all rational comprehension, I had to make do with laughter. And despite the laughter—amidst the tears—there were drugs, drinking, depression, and attempts at suicide. Mere laughter is too thin an armor for tilting with Marlon Brando.

A naïve young girl probing her way through the world meets the suave seducer. It is the fare of soap operas, of movie magazines, of daydreams: starlet meets star, Eliza Doolittle meets Henry Higgins, Little Red Riding Hood meets the Big Bad Wolf. Marlon is hero, preceptor, villain—and more. He is an amalgam of numerous distinct personalities. He could be the archetype of the contrasting forces that wrench at men: hedonism and asceticism, instinct and rationality, pride and humility. The geography of his mind ranges from the parochial to the global. He is larger than life although smaller than myth.

To the world Marlon is Superman—a man above men. To one who has peeked beneath his blue leotards, there are the stuffings of Clark Kent, shy, bewildered daydreamer. Clark Kent dreams of success, of power, and of Lois Lane. But Lois Lane has no time for him. She lusts for Superman who, in turn, is too preoccupied with leaping tall buildings and saving the world to dally with her. The Superman cloak confers strength, a distinct personality, and, above all, a sexual identity.

A studio publicity blurb asked: "What is there about Marlon Brando that attracts women? Will his half-man, half-beast quality of lovemaking replace the more subtle techniques of John Barrymore and Rudolph Valentino?" Ex-mistresses, ex-friends, ex-associates, and casual acquaintances relate a spectrum of *Rashomon* impressions through which, occasionally, a glimpse can be caught of his inner self. Some still love him. Some hate him. (One discarded paramour sought revenge by casting a voodoo spell on his front lawn.) None remain indifferent. Some sensed an animal magnetism. Others were attracted only by the movie-star image. He has been belittled by more than one woman as a lousy lover who leaves unsatisfied the appetites he arouses. Many felt humiliated by his treatment—"left like an orange split in half and squeezed dry of its juices." When all who have known him are recorded, it is still impossible to raise a composite model that won't crumble with the weight of another anecdote.

Regarding his sexual quiddity, Marlon admitted to Hedda Hopper: "When people tell me I've got sex appeal, I have to laugh. Girls never turn around to look at me on the streets. It's only when I'm identified as Marlon Brando the actor that women take notice. I prefer girls that like me for myself alone." Like most of his Clark Kent statements, the thought is bland and unrevealing.

Women who have shared Marlon's bed also share common characteristics: dark hair, dark complexion, and, preferably, sloe eyes. Marlon reserves his favors for Orientals, Latins, blacks, Polynesians, and Indians, both east and west. When I accused him of choosing "inferior" women as partners to satisfy his need for superiority feelings, he was incensed. "My mother was blonde," he said, thereby exposing—while still denying—the roots of his sexual fancy. At a later time he admitted he could not function sexually with light-skinned females; darker women pose no Oedipal threat.

On screen and off Marlon flaunted his dominance of women by humiliating them whenever they dared display an independent mien. In *Last Tango in Paris*, the American expatriate, Paul (Marlon), coerces his girl friend, Jeanne, into sexual and psychological degradations. The parallel to his noncinematic life is not coincidental. Marlon personally initiated much of the picture's sexuality (and obscenity). He had tyrannized many women before the celluloid Jeanne. I asked Marlon one time if he felt that women had less pride than men. He responded with one of his favorite aphorisms (a quote from the satirist Georg Lichtenberg): "It is a fine kind of pride women have that lies only half an inch from the rectum."

Marlon's sexual tutti-frutti comprise several shadier flavors.

3

Many of them melt, however, under the light of reality. I had heard most of the bizarre tales pinned to his backside: that he consorts with ducks, attends the Club Necrophilia (wherein bodies of deceased celebrities are rented out), and consults a "proctolist" (a "rectum-reader" whose soothsaying derives from anal creases). Marlon refused to admit or deny such gossipy yarns but seemed to relish their telling and may well have lent his hand to their construction if not to their fulfillment. As the creator and high priest of his own legend, he is compelled to nourish and encourage his creation. Coco Chanel once pointed out that "people with a legend end up being like their legend so as to reinforce their own celebrity."

"Super sex" is as much a part of Superman's raiment as his cloak. "Every night," Marlon said, "fifty million women get in bed to masturbate, thinking of sex with Marlon Brando." ("What do you think of that statement?" I asked a well-known movie-colony psychiatrist. "Ah," said that learned man, "a wondrous attempt to compensate for his feelings of penis inadequacy.")

It was difficult to discuss Marlon's sexuality with him. Despite his introspection, he shied from the subject like a Victorian virgin. Yet he would freely recount incidents from his childhood that signaled incipient sexual aberration. A weak, passive father and a domineering, aggressive, castrating mother (a Lois Lane type) derailed him early from the track of normality. He continually deprecated his father to me; Marlon, Sr., actualized an alcoholic womanizer as the model for his son to emulate. As a child Marlon frequently observed his mother convulsively drunk at home and in public. The effect on him was enduring.

One outgrowth of his unbalanced but unremitting sexuality was Marlon's penchant for motorcycles. As a penis equivalent, the motorcycle is unchallenged. ("I never felt better than with that big, hard thing between my legs," Marlon said.) Further, it is a penis that can be exhibited to the world in a noisy, obtrusive fashion no one can deny.

Occasionally, Marlon betrayed his Superman alter ego. He collected and pored over a number of books detailing the customs of ancient phallus-worshiping civilizations (principally Dravidian and Mayan). Stories of corybantic maidens impaling themselves on stone lingams would transport him into rapturous reveries. He attempted to feature an obtrusive fertility symbol in one of his motion pictures. A discreet film editor excised the scene—and staved off the censor.

"Scratch any actor," goes a Hollywood saying, "and underneath you will find an egomaniac." Undoubtedly, Marlon is arrogant, narcissistic, and stuffed with antic hay. It is a privilege reserved for him. No other actor has so altered the course and style of acting in the American theatre and in film. The pre-Brando screen hero was a dandified paragon of masculinity who, while winning the girl and trampling the villain, never turned his heart from virtue nor his better profile from the camera. It was Marlon who lifted the skirts of the cinema and showed us the guts, the muscles moving the flesh, the maggots in the mince pie. We believed him. He believed himself.

No other actor has shone so brightly in his constellation. He is a star hiding from his planets. James Dean, Paul Newman, Steve McQueen, and Warren Beatty have circled in his orbit. Scores of other well-known performers acknowledge his influence—Dustin Hoffman, Robert Redford, Jack Nicholson, inter alia. And as he spawned more and more emulators, he grew more and more exacerbated with them.

No other actor exceeds his zeal for creating life from a paper character. Were he assigned the part of a blind man, he wouldn't open his eyes for weeks—to absorb the reality of blindness. As an actor Marlon dissects each role with an almost forensic scrupulousness.

Director Edward Dmytryk, after working with him on *The Young Lions*, marveled: "Marlon's a chameleon. He slips in and out of characters as though they were costumes. It's hard to imagine a role he couldn't interpret." Another director agreed: "Marlon Brando can portray just about any character except 'Tugboat Annie' and make you believe it." This lavish praise from his fellow professionals and the even greater adulation bestowed by the movie-going public created a new term: "Brandolotry." It certifies that Marlon Brando is unique among public figures.

Marlon professes to despise the art of acting. While filming he has used earplugs to avoid hearing other actors, has ignored directors, argued for a change of role in midproduction, and has decamped from productions in progress. "I can't stand to be paid for posturing," he has often repeated, although such otherworldliness has never deterred him from cashing the checks. Harold Clurman once remarked that "Brando has developed an extraordinary series of rationalizations to justify his actions. One, he does what he does for money. Two, acting is neurotic, anyway. Three, movies are so powerful that by staying in them, he will be helping the world." Evidence suggests that Marlon's feelings toward acting are not really so cavalier. He owns prints of his films, and I have seen him sit for hours, running them through a projector in our home. It is not acting but the clash between pragmatism and theoretical ideals plus the inability to accept fame that perturbs him. "What a heavy burden is a name that has become too famous," said Voltaire.

The acting profession tends to attract those with uncertain identities. Writers and directors can accommodate the actor with a temporary identity, one that can be adopted for living and feeling. The actor is allowed—encouraged—to crawl inside someone else's skin. From that sanctum he can execute actions and reactions that garner the world's attention—that certify him as a special individual who leaves a unique imprint on events. This image may be unrelated to his self-appraisal. He may be submerging himself in the role to conceal his fear or hatred of himself. Volumes of psychology have been written on this theme; they are epitomized in the Hollywood adage: "All actors are nine years old."

Marlon has always viewed the world through a child's eyes. Possibly for that reason, among others, the actor's art is engrained in him as it was from childhood. Creative men, I conjecture, sense their direction at an early age, and they proceed in that direction gathering impetus as they gather knowledge and experience. Average men are more subject to the accident and circumstance of their environments. Einstein could not be kept from physics nor Michelangelo from drawing; Marlon's destiny led inexorably to acting.

Marlon insisted on the naturalness of his art while acknowledging the peculiarities of its practitioners. "We all carry in us the seeds of any character that we might play. We all entertain the full spectrum of human emotions. Acting is something most people think they're incapable of but they do it from morning to night." Subsequently, he admitted: "Movie stars aren't mature as people. No actor is. Ever meet an actor really worth talking to offscreen or offstage? Ever meet an actor who was a whole person without his image up there for you to fill in?"

As further proof of his absorption with acting, Marlon would often transfer his screen roles to his home life. His films offer a touchstone for the appreciation of the man. Scenes and lines of dialogue from his pictures surfaced later to be replayed in private acts and conversations. During the filming of *Sayonara*, he insisted that I be his personal geisha — scrubbing his back, fetching his slippers, and giggling behind a fluttering fan. At times he seems to confuse the more elusive and important qualities of life with his black-and-white image of it.

Yet the satisfactions of stardom have not escaped him. "It was like I'd been asleep, and I woke up here sitting on a pile of candy," he said after *A Streetcar Named Desire* detonated his fame. Discussing acting with a Hollywood columnist, he admitted, "If you're successful, it's about as soft a job as anybody would ever wish for. But if you're unsuccessful, it's worse than having a skin disease."

Many of Marlon's motion pictures reveal glimpses of his internal engine. Sadomasochistic elements emerge in *The Wild One*, *Last Tango in Paris*, and other pictures. *Last Tango*, with its anal slant, radiates a homosexual aura. Thus viewers felt removed from its sexuality; they could not identify with the sex portrayed. Films with much less graphic sex provide much greater titillation. Watching the screen's sex god engaged in sex proved disappointingly unerotic. The Superman thread also weaves through his films (*Viva Zapata!*, *Desirée*, *The Young Lions*, etc.). To survive beatings, turmoil, and physical and emotional pain proves that he is stronger than other men, that he is to be revered and respected. In life, Marlon has inflicted pain on himself by extinguishing cigarettes on his hand, puncturing his tongue with needles, and chewing a dozen live bumblebees (the rituals of primitive man to demonstrate manhood). I rarely knew if he were acting on screen or off. In life, as in his films, he masqueraded as a man above men.

Marlon, viewed in close-up, resembles a compilation of organic inconsistencies and ambiguities. Thus almost everything said about him is true, nearly true, or carries the semblance of truth. He can be magnanimous. He purports to follow the Confucian dictum, "Each of us is meant to rescue the world." He contributes to social and philanthropic causes, has trod the picket line, and marched for civil rights. He supports his illegitimate children and ex-mistresses without the impositon of legal obligation. He has been uncommonly kind to me when I was ill, depressed, or penurious. When I recovered and regained a measure of independence, his kindness evaporated. His compassion, seemingly genuine, was always the puppet of the circumstance.

He can be brutal. He has punched photographers with the temerity to request a pose. He has slapped and beaten women. He has shown callous unconcern at the death of a friend or employee. Within his being lurks the unregenerate soul of a Cro-Magnon.

"Brandolotry" flourishes through its hero's delight in shocking people. "That grubby Peter Pan," as an intimate refers to Marlon, has urinated on sidewalks, spat at a caged baboon, kept a pet raccoon as a habitual companion, toilet-trained an ocelot, and driven along Sunset Boulevard in a convertible, a trick arrow "skewering" his head. Such flamboyancies provide grist for the Brandoloter's mill. And Marlon caters to the mill, indulging his fantasy for the dramatic gesture whenever the curtain rises. He was once dining quietly with a girl friend when he was recognized despite—or because of—a ridiculous, setaceous, half-moon moustache and a stalk of celery wedged behind each ear. Several patrons approached his table for autographs, and Marlon's resentment exploded. He climbed onto the table, balanced a bowl of soup on his head, and danced a jig, scattering broken glass and crockery. "Here I am—don't look at me," he seems to be saying.

Marlon revels in the title "King of the Mooners." ("Mooning" is the enterprise of dropping one's pants at unexpected moments and baring one's backside to passersby; Marlon's tushy is available for public viewing in *Last Tango*.) In trying to understand the man I had married, I once questioned his psychiatrist on the subject of "mooning." I was told that baboons display their buttocks to other baboons as an act of submission. In Homo sapiens (or in those few who engage in such practice), the design would seem to be the reverse; however, the comparison with baboon behavior may be significant. Perhaps "mooning" is correlated to "rectum-reading."

The Hollywood exhibitionist syndrome has been long established: "I'm famous. I want my privacy. But if you don't notice me, I'll throw a tantrum." For a face known to the world, privacy is impossible. There is virtually no place to hide. The famous and the infamous either adopt a form of total removal—which suppresses their natural character—or they find ways to play games with their fame. Marlon is an inveterate game player.

His pranks, vulgarizations, and indifference to conventional social behavior and the personal feelings of others verge on the transcendent. He rationalizes his lobotomized version of the world by stubbornly running outside the reach of his society. "Conformity is death," he impressed upon me often. It is more than a maxim for him. It is a feverish imperative.

In counterpoint to his exhibitionism, Marlon is also a recluse, a monomaniac. "My personal feelings, my personal involvements, are not the business of the press," he said. "I don't want to share them with thousands of people that I've never known and never will know, and I don't want to be a pawn." But he does speak to the press and he does share his feelings. Then he regrets (or does he?): "I make a mistake in talking to anybody. What I have to say is either misinterpreted or misunderstood, and I always feel betrayed afterward. But I'm building up armor against this sort of thing so they can't hurt me anymore."

The primitive man in him struggles to shake off the bonds of civilization: "Personal freedom has always been terribly important to me, and I have carried aloofness as a sort of banner to my sense of freedom." For weeks at a time he

9

withdraws to a private island off Tahiti, barricaded against the world. Trespassers have been threatened with mayhem. I have a recurring dream of Marlon standing at the edge of his island, shouting "World, I'll give you twenty-four hours to get out!"

(The choice of Tahiti as a retreat, I believe, was not arbitrary. It symbolizes for Marlon a primitive, earthy environment inhabited by dark-skinned nymphs. It accords with his sexual and psychosocial attitudes.)

Neither in Tahiti—actually the island of Tetiaroa—nor in Hollywood does Marlon surround himself with the accouterments of great wealth—chauffeurs, valets, maids, or other personal attendants. "I don't want anyone to help," he told me when I first proposed to hire a maid. "My own needs are no one else's concern. I can take care of them myself. I'm a completely self-sustaining, enclosed system that works without input from anyone. I have my own entity." He might have added: "Look at how much more I do even though I'm famous and wealthy. I'm a man above men."

His Superman syndrome also accounts for Marlon's ambivalent feelings toward his children. Each of them—particularly our son, Devi—resembles his mother in color and countenance. It cannot be comforting for Marlon to contemplate that the genes of his dark-skinned women proved stronger than his. A Superman should have supergenes that produce little replicas of Marlon Brando. As a father, then, he is permissive. For he cannot demand perfection of his tainted offspring.

Marlon is not unaware of the clamorings of his psyche. Ten years of psychotherapy produced introspection if not insight. Regarding his lengthy analysis, Marlon reported, "I don't say I've found happiness but I've certainly lost chronic misery. Happiness comes to you from time to time; it isn't something you put on like a hat and wear forever. But I'm considerably less restless—less at odds with things. I've also lost my kind of zest for traveling—or running away. I don't feel obligated to go tearing off to India or Bangkok." That achievement is a shabby capstone to a ten-year project.

What, then, can penetrate to the essence of Marlon Brando? What can move him? For a man who has been on display for over thirty years, it is astonishing that no answers are available. The world doesn't know. His friends don't know. Marlon doesn't know—and doesn't want anyone to find out. Only kryptonite could pierce Superman's skin. Marlon's bane is likely some equally arcane substance.

Marlon is now balding, paunchy, and sprouting toes (at least) of common clay. He has, by cinematic imprimatur, metamorphosed from Superman into Superman's father. He remains an egomaniac, a rock upon which other egos founder. He is a Chinese box, an iconoclast without icons, a Messiah without a god. He is a genius without taste. He is a frightened, lonely child.

But he still has the world for support. He can look out into millions of eyes and confirm that Marlon Brando really exists.

# Two

**I** saw Marlon Brando for the first time in October 1955 while lunching in the Paramount Studio commissary. The meeting was not notable for stirring a sudden emotional surge. No bells rang. No glances were transfixed across a crowded room. If bells had rung, they would have been drowned out by the din; the Paramount commissary was a crowded, clamorous cavern whose acoustics reminded me of the Bombay railway station.

Wooden cafeteria tables with legs of varying lengths constituted the commissary's partitioning efforts. I was seated at one of them with Harry Mines, the studio publicist, and A. C. Lyles, assistant producer for *The Mountain*—the motion picture I was then engaged in—and later the producer of countless Westerns (*Law of the Lawless*; *Raymie*; etc.). With only a week's acclimatization to American customs, the scene in the commissary struck me as a Dantesque tableau. Faces familiar from the screen were omnipresent, animated, wolfing prodigious quantities of food as if the studio accountant were threatening to reduce future rations, shouting in competition against the background hubbub. Seemingly unrelated bodies attached beneath the faces, gesturing, costumed in incongruous and anachronistic garb—Roman tunics, Elizabethan bloomers, and eighteenth-century lace ruffles in a single coterie. I was wearing a dark red sari with gold trimming, apparel that usually attracted attention on the streets. Here it seemed almost retiring.

An adjoining table had captured Pearl Bailey and George Sanders, two actors whom I had already met, and with whom I later became close. The two were convulsed over the antics of a man at another nearby table. This man, I became aware, was staring at me—staring, that is, when he was not alternatively occupied with kissing and nibbling at the nape of a blonde (subsequently identified to me as Eva Marie Saint) seated beside him. Ripples of attention were expanding from the source of the staring and nibbling.

Finally, A. C. Lyles left our table, conferred briefly with Pauline Kissinger, chargé d'affaires of the Paramount commissary for thirty-five years to its closing, and was introduced by Pauline to the starer. Evidently the man expressed a desire to meet me, for he then followed A. C. back to our table.

"This," I understood A. C. to say, "is Marilyn Bongo." Through the commissary noises and in the exotic environment, it sounded reasonable.

"Hi," the man said. Somehow I had expected a statement more profound. The voice sounded like a caterpillar squiggling through a soda straw. The face, with an incipient heaviness about the jawline, reflected a wistfulness, an open sensuality, a sensitivity, and an ineffable indifference. The bluish-gray eyes lay in ambush behind a ciliary curtain, promising power in reserve, an inexhaustible force. He had the features of a man whose inner turmoil was preparing an organized escape.

I smiled. He shuffled his feet. I nodded. He executed a shallow, awkward bow, reshuffled his feet, and retreated to his table.

Such was the momentous meeting. I had seen none of his films and did not recognize him. He seemed unsure, unprepossessing, a blank page—and yet a volume of prose. His T-shirt and blue jeans only underscored that impression.

After the excitement that the incident engendered among the onlookers died down, I put it out of mind. Later that afternoon when I was leaving the set of *The Mountain*, Harry Mines brought it up again. "Remember that gentleman who was sitting at the next table during lunch? Well, he would like to take you out."

I gave Harry some noncommittal answer. At that time I was dating an Italian jet pilot named Enrico Mandiaco. While the intent of our relationship was yet unresolved, I felt no particular impulse to venture another man. Indeed, I still felt a degree of trepidation about the trustworthiness of the American male.

There the matter rested for about a week. It was raised again by a telephone call. "This is Marlon Brando," the voice avowed, "do you remember me?" Like a schoolboy, he cited the commissary episode to identify himself.

A diffident invitation to dinner followed. The lack of aggression, the obvious sincerity, made it tempting. Yet my remaining insecurities gave pause. (In certain regions of the world America's reputation remains that of the previous century's frontier morality.) In retrospect it seems prudish, but I then considered it an impropriety to be alone with an "eligible" stranger, and I told him so. Perhaps it was more prudence than prudishness; in India the *amah* provides more for discretion than for protection. Marlon was not at all surprised by such an old-fashioned attitude. He would be charmed, he said, to furnish a chaperone. And he did. And we began.

Looking back, I often wondered whether we are governed by a predestined fate, as many Eastern philosophies assert, or whether, as science insists, chaotic chance dominates. In the beginning it was difficult to credit fate with so trivial a concern. Yet from that inauspicious start events continued, like Banquo's ghost, to haunt our lives.

If the meeting in the commissary were indeed predestined, the paths leading to it began far apart and traveled an improbable convoluted course. For me the starting point was Calcutta, India, the thirtieth of September 1934.

An unregistered alliance between my father, Devi Kashfi, a professional architect, and my mother, Selma Ghose, brought me into the world at a time of mounting British-Indian conflict. When I was two, my mother espoused an Englishman, William Patrick O'Callaghan, thereby provoking disapproval from her family. Marriage to an Englishman was then, to many, an upward step to social prestige. To others with more nationalist fervor, it was a censurable act. Because of our familial discord and because of the social unrest in the cities, both arising from the clash of the two cultures, my half brother, Bosco (two and a half years younger), and I were removed to the mountain redoubt of Darjeeling in the north of India. There I attended school at the Kurseong Roman Catholic convent.

I can recall, from the ages of five and six, being sent by train to visit the family in Calcutta, a journey that covered two days along the narrow-gauge (two-foot) tracks of the Darjeeling Himalayan Railway after descending the mountain by *téléphérique*. The route, frequently blocked by landslides, spiraled alongside precipitous ledges and across hypnotic gorges. It included the world's highest station (over 7,000 feet) and probably the world's tightest loops. A retinue of geriatric wagons-lit, moldy coach cars, and bare wooden stock made up the train—a toy train for the climb north from Siliguri—and served to preserve the nineteenth century well into the twentieth. Seated demurely on the leather upholstery of the first-class carriage, an address label pinned to the shoulder of my pinafore, I spoke only to the resplendently uniformed conductor who, after each stop, officiously registered my continued presence.

By 1940 the jewel of the British Empire had become both tarnished and slippery. Caught between excesses of magnificence and squalor, past grandeur and subsequent oppression, the subcontinent struggled with a ruinous schizophrenia. The belief that the British were assigned a God-sanctioned mission to civilize India had been shattered by the 1857 Rebellion but its echoes still reverberated across the land. British and Indian societies coexisted on opposite sides of a one-way glass barrier, rendering the Indian side invisible to the British. I remember, during one visit to Calcutta, my first exposure to the racial regulations practiced by the British. My half brother and I were on an outing in the city with our governess when we passed a children's park. Bosco had to be restrained by the governess from rushing toward the swings and slides. It was explained to us that the park was reserved for British children. Signs warning "No Indians Allowed" were a common sight in Indian cities.

I was relatively insulated from the upheaval of independence in 1947. I had thought romantically of running off to join the "Monkey Brigade," a children's army of many thousands who served as couriers and attendants in the independence movement. Strict supervision within the convent suppressed the possibility of translating such thoughts to action.

Although not the most saintly child in the Kurseong convent—I delighted in scooping jellied aspic into the nuns' pantalets—I graduated on schedule and was rewarded by my father with a sea voyage to Rio de Janeiro. My only strong recollection of that trip was meeting the Brazilian architect Oscar Niemeyer, then a consultant to Nova Cap, the firm hired to create the new capital, Brasília. He was shortly to astonish the world with his combination of inventiveness and architectural virtuosity.

At eighteen I was packed off to England to the London University of Economics. My mother and stepfather had taken up residence in Ogmore-by-the-Sea, a small resort town on the coast of Wales, close enough to afford occasional visits. Mostly, I spent the time studying, riding the double-decker buses to and from the university, rarely venturing far from my flat off Montague Square.

My first serious romance was responsible for my leaving the university. Rico Mandiaco was a suave, charming Italian who proved irresistible. He swept me off to Rome to meet his parents and to have his skinny Indian girl friend padded with the family pasta. On our way back to London we stopped for the weekend in Paris. There I was the victim of one of those B-movie coincidences that would tax even the most gullible. While strolling with Rico along the Rue de la Paix, I literally bumped into my father. My last letter to him told of how I was busy studying in London. I assumed he was still in India. We were both so disconcerted at discovering each other in Paris that no words were exchanged. He was probably shocked not so much at finding me with a man as that I had lied to him. Upon arriving back in London I found my allowance to have been precipitately severed. Thus ended my academic career.

Modeling jobs in Soho provided a meager living for a few months. In the summer of 1955 Rico escorted me to a party where I met the Paramount Studio representative in Europe, Richard Mealand (whose talent scouting uncovered Audrey Hepburn, among others). I had never been to America and was quite curious about Americans. Mealand seemed to typify the species—brash, confident, enthusiastic; he proceeded to paint an exciting picture of his country for me.

Then he said: "Look, Paramount is doing a picture in France that calls for an Indian girl. The star has casting approval, and he is very difficult. We've interviewed seventeen girls so far, and they have all been turned down. The part requires you to speak only Hindi—no English. And the acting is only to react against the star. If you're interested, I can arrange an interview in Paris."

There was no sensible reason for refusing the offer. I couldn't type, take shorthand, or offer other secretarial skills. Modeling as a profession ranks high on insecurity.

Harry Mines, the Paramount publicist, met me in Paris, arranged for a room at the Hotel Raphael where the production company was staying, and introduced me to Edward Dmytryk, producer/director for the film. Dmytryk asked me to read the script, which was titled *The Mountain*; the plot (derived from an actual event) concerned an aircraft crash on a mountain peak, the sole survivor being a beautiful Indian girl. I was then escorted by Dmytryk to the hotel suite holding the star of the picture. We entered the main room and stood waiting; the door to the bedroom opened, and out bounded a huge, ursine, Pickwickian specter—Spencer Tracy. Before I had a chance to collapse from fright—no one had told me the star's name—he surrounded me in a smothering embrace, lifted me off my feet, turned to Edward Dmytryk, and proclaimed: "She's the one. Pack the bags. We're rolling."

In such a manner did I become an actress. Later, when I came to know him well, I asked Spence why he had spontaneously conferred his blessing on me; his answer was never more than a toothy Irish grin. Possibly, since the script enjoined him to carry the Indian girl down the mountain, he deemed my lightness an influential factor. At the time I weighed an even seven stone (ultimately, Spencer had to carry the extra ten pounds that I added on location).

Edward Dmytryk offered a less enigmatic explanation. He subsequently told a journalist: "We chose her because she was intelligent and because she looked as though she had the potential of being a good actress. She's got great skin and eyes. I wasn't certain if she was all Indian but I really didn't care. She had a complexion that indicated strongly that she had Indian blood. I heard later that she had light hair as a little girl; perhaps she dyed it black to look more like a full-blooded Indian. But that didn't matter to me either. All I cared about was whether she was right for the part. And she was."

Locale for the picture was Chamonix, a small village under the shadow of Mont Blanc in the French Alps. From the onset an ill fate visited the filming. The funicular to the mountain peak stalled whimsically, suspending cast and crew two hundred feet above the jagged terrain. Bad weather was responsible for endless postponements. Scenes were restaged from the peak to the lower slopes. Still the funicular and the weather refused to cooperate. Tracy's celebrated temper boiled over with each perversity. Spencer was eternally a perfectionist. He would tolerate no laxity either with me, with his costars— E. G. Marshall, Claire Trevor, Robert Wagner—with the director, with the technicians, or with the elements. When men or gods displayed a flaw, his rage could be volcanic. Hyperbole suggested that burying his head in a snowbank would melt enough drinking water for the entire company.

Late in the summer one of the professional mountain climbers who substituted for the actors in long shots fell into an ice crevice (his body was not recovered until the following spring). His death proved to be the tragic squeeze that cracked the egg. It was decided to abandon Chamonix for the more predictable purlieus of the Paramount sound stage. I was included in the move although I had finished most of my scenes. Movie moguls never disclose their reasoning.

I had always traveled throughout Europe on an Indian passport. The United States, however, imposes a low quota for Indian citizens; queueing time for admission can extend to several years. On Spencer's advice—he had seized the role of my knightly champion—I obtained a British passport using my stepfather's name, O'Callaghan. Subsequently, with marriage to Marlon Brando, the press uncovered this nom de convenance and concluded, with journalistic fervor, that I was an Irish lass masquerading as an Indian.

We flew to New York for a three-day rest before proceeding to Hollywood. At the New York airport we were detained by the press with the traditional nonsensical questions: "Who was my favorite movie star?" "What, if anything, did I wear to bed?" "What perfume did I favor?" Etc. American reporters were less ill-mannered than their British colleagues. In the presence of Spencer Tracy, at least, they were more subdued. One paper reported that I had browned my skin by daily bathing in coffee. Percolated or instant was not specified.

My memories of New York typify those of the first-time visitor: forbidding skyscrapers, pulsating throngs, the Rockettes, Macy's, and first bite of a mysterious and tasteless concoction known, for equally mysterious and tasteless reasons, as a "hot dog." Broadway theatres proved disappointing—less glamorous than their West End counterparts. Times Square also disappointed; its ambiance felt tawdry, commercial rather than exhilarating. I shopped for my first dress, being accustomed only to saris.

Los Angeles was a city like none other I had seen. It was the cutting edge of a culture only vaguely American. It was not tethered to the ground but floated freely like a sculptured cloud of dry ice, a Camelot fenced by palm trees to guard its denizens from straying over the edge. Inside the cloud gaudy neons and billion-candlepower searchlights bruited metastasized food dispensaries disguised as doughnuts, hats, trains, or tepees—a Raymond Chandler novel raised up as a movie set (complete with pink and blue bathtubs!). The occasional bodies in motion either were movie extras or acted as if they were.

Some years later a cold economic wind struck the set and blew the city back to earth. Only then did I perceive that there were real people living on the other side of the looking glass; only then did I find the rabbit hole to reach them.

I had scarcely stepped from the plane when I was drawn into the routine of moviemaking: morning calls at eight o'clock, through by five. Legendary names materialized into human beings. My first day on the Paramount lot I lost my way to the makeup room. A charmingly overwhelming lady named Pearl Bailey found me wandering about, piloted me by the elbows like a tricycle, and became a staunch, helpful friend. Bob Hope and Eva Marie Saint were introduced. George Sanders became friendly. Sanders was an accomplished pianist; a piano was always installed for his use near his dressing room. Within a short time the mystique of the motion-picture personality eroded. Stars became people. Acting became a job.

While a film is in production its participants tend to be insular, to cohabitate beyond the confines of the set. The nonparticipant is an intruder, an inhibitor of expression. Thus it came to pass that I lunched each day in the Paramount commissary, secure and shielded by allies in the same drama. Thus it came to pass that Marlon Brando was also in the Paramount commissary. And thus came to pass all the rest.

My knowledge of Marlon Brando's life before we met derives mostly from his friends, his family, and secondhand accounts. With few exceptions (mostly relating to personal responses and sexual experiences), Marlon avoided discussing what he called "ancient history." "Never look back," he quoted Satchel Paige's sage advice, "they may be gaining on you."

As my relationship with Marlon grew more intimate, as our emotional bond intensified, as I began to experience his idiosyncrasies, I became less inclined to accept his philosophy of divorcing past and present. "What's past is prologue," quoth Antonio, and, he might have added, is essential to an understanding of the acts that follow. Further, a woman is inherently motivated—by more than casual curiosity—to fathom in the fullest sense the man she loves. Marlon's "ancient history," I discovered, indeed foreshadowed the man and his measure. I uncovered more characters, more sexual escapades, more comedies, and more capsulated dramas than Scheherazade could make up in a second thousand nights. Worse, they were all true.

Marlon Brando began on April 3, 1924, in Omaha, Nebraska. If the Good Faerie hovered over his cradle, there was also a grinning imp drooling on his face. He was the third and last of three children born to Marlon, Sr., and Dorothy Pennebaker Brando. Marlon, Sr., a sales representative for National Carborundum, was, in retrospect, described by his son as a "strict, argumentative bastard." Although father and son became reconciled later in life—particularly after Dorothy Brando's death—the father's indifference to Marlon as a child undoubtedly steered the boy to his mother and planted the seed of his ambivalent feelings toward women and his tangled sexuality. Known as "Bud" to distinguish him from his father, he insisted upon being addressed as Marlon as soon as he was old enough to issue a direct challenge. When he became famous, he acquired the effrontery to suggest his father change his name. "Goddamn it," said Marlon, Sr., ever on the defensive with his son, "I had it first."

Marlon's mother ("Dodie" to friends and acquaintances), an attractive but disoriented woman with blonde hair coiffed into bangs, adhered to the then progressive theory for raising children: permissiveness, minimum discipline, minimum direction, and encouragement of free expression ("don't inhibit their little psyches"). She was described years later by actress Stella Adler as "a very beautiful, a heavenly, lost, girlish creature." Dodie was quite willing to accept undivided responsibility for superintending her only son and so sheltered him from his father's authority that he was unable to develop a normal masculine sense of security. This situation naturally provoked bitter disputes between the parents and left the Brando household bristling with tension.

Jocelyn ("Tiddy") and Frances ("Fran") were Marlon's two elder sisters. All three children resembled their mother, both in appearance and in temperament, a resemblance that fostered unbalanced emotional attachments. Sibling rivalry for their mother's affections led the young Brandos into a continuing competition, which Marlon, as the youngest and sole male offspring, entered with an endemic vantage. Tiddy recalled that "Marlon was a blond, fat-bellied little boy, quite serious and very determined. He was Mama's pet. He could do no wrong. We couldn't compete." With his father absent on frequent trips, Marlon reinforced his dominance. "I owned the only pair of balls in the house," he boasted.

No one in the family could disagree. Thirty years later Tiddy remembered that "even when he was going to kindergarten, Marlon had strong ideas of his own. I had to see that he got there. You may not believe it, but I actually had to put him on a leash. Otherwise he would run away."

Competition branched out to other people, other areas. Childhood friends were coerced into contests such as "Who can eat fastest?" "Who can hold his breath longest?" "Who can climb the fence quickest?" When Marlon won—and his determination usually brought him victory—he would squeal with childish glee. When he lost, his relationship with the victor cooled rapidly. Even in his mature years Marlon continued creating competitive situations that he could win; friendships—and love affairs—became predicated upon playing *his* game and letting *him* win. Our son Devi often complained to me, "Why do we always have to play the games Daddy wants to play?"

As the family moved from Omaha to Evanston, Illinois, to Minnesota, and in 1936 for an extended period to Libertyville, Illinois, Marlon attended a succession of schools. At each, he showed himself to be an unattentive, uncaring, and unruly pupil who spent more time daydreaming and sitting in the principal's outer office than listening to his teachers. Wally Cox, an elementary school classmate and lifelong chum, claimed that Marlon held the school record for fistfights and arguments. Yet his ability to sass his teachers, to flaunt a feigned sense of innocence, and to return from the principal's office as an unsubdued rebel reinforced his stature as an object of admiration to more restrained students.

The opposite facet of Marlon's embryonic personality was a surprising tenderness for life. He brought home wounded birds, snakes, and squirrels to nurse back to health. He attempted to embalm and consecrate a dead chicken out of respect for its former egg-laying capacity. The thought of hooking a fish revolted him.

In the poverty of the depression, any passing vagrant might be found by the young boy and invited home for a meal. At age eight he stumbled over a sick, hungry woman lying near Lake Michigan; violent tantrums finally persuaded his parents to subsidize her recovery in a nearby hotel.

At the beginning of his junior year in Libertyville's Fremont High School, Marlon was expelled for smoking on the school grounds, a minor crime that, when added to his other pranks and troublemaking, proved to be the drop that broke the dam. Marlon remained unperturbed, however. He seemed content to devote his waking hours to pounding on his set of trap drums. (Marlon fancied himself a talented drummer and attempted without success to organize a small band.) Perhaps it was the incessant noise that finally cracked his father's inattention. Marlon, Sr., demanded that his son be sent to a military school for discipline and, in the quarrels that followed with Dodie Brando, for once he prevailed.

In the spring of 1942 Marlon was enlisted into the Shattuck Military Academy in Faribault, Minnesota. It was hate at first sight. The "military asylum," as he referred to the academy, merely challenged his ingenuity and resoluteness as a prankster, an exhibitionist, and an unrepentant anarchist. He would soak tennis balls in acetone, light them on fire, and bounce them around the parade ground, where they deposited spots of flame at each bounce. He once spent an entire night stuffing a classroom to the ceiling with crumpled newspapers. He instigated the dismantling of an instructor's automobile and its reassembly in a third-floor office. In less than a year he achieved his goal of expulsion. The shaken school authorities capitulated when Marlon took to emptying a chamber pot out the dormitory window onto passersby while, in eighteenth-century French fashion, calling "Gardez loo!"

"I hated it every day I was there," he said later. "The school officials were pricks. They made you show respect—like the warden in a penitentiary. I also hated their goddamn clocks. The goddamned bell clanged every half hour. One night I climbed up the tower and cut off the clapper. Then I busted it on the ground."

Nineteen-year-old Marlon was back in Libertyville, aimlessly slouching around his home. When not beating his trap drums listlessly or slubbering through an odd job, he would ponder the few courses open to him. No profession, no skill offered an appeal. The war never penetrated his consciousness. ("I watched the war in the Trans-Lux theatre at 42nd and Broadway," he said.) He had been classified 4-F, presumably because of a knee injury suffered during a high-school football scrimmage. I could never detect an irregularity with his knee, however, and the alleged impairment never affected his actions.

Dodie Brando had long been associated with the acting profession; she often referred to herself as a frustrated thespian. In the twenties and early thirties she was a member of the respected Omaha Community Playhouse, a semiprofessional theatre group that lent early impetus to Henry Fonda, Dorothy McGuire, and other talented actors. Henry Fonda was Dodie's special protégé, a recipient of her encouragement and sponsorship. Marlon remembered that as a teenager he had met Fonda and was impressed with the man and with the idea of acting. Both of Marlon's sisters were quondam actresses. Tiddy moved to New York after her college graduation and landed bit parts in several Broadway productions. Fran, after braving a number of amateur acting groups, joined her sister in New York where she enrolled in the Art Students League. Dodie Brando managed periodic visits to her daughters' lodgings to aid and supervise their endeavors.

Marlon maintained that he never deliberately pursued an acting career but drifted into it when his true calling failed immediately to identify itself. Even today he persists in the notion that a meritorious vocation more suited to his talents and inclinations will arise and beckon to him. "Acting," he told Dick Cavett in a television interview in the summer of 1973, "is just a living."

A more perceptive interpretation of Marlon's foray onto the roulette wheel of acting would credit his competitive drive to surpass his sisters' accomplishments in their own field. With his mother lavishing her time and energies on his siblings, the incentive to regain pre-eminence in her esteem must have been intense. In the summer of 1943, impelled by an Oedipus complex, a sibling rivalry, and the drive to substantiate his manhood, he entrained for New York to proclaim his presence to the world.

At first the world appeared regally indifferent to his proclamation. Days were occupied with the fruitless search for bit parts, with a mélange of menial and doorstep jobs (elevator operator, doorman, busboy, milkman, encyclopedia salesman), and with absorbing the multiflavored palate of New York. Nights found him sprawled out, fully clothed, on the couch in his sisters' apartment. Probably thousands of drifting, indigent young men were tramping the streets of Manhattan the same time as Marlon, sleeping on a friend's or relative's couch, scratching at creation for a few dollars. Whatever quality distinguished Marlon from all the others, it was soon to emerge.

In the autumn Marlon joined the Dramatic Workshop of the New School for Social Research. Founded and directed by the German expressionist director Erwin Piscator, the Dramatic Workshop featured avant-garde staging of plays with social content. Along with the Actors Studio, the Workshop was the foremost exponent of the Method school of acting in America. Workshop alumni such as Shelley Winters and Maureen Stapleton were Marlon's contemporaries. Piscator's teaching staff, all professional and successful actors, included the incisive and astute Stella Adler who was assigned as Marlon's instructor. Stella, daughter of Jacob Adler, the legendary acerbic personality of the Yiddish theatre, and sister of Luther Adler, had been a dedicated trouper since the age of four, performing first with her father and then as leading lady in hundreds of roles on and off Broadway. After a go at Hollywood in several mediocre films, she returned to direct several Broadway productions without notable success and then was engaged by Piscator as a faculty member. A disciple of Konstantin Stanislavski, the renown director who founded the Moscow Art Theatre, Stella followed her master in teaching that true acting emanates from an inner emotional reservoir. The Stanislavski actor not only interprets dialogue and action but mirrors the underlying motivation and conflicts of the character he portrays.

Both the method and the teacher suited Marlon's temper.

For the first time ever, he focused his thoughts and accepted advice. In the New School's other classes he studied French, philosophy, dancing, fencing, and yoga exercises. Almost from the beginning he captured the star pupil ranking. Director Piscator noted that "he has an inner rhythm that never fails." Stella Adler was even more impressed with his innate abilities: "Marlon never really had to learn to act. He knew. Right from the start he was a universal actor. Nothing human was foreign to him. He had the potential for any role. It's incredible how large the scale of his emotions is—he has complete scale. And he has all the external equipment—looks and voice and power of presence—to go with it."

Twenty years later she remained a consistent partisan, telling a journalist: "I taught him nothing. I opened up possibilities of thinking, feeling, experiencing and, as I opened those doors, he walked right through. He never needed me after that. He lives the life of the actor twenty-four hours a day. If he is talking to you, he will absorb everything about you— your smile, the way your teeth grow. His style is the perfect marriage of intuition and intelligence."

Tall and rough-hewn, Stella Adler was known as "Mother Earth" to her students. Twenty-two years older than Marlon, her magnetism as a mother-surrogate was high gauss. At that time Marlon had not yet fashioned the security to approach comely damsels; "even in school," his grandmother is quoted as saying, "Bud always fell in love with the cross-eyed girl." His attachment to the matriarchal Miss Adler was brief and not fully gratifying. When it was over, he reacted with a typical Brando pirouette—he courted her daughter, Ellen.

Marlon's recollection of his Dramatic Workshop days suggested that his progress was not uniformly smooth: "One summer we had a season of stock with German director Erwin Piscator, who was trying to start something called Epic Theater. He vas der meister und ve vere der shtudents, und der girls vere not supposed to see der boys after hours. So one night he caught me necking with one of the girls in the company but all he said was, 'Ja. So. Brrrando.' The next day it was 'Oudt! You are oudt of zis company!' and I left."

One of Marlon's girl friends at the Workshop was Elaine Stritch, who was to play the part of Ruth in the television version of *My Sister Eileen*. In December 1960 she reminisced to an interviewer: "Every Saturday night he was taking out the ugliest girl in the class, the one with the buck teeth. It was his idea of generosity. I was the last girl he asked. He made me wait, see? Then he said, 'Where do you want to go? How about the Public Library?' We went and looked at books—he put on a show about how intellectual he was. Then he took me to a strip joint. He said, 'This is a part of life you should know about.'"

During his apprenticeship at the Dramatic Workshop, Marlon flitted through a series of shabby apartments, mostly in the Greenwich Village area. He was often evicted, either for overdue rent or for the disturbance his bongo drums created in the early morning hours. Some of the apartments were shared with Wally Cox, then studying industrial arts at NYU. (The future Mr. Peepers didn't enter show business until 1948 when, encouraged by Marlon and others, he debuted with a nightclub act.) Cox's friendship with Marlon waxed and waned periodically throughout his life. When the subject of Marlon Brando arose, Cox offered little enlightenment about their relationship, as have Marlon's other confidants. Cox's one public quote flattered his roommate embarrassingly: "a creative philosopher, a very deep thinker. He's a real liberating force for his friends."

The two grade-school chums carried on a bohemian lifestyle. A guest at their brownstone apartment on 52nd Street (one of their uptown quarters) depicted the cluttered scene as a "surrealist junk shop." Once Marlon and Cox, resolving to clean up the mess, painted one wall; then for the next twelve months, canvas, buckets of paint, and brushes lay on the living-room floor. They and the stream of visitors simply stepped around them.

One of the Manhattan apartments that held Marlon for a brief term was equipped with a fire-prevention sprinkler system. Repeatedly, Marlon would hang up his clothes to dry in the kitchen. He would turn on the stove burners to expedite the drying, leave the apartment, and return to find the sprinklers exploding and the rooms flooded. If Marlon could not be relied upon to profit from experience, his landlords could.

Wherever Marlon lived, with or without acknowledged

roommates, his apartment offered a haven for fellow actors, fellow bohemians, or anyone who could locate his address. The famous and the hopeless were equally sheltered under Marlon's aegis. Shelley Winters dropped in frequently, her ample maternal instincts aroused by Marlon's semblance of helplessness. She cleaned his rooms, darned his socks, and thoroughly mothered him.

Across 52nd Street stood the fashionable Leon and Eddie's. Its management was persistently annoyed by the eyesore of Marlon's parked motorcycle blocking the entrance. Marlon, in turn, was annoyed by the management's refusal to admit him in T-shirt and jeans. Marlon resolved the dispute by collecting a bucket of horse manure from Central Park and hurling its contents from his apartment window onto the restaurant's frontage, shouting, "Beware the flying red horse!"

Horse manure provided an abiding resource for Marlon's expression. An amateur violinist who frequented Marlon's apartment to perform found his instrument, one evening, to be heavier than usual.

"Why, it's filled with horseshit!"

"Yes," said Marlon, with nonchalance, "that's precisely what it sounds like."

Despite the exhibitionist pranks, Marlon began sinking more and more into the lower half of his manic-depressive cycling. He would withdraw into himself, unresponsive to attempts at rousing him. For hours he might sit brooding— while a boisterous party pranced around him—staring blankly, unfocused, into another dimension. It was evident to those few of his acquaintances who possessed a modicum of insight that he was nearing a state of melancholia. It became evident to Marlon himself.

Fearing to take the fall onto the psychiatrist's couch, Marlon aroused himself from his fits of depression whenever the Dramatic Workshop staged a production. It was Piscator's practice to produce a series of classical plays (Shakespeare, Shaw, Molière) in his theatre and to direct a summer stock group. Marlon commanded major roles in these productions, acquiring his first favorable reviews from the occasional critic who bothered to attend.

He also acquired his first casting agent, Maynard Morris,

who had seen a Workshop performance and sensed the depth of talent in the young actor. Morris dispatched Marlon to the major film studios for screen tests. Marlon flunked. He was not suitable for motion pictures, decreed one studio executive, with a nose that "dribbled down his face like melting ice cream." Morris persisted and wheedled an audition for his client with Rodgers and Hammerstein who were casting for their production of John Van Druten's play, *I Remember Mama*. Despite a woeful, mumbling performance by Marlon, the auditioners too sensed the dynamic reserve below the surface and awarded him the secondary role of Nels, eldest son of the Norwegian immigrant family in first-of-the-century San Francisco.

For his *Playbill* biography, Marlon provided the salient points of his background. He had been born in Calcutta, educated at Shattuck Military Academy, and studied drumming technique under a disciple of the famous East Indian dancer, Shan Kar. He was devoted to his Great Dane, who thrived on dehydrated cubes of dog food, and to the philosophies of Schopenhauer and Spinoza, not necessarily in that order. "Why did you say such things?" asked a friend. "Why not?" said Marlon, "it could have been true."

In addition to the scattered accolades he earned in his maiden venture on the Broadway stage, Marlon collected two more influential admirers—the play's director, Bobby Lewis ("He was so real I found myself forgetting he was an actor and that I had ever met him"), and an MCA actors' representative, Edith Van Cleve ("Watching him on stage, I tingled all over with excitement"). Bobby Lewis was instrumental in recruiting him for the Actors Studio. Miss Van Cleve, another mother figure (she was then forty-five years old), signed him to a contract and proceeded to mastermind his rise to theatrical fame.

Success with the long-running *I Remember Mama* interfered little with Marlon's other activities. He continued his classes at the Dramatic Workshop with Stella Adler. He continued his open-house policy for every offbeat character in the neighborhood. He continued his pranks, his brooding and despondency, his sexual affairs with older women, his all-purpose T-shirt and jeans. With a $75 weekly salary from the show, he moved into a West End apartment—a fourth-floor walk-up—and invited his mother to share it.

Dodie Brando readily forsook her husband for her son. All but the veneer of her marriage had long since dissolved, and she was suffused with maternal pleasure over Marlon's ascendancy. Yet the strains of living together proved intolerable for both mother and son. Marlon's submerged sexual longings for his mother had to be vented. Because of the ingrained incest taboo, Oedipal intercourse could be realized only vicariously. He urged an actor friend, Carlo "Freddie" Fiore, with whom he shared casual adventures ("Freddie is a left-handed homosexual," Marlon described him to me) to seduce his mother; Fiore claimed he rejected the invitation—reconfirmed by Dodie herself—out of friendship for Marlon. On the other side, Dodie's drinking, possessiveness, and neurotic posturings were more than Marlon could suffer. He had already scored the winning goal by appropriating his mother from his father's dominion. After two months he evicted her.

Twelve years later, coaxed into an alcoholic fog by Truman Capote in a Tokyo hotel room, Marlon maundered about his feelings for Dodie: "My mother was everything to me. A whole world. I tried so hard. I used to come home from school . . . There wouldn't be anybody home. Nothing in the icebox. Then the telephone would ring. Somebody calling from some bar. And they'd say, 'We've got a lady down here. You better come get her.' I thought if she loved me enough, trusted me enough, I thought, then we can be together in New York; we'll live together and I'll take care of her. Once, later on, that really happened. She left my father and came to live with me. In New York, when I was in a play, I tried so hard. But my love wasn't enough. She couldn't care enough. She went back. And one day, I didn't care anymore. She was there. In a room. Holding on to me. And I let her fall. Because I couldn't take it anymore—I watched her break apart in front of me, like a piece of porcelain. I stepped right over her. I walked right out. I was indifferent. Since then, I've been indifferent."

After a year of _I Remember Mama_, Marlon was sated with the play and eager for other roles. Edith Van Cleve arranged an audition for *O Mistress Mine*, an Alfred Lunt and Lynn Fontanne comedy. As usual, Marlon slouched onstage unshaven, unkempt, and uncooperative.

Lunt handed him the script. "Pick out a few lines and read them," he suggested.

Marlon squinted for several moments, then threw the script into the fifth row. "I can't do it," he declared, either from lack of desire or lack of vision. (He refused to wear obviously needed glasses.)

"Try something from memory," said Lunt, ever helpful.

Marlon thought and struggled and strained. Finally he emoted: "Hickory dickory dock, the mouse ran up the clock."

It wasn't quite enough. (The story became a Broadway legend, although Lunt later denied its authenticity.)

Marlon left for a two-month vacation in Paris, his first view of Europe. In later years he was to return often to the French capital to "cleanse my sinuses." He moped about the city enriching his classroom French, observing the postwar renaissance, sampling French sexuality, and, as always, absorbing the mannerisms of the people.

Returning to New York, he rejoined Wally Cox in residence and costarred (with Karl Malden) in Maxwell Anderson's play, *Truckline Cafe*. The role was cajoled for him, over the objections of Edith Van Cleve, by Stella Adler, whose husband, Harold Clurman, was co-producing with Elia Kazan.

"Gadge" Kazan (a corruption of "gadget") was to exert, for a time, an intimate influence on Marlon's life; for many years he was the only person to direct Marlon through more than one motion picture. His introduction to the embryonic star was not auspicious. At the first reading of *Truckline Cafe*, Marlon contributed his usual inarticulate rendition. "Speak up, Marlon!" Kazan shouted from the rear of the theatre. "Stop mumbling! If this thing is going to lose money, I want to hear what I'm losing it on."

A disastrous production with a cast of thirty-five, *Truckline Cafe* crashed into oblivion after two weeks on Broadway. (The program for the play revealed Marlon's birthplace as Bangkok, Siam.) Pauline Kael, film critic of *The New Yorker* and later Marlon's most uncritical admirer, was initially unsympathetic: "Arriving late at a performance, and seated in the center of the second row, I looked up and saw what I thought was an actor having a seizure on stage. Embarrassed for him, I lowered my eyes."

Others also failed to discern Marlon's camouflaged talents. Clifford Odets, brought by Stella Adler to the Workshop to observe her prize pupil, reported: "I saw the boy in her classrooms, and the genius Stella was talking about was not apparent to the naked eye. He looked to me like a kid who delivers groceries."

Next in Marlon's theatrical career came a revival of George Bernard Shaw's *Candida*, starring Katharine Cornell, "The First Lady of Broadway"; the play toured throughout the summer of 1946 with Marlon as the young poet, Marchbanks. In the autumn he joined Paul Muni, one of the many outstanding graduates of the Yiddish theatre, in Ben Hecht's drama, *A Flag Is Born*. Directed by Stella's brother, Luther Adler, the play was an anti-British, Zionist propaganda piece. Marlon undertook his participation as contributing to a noble cause. (Proceeds went to the Repatriation Fund for displaced Jewish refugees.) It marked the first of many attempts to invest his actions with a philanthropic guise. I think Marlon was sincere in this and other causes he later espoused. But sincerity for Marlon is like a signal flare—it shines intensely for a moment but is soon lost in the night.

After the rupture with his mother, Marlon shifted his sexual attentions toward younger females (although acceptance by Marlon required of each girl at least one personality trait common to his mother). Stage-door nymphs were ever anxious for quick carnality with the rising young stars of the theatre, and Marlon was pursued by the greatest numbers. Without effort, he gathered an ardent harem of voluptuaries. And whenever he wearied of a particular harem, he simply moved without announcement to another apartment.

"I'd like to have a houseful of women," Marlon admitted, "one for every occasion. One for a picnic, one for the beach, one to screw in bed, one to screw standing up."

A new play claimed much of his energy. Edith Van Cleve had contracted him as Tallulah Bankhead's leading man in Jean Cocteau's fantasy, *The Eagle Has Two Heads*. (A peasant plots to assassinate his Queen, falls in love with her, and dies after dispatching her anyway.) Mixing Bankhead and Brando, it developed, was akin to locking two bantam cocks in the hen house.

The histrionic Tallulah (an intimate friend of Miss Van Cleve) was no advocate of the Stanislavski method. "Any actor who loses himself in a part," she said, "is a stupid ass." Marlon's quixotic rehearsal techniques quickly unnerved her. She counterattacked with sexual overtures. However, Marlon had discarded his maternal-sex phase and rebuffed her propositions. (Tallulah was then twice Marlon's twenty-two years.) The lady who had turned cartwheels without benefit of panties was upstaged both in and out of the theatre. The two spied each other in an elegant uptown restaurant crowded with lunching society people. "Tallulah!" boomed Marlon, as if projecting to the upper galleries, "how the fuck are you?" Three ladies spilled their soup, and even Tallulah was nonplussed.

Opening night of the out-of-town trials proved Marlon's last with the play. In the first act Tallulah's part involved a lengthy soliloquy while Marlon's task was to stand inconspicuously in the background. Instead, Marlon picked at his nose, zipped and unzipped his fly, dusted the furniture, leered at the audience, and waved at a stagehand in the wings. Tallulah couldn't wait for the curtain to fall before pitching him out of the show, which was unanimously panned and closed after twenty-nine performances.

Tallulah never spoke to Marlon again. Despite her natural gift for outrage, she had been outpointed. Her final comments were mild, considering the provocation: "He drove me to distraction, always picking his nose, pausing too long, and scratching his balls. That's where I'd like to give him a good kick."

Marlon presented his version to columnist Earl Wilson: "Tallulah considered me a weirdo. I got bounced from her show. The play was no good. Every day they had the janitor in to help rewrite the script. Tallulah didn't like me much. She always wanted to go out and order champagne. Then she'd say, 'Oh, do let's paint the walls with fish.' I just about left my mind."

Marlon's reputation as a spontaneous troublemaker gained

him several months of unemployment. Stories spread by *Eagle* cast members impressed every New York producer despite Miss Van Cleve's valiant defenses of her client. Marlon flew off to Paris to let the resentment subside. "I couldn't stand to stay there among all the unpleasant thoughts," he insisted.

He returned in the early summer of 1947, his erratic behavior not noticeably repressed. He ranged about the streets of New York wearing a rubber horror mask. A reporter noted him sawing at a violin on West 50th Street, accompanied by a notorious madman who wore a sign around his neck identifying him as "the world's greatest deaf piano-tuner." He glided through dancing lessons at the Katherine Dunham Studio, fencing lessons at the New School, and classes in the Stanislavski Method at the Actors Studio. No acting offers materialized.

Edith Van Cleve had exhausted her Broadway and Hollywood contacts—pressing for a Brando role—when she was handed a copy of Tennessee Williams's *A Streetcar Named Desire*. She immediately recognized the part of Stanley Kowalski as ideally befitting Marlon's talents. When Marlon read the script, he agreed for once with his agent. The producer, Irene Selznick (the daughter of Louis B. Mayer and first wife of David O. Selznick), did not agree. Nor did the director, Elia Kazan. Mrs. Selznick announced that she had signed John Garfield. After thorough deliberation, Garfield concluded that the role of Stanley Kowalski was overshadowed by that of Blanche Du Bois, and he withdrew. Burt Lancaster was next in consideration but was committed to another project.

With the casting deadline nearing, Miss Van Cleve's perseverance cracked the resistance to Marlon. Kazan and Mrs. Selznick agreed to an audition. Miss Van Cleve refused. She had a vision of Marlon shuffling onstage, attired in kimono, false buck teeth, and horn-rim bifocals to read Kowalski with a Japanese accent. It was finally resolved that Marlon would be signed without an audition if the playwright approved.

Tennessee Williams was then occupied in polishing his play, secluded in a beach cottage in Provincetown, Massachusetts. Again without funds, Marlon hitchhiked from New York to Cape Cod. The two similar temperaments—artistically, sexually, psychologically—found no obstacle to a mutual understanding. Marlon captured the part without a serious skirmish.

Williams's memory of the episode is detailed: "I first met [Marlon Brando] in 1947 when I was casting *Streetcar*. I had very little money at the time and was living simply in a broken-down house near Provincetown. I had a houseful of people, the plumbing was flooded, and someone had blown the light fuse. Someone said a kid named Brando was down on the beach and looked good. He arrived at dusk, wearing Levi's, took one look at the confusion around him, and set to work. First he stuck his hand into the overflowing toilet bowl and unclogged the drain, then he tackled the fuses. Within an hour, everything worked. You'd think he had spent his entire antecedent life repairing drains. Then he read the script aloud, just as he played it. It was the most magnificent reading I ever heard, and he had the part immediately. He stayed the night, slept curled up with an old quilt in the center of the floor."

*Streetcar* opened in Broadway's Barrymore Theatre on December 3, 1947. In addition to Marlon, the original cast included Jessica Tandy, Kim Hunter, and Karl Malden. After his usual distracting, disrupting rehearsal techniques had alienated his costars, Marlon settled into performing his role with a power, energy, and virtuosity that remains unsurpassed. The production gained the New York Drama Critics' Award and the Donaldson Award. Tennessee Williams received the Pulitzer Prize for his writing. Marlon passed from the enfant terrible of Broadway to an established actor of national renown.

The critics vied for expansive superlatives. Marlon was "astonishingly authentic," "the greatest actor America has produced," "unbelievably profound"; his "puissant sexuality" overwhelmed the audience. Indeed, Marlon's sexuality in the being of Stanley Kowalski provided a new experience for the theatre. Truman Capote, in his famous portrait for *The New Yorker* in 1957, captured the sexual overtones: "It was a winter afternoon in New York.... He was still relatively unknown; at least I hadn't a clue to who he might be when, arriving too early at the *Streetcar* rehearsal, I found the auditorium deserted and a brawny young man stretched out atop a table on the stage under the gloomy glare of work lights, solidly asleep. Because he was wearing a white T-shirt and denim trousers, because of his squat gymnasium physique— the weight-lifter's arms, the Charles Atlas chest (though an opened 'Basic Writings of Sigmund Freud' was resting on it)— I took him for a stagehand. Or did until I looked closely at his face. It was as if a stranger's head had been attached to the brawny body, as in certain counterfeit photographs. For this face was so very untough, superimposing as it did, an almost angelic refinement and gentleness upon hard-jawed good looks; taut skin, a broad, high forehead, wide-apart eyes, an aquiline nose, full lips with a relaxed, sensual expression. Not the least suggestion of Williams's unpoetic Kowalski. It was therefore an experience to observe later that afternoon with what chameleon ease Brando acquired the character's cruel and gaudy colors, how superbly, like a guileful salamander, he slithered into the part, how his own persona evaporated."

I was never so fortunate to see Marlon perform onstage. I have felt, with others, that the stage offers a more suitable medium for the deployment of his talents than does the motion picture. Actors, directors, producers, and theatregoers have exclaimed to me of Marlon's virtuosity as Stanley Kowalski. William Redfield wrote that "this performance . . . is the finest I have seen given by an actor in the twenty-nine years I have been going to the theatre—and I saw it seven times." Another friend told me, "He could take a sentence, wind it up like the gauchos' bolas, and hurl it forth to strangle the audience. He knew what to treasure and what to throw away, what to conceal and what to reveal, with depth below depth, what to whisper and what to shout."

The extent to which Stanley Kowalski commandeered Marlon's life has been debated by his enthusiasts, his detractors, and Marlon himself. Certainly he adopted Kowalski's careless attire—he accomplished for T-shirts what Brigitte Bardot did for French bikinis. And certainly his humiliation of women and his compulsion to dominate his surroundings paralleled the boorish, brutish, inarticulate Kowalski's nature. One afternoon, when *Streetcar* had been running for two months, Marlon and a friend (Bob Condon) were strolling through the Central Park Zoo. They paused in front of a baboon's cage. The baboon objected to Marlon's stare and spat on him. Marlon spat back, striking the animal squarely in the face. The baboon was horrified at this unexpected, nonhuman deportment and retreated, cowering, to the rear of its cage. "If more people did that, it would teach that damn ape some manners," said Marlon. Kowalski couldn't have done it better.

Marlon denied it: "People have asked me if I'm really Stanley Kowalski. Why, he's the antithesis of me. He is intolerant and selfish. Kowalski is a man without any sensitivity, without any kind of morality except his own mewling, whimpering insistence on his own way. I can't think—I can't believe—that we are here for one terrible, gnashing, stomping moment and that's all."

Still, the Jekyll-Hyde specter must have haunted him. At the suggestion of Elia Kazan who delivered him to his own New York psychiatrist, Dr. Bela Mittelman, Marlon entered analysis. He was to continue sporadically for the next ten years.

"I was afraid of analysis at first," he said. "Afraid it might destroy the impulses that made me creative, an artist. A sensitive person receives fifty impressions where someone else may only get seven. Sensitive people are so vulnerable; they're so easily brutalized and hurt just because they are sensitive. The more sensitive you are, the more certain you are to be brutalized, develop scabs. Never evolve. Never allow yourself to feel anything, because you always feel too much. Analysis helps. It helped me."

If it really helped, it was not apparent to the lay observer. Marlon's onstage antics continued with his offstage posturing. During one performance, while Jessica Tandy as Blanche was the presumed focus of attention, Marlon turned to the audience stone-faced and stuffed a cigarette up each nostril. Miss Tandy called him an "impossible psychopathic bastard." He dismissed her with a galloping non sequitur: "She doesn't like peanut butter."

As the play's run lengthened, Marlon varied his interpretation of the role. He invented lines and added bits of stage business. Producer, director, and actors were horrified, but

Tennessee Williams insisted Marlon's alterations improved the play. After that, Marlon remained beyond criticism.

Outside the theatre, a woman columnist walked up to him and said in a sugary voice: "Why, Mr. Brando, you look just like everybody else." Marlon stared at her a moment in silence, then without a word he turned to the nearest doorway, unzipped his fly, and urinated on the walk.

*Streetcar* continued playing to packed houses. Marlon continued his shenanigans, one of which ended with his nose broken. Between his scenes onstage, he would box with the stagehands or spar with a punching bag hung in the theatre's boiler room. (Sounds from the scuffling would drift up to the stage, distinctly audible to the audience.) While holding the punching bag for a young prop man named Ronnie Green, Marlon was the recipient of a miscarried blow. The nose was not set properly. Yet it was his fortune that the misshape merely lent a more interesting, rugged resource to his countenance. Producer Irene Selznick commented: "I honestly think that broken nose made his career—especially in the movies. It gave him sex appeal. Previously, he was just too beautiful." Marlon agreed. "I should have gone to a plastic surgeon," he said when I questioned him about the incident, "and had it twisted when I was sixteen."

Toward the end of his engagement as Stanley Kowalski, Marlon's preoccupation with fecal matter rebounded against him. He complained more and more irately to the propman that the chicken supplied for the dinner scene was becoming less edible with each performance. One evening he stomped offstage and bellowed: "That chicken is godawful. I'd rather eat dogshit." The next performance, when he sat down at the table onstage, that was precisely what he found on his plate.

Marlon's contract for *Streetcar* (at $550 weekly) expired in June 1949. With recurring incidents of memory blackouts onstage, he declined to renew it in favor of a hiatus from the theatre. Deserting his two steady girl friends, dancer Tony Parker and "official fiancée" Cecilia D'Arthuniaga, he sailed off for "a nice long shlunk in Paris."

While Marlon was fraternizing with the Left Bank beatnik community, Edith Van Cleve was selling her client to the movie studios. MGM was preparing a film—from Carl Fore-

man's screenplay, *The Men*—about the readjustment problems of a paraplegic war veteran. The studio, previously apa-
thetic to the Brando mystique (he had stood working a Yo-Yo
during his last screen test), was now eager to exploit his
name; an offer of $40,000 was extended for Marlon to star in
*The Men*. By then Marlon had lost his passport, his available
funds, and much of his cocksureness to the local predators; he
was reduced to panhandling in Montmartre. In exchange for
passage home, he agreed to the MGM proposal without—for
the first time in his career—reading the script. (The next time
was not until 1965 when Charlie Chaplin signed him for *A
Countess from Hong Kong*.)

Marlon stepped off the train in Los Angeles carrying his
worldly possessions in a small canvas handbag. The bag contained two pairs of blue jeans, four T-shirts, two pairs of
socks, and a copy of Spinoza's *Tractatus Theologico-Politicus*.

Over the next few years in Hollywood he would achieve a
reputation for infantilism unsurpassed in a profession not
noted for its mature practitioners.

Escorted around the filmland scene by MCA agent Jay
Kanter, Marlon promptly antagonized the establishment.
Throughout one meeting with studio executives, he stood
holding a fried egg in one hand. For an interview with Hedda
Hopper, he contributed two grunts in response to an hour's
questioning. He referred to Hedda as "the one with hats";
Louella Parsons was "the fat one." He told one reporter that
his parents were destitute Polish displaced persons, another
that his daily diet consisted mainly of gazelle's eyes. He var-
iously claimed as his birthplace Bangkok, Outer Mongolia,
or the Gobi Desert. He snorted at the "putrid glamour" of
Hollywood, the "funnies in satin Cadillacs." "The only reason
I'm here," he insisted, "is because I don't have the moral
strength to turn down the money." He delivered his verdict on
film producers: "If you can make money for them, they'll let
you shit on their living-room rug. And thank you for it."

He summed up his feelings of the industry's clamor for his
talents: "Hollywood is a frontier town in lotus land ruled by
fear and love of money but it can't rule me because I'm not
afraid of anything and I don't love money. People around here
are trapped by success and wealth. You can't get inspired

here. Hollywood is like one big cash register ringing up the money all day long."

The gossip columnists, accustomed to fawning, servile actors, reciprocated. "Lolly" Parsons wrote: "As far as I'm concerned, he can drop dead. But really, darling. He has the manners of a chimpanzee, the gall of a Kinsey researcher, and a swelled head the size of a Navy blimp, and just as pointed . . . . As far as I'm concerned, he can just ride his little motorcycle right off the Venice pier." Less caustic columnists dubbed him "The Slob," "The Male Garbo," "A Dostoevskian version of Tom Sawyer."

For several weeks Marlon slept on a couch at the Eagle Rock home of his aunt, Mrs. Betty Lindermeyer, a sweet, ingenuous lady who never fathomed her nephew's eccentricities. Before shooting began on *The Men*, he moved into the Birmingham Veterans' Hospital rehabilitation center to live as a paraplegic. After a month without using his legs he found it difficult to walk, such was his immersion in the role. His dedication was rewarded in a brilliant, convincing presence on the screen (although the picture proved more a *succès d'estime* than a commercial triumph; it was released just as the Korean war erupted). And to the surprise of all concerned, he demonstrated the same dedication on the set, completing the production without tantrums, tricks, or upstaging the other actors.

Fred Zinnemann, *The Men*'s director, could muster only laudable comments: "Marlon is a combination of idealism and shrewdness. He knows exactly what he's doing. And he's all that a director could desire in an actor. Yes, Marlon's not only a great character but he's a great actor."

Back in New York, Marlon had barely unpacked—his assets had expanded to fill two suitcases—when he agreed to repeat his *Streetcar* role in the motion-picture version (opposite Vivien Leigh as Blanche with Elia Kazan directing). In the three months before rebounding west in the summer of 1950, he acquired an apartment with Wally Cox, acquired two more devoted girl friends, acquired a pet raccoon, and returned sporadically to the Actors Studio (where Lee Strasberg had succeeded Bobby Lewis) to participate in house productions and to the New School for French lessons.

41

Stanley Kramer, *The Men*'s producer, visited Marlon during this period and described him to an interviewer: "You can bet on Brando. He's mad but great. I don't know how often he washes or brushes his teeth. He's now living over a 52nd Street jive joint and studying conversational French at the New School. He can't even handle conversational English. But when he cries before a camera he destroys you. What an actor! Absolutely no ceiling to him."

The pet raccoon, Russell, accompanied him everywhere—on the streets, in classes, to the toilet (where Marlon induced him to urinate in the bowls), and to nightclubs (where he was deposited with the hatcheck girls). During a cross-country tour to publicize *The Men*, Marlon and Russell arrived at the Chicago airport. They were greeted by a United Artist PR man who inquired if he could provide any service for the star of the picture. "Yeah," Marlon said, "can you tell me where I can get my raccoon fucked?"

Because of Russell's penchant for nibbling on sleeping bodies, Wally Cox presented an ultimatum: "Either Russell goes or I go." Cox found a new apartment, his nose and other appendages chewed but still intact.

Marlon's subdued behavior on the set continued through the filming of *Streetcar*. Except for dangling black rubber spiders in the script girl's face and burning obscene words into the scenery, he concentrated on acting. Russell, on the other hand, scurried around the set, knocking over light reflectors, biting cables, and scratching at anyone who approached Marlon. "He was," noted one technician, "taking over where his master left off."

Whether because of Russell's antics or his own aloofness, Marlon was disliked by the crew of *Streetcar*. Mostly, when not on camera, he confined himself to his dressing room, occupied with a black girl who had been hired as an extra on the picture. "She gave me a dose," Marlon grumped to me years later.

Despite censorship problems, the picture proved a commercial and artistic success. Chief censor Joseph Breen demanded compliance with the fig-leaf propriety of the production code: eliminate the homosexual overtones, diminish the force of the rape scene, and punish Stanley for the rape by the loss of his wife. The film's scheduled premiere at Radio City Music Hall in the spring of 1951 was canceled when the Legion of Decency threatened to condemn it (Catholics attending would then be guilty of a sin). To placate the Legion, a musical background deemed "too carnal" was changed, and the words "on the mouth" were excised from Stanley's line, "I would like to kiss you softly and sweetly on the mouth." Such efforts at thought control and dictatorial righteousness seem particularly atavistic in light of current films with unrestricted sexual explicitness.

*Streetcar* raised a host of Brando imitators in torn T-shirts and distinction for Marlon as "The Slob," leader of legions of the unwashed. Marlon added to this reputation in his public statements. When a reporter inquired of his bathing habits, he replied, "I spit in the air and then run under it." The picture earned Marlon an Oscar nomination. Humphrey Bogart won (for *The African Queen*) although Marlon was expected to triumph; the industry was obviously loath to reward a member who reviled it for its "dishonesty" and money-mindedness.

Over the next several years Marlon adopted a pattern of withdrawing to New York between pictures. "A return to reality," he called it, steadfastly refusing to look beyond the Hollywood façade.

*Streetcar* was succeeded by *Viva Zapata!* with Marlon, again under Elia Kazan's direction, as the Mexican revolutionary leader. In preparation, Marlon moved to a small village in Sonora to study Mexican culture and speech patterns. As part of his makeup, plastic rings were fitted into his nostrils to flatten his nose; his eyelids were glued upward; and he wore brown contact lenses. To safeguard the lenses when not in use, Marlon stored them between his gum and his lower lip. Inevitably, he swallowed them; the shooting schedule was delayed until his New York optometrist was located, a duplicate set made and flown from New York to the filming site in Roma, Texas, by an MCA agent.

On the *Zapata* location, Russell again was cast as companion and surrogate cutup. The raccoon scratched at Jean Peters, Marlon's leading lady in *Zapata*, and tore at her clothes. Miss Peters had acquired a new Cadillac and invited Marlon for a ride. Russell was not impressed, and urinated over the leather seats. Marlon's light efforts at romance with Miss Peters were doused.

Anthony Quinn was costarring in the role of Zapata's brother, Bufemio. Since Quinn had played Stanley Kowalski in the road company *Streetcar,* a version directed by Harold Clurman, the suspicion arose that he and Marlon would fall into an unhealthy competition—a competition that would be exploited by Kazan. Marlon immediately quelled such notions by challenging Quinn to a pissing contest on the banks of the Rio Grande. Whether the idea for the contest derived from Russell or from Howard Hughes (who used his micturation prowess to win several wagers) was not revealed. Nor was it disclosed whether Marlon or Quinn outdistanced the other.

It was a bit actress in the picture who set Marlon's libido racing. Movita, a dark-skinned, high-cheekboned Mexican, several years older than Marlon—six to sixteen years older, depending on which studio biography is accurate—had played Franchot Tone's sweetheart (under the name of Maria Castenada) in the 1935 film version of *Mutiny on the Bounty.* Her career since then had sagged monotonically. For Movita—and for Marlon—their meeting was sex at first sight. She accompanied him back to Hollywood to share his rented bungalow. They remained intermittent lovers for eleven years, at which time Movita became the second Mrs. Brando.

Despite the high salary he commanded ($75,000 for *Streetcar,* $100,000 for *Zapata*), Marlon's mode of living hadn't perceptibly benefited. He had brought his father to California to manage his finances and was restricted to $100 weekly expenditures. Marlon's hatred for his father had not abated. He once explained to me that he had assigned his father as financial adviser out of filial obligation. But another time he ascribed it to masochism. A psychiatrist insisted that his father's presence was needed as reaffirmation that Marlon had won the battle for Dodie Brando's affection. In any event, the elder Brando employed his power to dampen some of Marlon's wilder affairs and, later, to interfere in our marriage. "Romance without finance is a nuisance," he used to mutter, and pulled tight on the purse strings.

In 1952 Marlon patched up his ties with Wally Cox and shared another New York apartment with his most intimate and steadfast friend. (Russell, who had taken to urinating on people's legs, was banished to an Illinois farm.) *Zapata* had gained him a second Oscar nomination but no Oscar (which was awarded to Gary Cooper for *High Noon*; Anthony Quinn won Best Supporting Actor for his part in *Zapata*). He rejected film offers until the summer when he signed for the role of Marc Antony in *Julius Caesar*. If skeptics still dubbed him "The Slob," he would rebut with a rapier. No slob could play Shakespeare.

Marlon's normal diction did not impress the critics as Shakespearean timbre but with the intensity he could muster when motivated, he spent weeks studying tapes of John Gielgud, cast as Cassius in the picture, Ralph Richardson, Laurence Olivier, Maurice Evans, and John Barrymore (his longtime idol), shaping the rhythms and resonance of Shakespeare's blank verse. Sounding somewhat like Polonius, Marlon insisted that anything Olivier et al. could do, he could do better. When the cameras rolled, director Joseph Mankiewicz, who had selected Marlon as Marc Antony, was impressed: "When Brando goes into a role, he plunges in like a deep-sea diver. If he was going to play a blind man, he'd go around for weeks with his eyes shut. If he was going to play a man with his right arm missing, he'd do everything lefty until he got the hang of how it felt."

Although Marlon's performance provoked controversial responses from others, it was defended by John Gielgud as "commendable." Marlon returned the compliment severalfold. Speaking of Gielgud's mastery of Shakespeare, Marlon said, "He's good in the movie—damned good. Now and then I can hear his metronome clicking away, but he sure knows his way around the meanings. I liked him very much. He made me laugh." (Lee Strasberg agreed: "When Gielgud speaks the verse, I can hear Shakespeare *thinking*.")

When box-office returns for *Julius Caesar* proved disappointing, Marlon was encouraged by several British actors to study in England under the auspices of the Old Vic. He declined. It is simple to fault him for not seizing the opportunity—actors either expand or contract—and I would never have met him had he done so—but his reasons, as usual, hinged on more complex fulcrums than a critical point in his acting career. Perhaps eccentricity had already become an asset and had to be fed.

Early in 1953 came *The Wild One*, the picture that entrenched Marlon as a hero of the youth cult. When his film persona is asked "What are you rebelling against?" and the character replies "What have you got?", he threw a spotlight on a previously dark recess of the American social experience. Millions of young men identified with the brutal, leather-jacketed Johnny portrayed on the screen. Torn T-shirts were discarded as sales of leather jackets and motorcycles soared. (Marlon had charged about on a cycle since his first days in Hollywood; when the activity became a fad, he abandoned it.) *The Wild One* triggered a mania for motorbike movies which persisted through *Easy Rider* and beyond.

(It also opened a lasting feud between Marlon and Lee Marvin who played a rival gang leader. Henceforth, Marvin spread tales about a "Marvin Brandy" while Marlon made reference to a "Lee Moron.")

Marlon pursued the character of Johnny with his usual dedication. Producer Stanley Kramer had hired groups of motorcyclists to mingle with the actors, and Marlon devoted much of his time in their ranks. His efforts secured a convincing performance—despite pressures from the Breen office to dilute the film's social commentary. (The original script was declared "socially dangerous.")

After *The Wild One* Marlon issued the first of his periodic retirement announcements. "I have a thousand head of cattle on my ranch in Nebraska," he said, "which will soon bring me an income of $80,000 a year. (Marlon, Sr., had invested in the Penny Poke Ranch in Broken Bow, Nebraska.) That's enough. I'll just sit back and enjoy life."

He didn't, of course. He played the straw-hat circuit through the New England states (Shaw's *Arms and the Man*)—his final stage appearances. He was brilliant once or twice a week, then threw away his other performances. To his friend and co-actor William Redfield, he said, "Man, don't you get it? This is summer stock." When he didn't care, the audience knew it. But Marlon was now beyond concern for audiences.

After summer stock he indulged himself with another trip to Paris and another sojourn of bohemian living on the Left

Bank. Then came the picture commemorated by his first Oscar, *On the Waterfront,* and one of the finest performances ever by an American actor on the screen.

The controversial film about crime and corruption among unionized dock workers was initiated by Elia Kazan. Independent producer Sam Spiegel provided capital backing—under the name of S. P. Eagle to shield himself from union displeasure. (Kazan too was threatened and protected himself with a bodyguard.) Frank Sinatra, following his comeback performance as Maggio in *From Here to Eternity,* coveted the role of *Waterfront's* coarse-grained stevedore, Terry Malloy. Kazan and Spiegel had accepted Sinatra when Marlon arrived on the scene. Whether he truly perceived the potentialities of the part or whether he was spurred by the challenge of vanquishing Sinatra, Marlon resolved to appropriate Terry Malloy for himself.

To dissuade a producer and director from a contract with Frank Sinatra ranks as a virtually insurmountable task. Marlon achieved it—impaled by an idée fixe, his determination bulldozed any barricade. He was signed to star in *On the Waterfront.*

Sinatra stopped talking to Spiegel—except through his attorneys. His suit asked $500,000 for breach of contract.

Marlon began lounging about the New York dock fronts, acquiring the stevedore mannerisms and Bronx accent essential to his performance. Kazan lauded him as "the best actor in the world today" and with reasoned sentiment added, "Marlon is one of the gentlest—possibly the gentlest—person I have ever known." As he accepted the Oscar for best actor of 1954, Marlon seemed to justify Kazan's opinion—and disappoint those who anticipated his hurling the statuette into the balcony—by meekly mumbling: "This is a wonderful moment for me and a rare one . . . and I'm certainly grateful." He was to prove less gracious eighteen years later.

During *Waterfront's* filming, Marlon's attentions centered on Anne Ford, a twenty-four-year-old blouse designer. Afterward she told her story to *Glamour* magazine, painting him as a noodle-brained simpleton: "[He came through my front door] shirtless, danced the entire length of the room, made a demi-disappearance behind the opposite door, and exited with a graceful arabesque kick—without a word of greeting or a glance my way.... [His] conversation, often over the phone, consisted of abstract flights of fancy. Once he announced that he was a crow, and about to go off on his midwinter flight to Florida. 'I'd like to drop you a postcard,' he said, 'but these claws make it so difficult to hold a pen.' "

In Hollywood his escorts included Pier Angeli, Susan Cabot, and Shelley Winters. Liz Renay, in her memoirs, was one of the few to award him a "high bedroom rating." He briefly courted his agent Jay Kanter's wife, Roberta Haynes (a Polynesian beauty who had played opposite Gary Cooper in *Return to Paradise*). Miss Haynes quickly divorced her husband but nonetheless went unrewarded. What many ardent belles regarded as a serious romance, Marlon viewed as nugatory. Women, for him, were mostly objects to be caught and then ejected lest they hinder the new catch. ("I hold all my broads at the end of a long bamboo pole with a strap that fits around their necks. They can't get too close and they can't get away.") One exception was Rita Moreno, a Puerto Rican dancer who shared his erratic disposition and passionate admiration of Afro-Cuban rhythms—especially on the bongo drums at four o'clock in the morning. For over a dozen years Miss Moreno engaged in remote combat with me, with herself (attempted suicide), and with other pretenders to Marlon's affections. While I must modestly award myself the gold medal for stamina in the Marlon Brando wars, Miss Moreno can claim the silver.

Typically, while Marlon was enhancing his stature as a womanizer, he was presenting another face outside the bedroom. Kazan recalled that during that period he carried a veil of insulation with him wherever he went: "At parties [Marlon] was very self-effacing. He would crawl along the wall and lie down on the first empty piece of floor he could find.... I never once saw him approach a girl." (At possibly the same party Kazan attended, another friend of Marlon's noticed him moping in a corner and consoled him with a pat on the head. "Why are you so worried, Marlon?" he said, "after all, you're the only genius here." Marlon brightened perceptibly.)

In signing his contract for *Zapata* with Twentieth Century-

Fox, Marlon had ceded to that studio options on his future services. After *On the Waterfront*, Fox assigned him to *The Egyptian*, Darryl F. Zanuck's multimillion-dollar ostentation. At the first rehearsal Marlon discovered that he loathed the picture, the director, Michael Curtiz (*Casablanca*), and the leading lady, Bella Darvi (Zanuck's inamorata). Further, he had been invited by Joshua Logan to play, instead, the lead in the film version of *Mister Roberts*. ("I'll do it," Marlon promised. "Somehow I'll find my way out of this Egyptian pile of camel dung.") He left the set and retreated to New York and the security of his psychiatrist, Dr. Mittelman (who announced that Marlon was under his care as "a very sick and mentally confused boy"). Fox proposed that Dr. Mittelman—in return for due remuneration—desert his practice to attend Marlon during filming of *The Egyptian*. Dr. Mittelman refused. The studio then suggested that its own medical experts would coddle Marlon's psyche. Marlon deigned no reply. He was thereupon served with a summons for a Fox lawsuit asking $2 million for breach of contract. The process server knocked at the door of Marlon's Manhattan apartment and announced, "I have the notice of your nomination for an Academy Award." The door swung open.

Fox dropped its legal action only when Marlon agreed to a different historical romance, *Desirée*, in which he was cast as Napoleon. He expressed his disgust with the script, but his professionalism triumphed; he devoured Napoleonic histories and tacked up a portrait of the emperor in his dressing room. He applied putty and cosmetics to transform himself into a striking resemblance to a brooding, destiny-conscious Napoleon. "I just let the makeup play the part," he said. Nonetheless, the results left him frustrated: "I tried to get humor into the characterization. I guess I didn't succeed; the picture depressed me."

When I saw the picture, I was equally appalled by the awkward, expository dialogue and by the camera angles that emphasized Marlon's fat buttocks bulging against snug, silk breeches.

(While engrossed in his research Marlon read a postmortem psychoanalysis of Napoleon describing him as a "phallic, narcissistic type suffering from a castration complex and organ inferiority, and with sadomasochistic tendencies [especially sado]." Whether Marlon accepted the obvious transfer to his own personality, I never learned. But the phrase found a target, and he committed it to memory.)

Marilyn Monroe, then married to Joe DiMaggio, was filming *There's No Business Like Show Business* on a nearby Fox set. She paid a neighborly visit to Marlon and her friend Jean Simmons (portraying the title role of Desirée). Marlon and Marilyn had been previously introduced by Kazan in New York. They exchanged champagne toasts and promised each other a film project pooling their talents. Marilyn suggested they consider the roles of Lord and Lady Macbeth. No one present could muster an audible opinion. (Some years later I lived next door to Marilyn Monroe and observed her struggling to shed the image of a windup doll with a plastic smile and a pullover naïveté. By then I was divorced from Marlon, and Marilyn was desperately preoccupied with psychoanalysis.)

Midway through the filming of *Desirée*, Dodie Brando fell ill while visiting her sister, Mrs. Lindermeyer, in California. She was rushed to the Huntington Memorial Hospital where she died the thirty-first of March 1954. His mother's death provoked a profound grief in Marlon, I believe, despite the disillusionment from her drinking and possessive neurosis. It marked his transition to a more introspective mood. Yet he told Clifford Odets at the time: "She wasn't there when I needed her."

A *Time* magazine correspondent interviewing Marlon on the *Desirée* set (for a forthcoming cover story titled "Too Big For His Blue Jeans?") was told: "I'll be damned if I feel obliged to defend myself, but I am sick to death of being thought of as a blue-jeaned slobbermouth and I am sick to death of having people come up to say hello and then just stand there expecting you to throw a raccoon at them. I have always hated the fact that I have been obliged to conform. I agree that no man is an island, but I also feel that conformity breeds mediocrity. I think this country needs, in addition to a good five-cent cigar, a little five-cent investment in tolerance for the expression of individuality.

"When I came to Hollywood I had a rather precious and coddled attitude about my own integrity. It was stupid of me to resist so directly the prejudice that money is right. But just because the big shots were nice to me, I saw no reason to overlook what they did to others and to ignore the fact that they normally behave with the hostility of ants at a picnic. The marvelous thing about Hollywood is that these people are recognized as sort of the norm, while I am the flip. These gnarled and twisted personalities see no other way to live except on a pedestal of malicious gossip and rumor to be laid on the ears of unsuspecting people who believe them.

"Well, I really did feel I have every right in the world to resist the stupid protocol of turning my private life into the kind of running serial you find on bubble-gum wrappers. You can't just take sensitive parts of yourself and splatter them around like so much popcorn butter."

His new mood led Marlon—for a time—to seek less transitory relationships with women. At a New York theatrical party hosted by Stella Adler, he met a young (nineteen), petite (5 feet 1 inch), black-eyed, dark-skinned girl, Josanne-Mariana Berenger, the stepdaughter of a French fisherman. Mlle. Berenger moved in with Marlon for several months. When she could no longer tolerate his periods of depression, she retreated to her home in Bandol near the French Riviera. Marlon arranged to meet her in Paris, from whence they drove to Bandol where Marlon formally petitioned her stepfather for her hand and called a press conference to announce marriage for the following year. Docking in New York in October 1954, the couple reaffirmed their engagement to the press ("This is not just a publicity stunt!"), then separated. Reporters uncovered Mlle. Berenger's "past": at seventeen she had been a nude model for the painter Moïse Kisling. A Paris department store displayed the Kisling nudes, and the French delighted in ogling the charms of Marlon's fiancée. The store insisted it was rejecting Marlon's offer to purchase the paintings "at any price."

Josanne followed Marlon's trail to Hollywood, failed to obtain an acting job, and posed nude for some girlie magazines. For over a year she insisted that marriage was imminent.

Then she abandoned the pretense and drifted back to France. When I asked Marlon about her, he answered only: "She had bad breath."

Elia Kazan had been working to secure Marlon's services for *East of Eden*. Marlon's commitment to Fox, however, precluded his participation. Kazan turned reluctantly to James Dean, a Brando surrogate. Marlon had met Dean four years earlier when the latter was studying at the Actors Studio. Dean, seven years younger than Marlon, idolized him as a model for both his acting style and his personal behavior. A bisexual, Dean defended his practice casually: "Why should I go through life with one hand tied behind my back?" In *Rebel without a Cause*, Dean sulked, indulged in Mr. Magoo imitations (his costar was Jim Backus), and played his bongo drums in his dressing room instead of answering set calls. Marlon was more embarrassed than flattered by such adoration ("Dean is a lost boy trying to find himself") and may have resented the threat of competition. He told me he had refused to answer the telephone whenever Dean called (which was frequent) or had maintained—with his falsetto voice— that "Mr. Brando is not at home."

Dean finally cornered Marlon at a Hollywood party given by Ella Logan for Sammy Davis, Jr. Dean appeared in a leather jacket and motorcycle helmet, Marlon in a dark suit and tie—"probably to show me up," muttered Dean. He also complained to Sammy Davis that Marlon had been avoiding him. Marlon recommended that he consult a psychiatrist. Instead, on September 30, 1955, Dean slammed his silver-gray Porsche, a car he had dubbed "the little bastard," into another automobile on a highway near Paso Robles, California. He died as he had lived: at eighty miles per hour. Two young German girls committed suicide, leaving the message that "a world without Jimmy Dean isn't worth living in."

After *Desirée*, Marlon again declared for retirement. There would be no time for acting in his schedule of macaronic pursuits. His retraction came a week later. "I don't always feel the same way two days running," he admitted. "I get excited about something, but it never lasts more than seven minutes. Seven minutes exactly. That's my limit. I never know why I get up in the morning."

Rather than retiring he began seeking a lighter vehicle for his next picture and found it in Samuel Goldwyn's *Guys and Dolls*, a musical interspersed with contrived Runyonesque dialogue. "I'm tired of the 'screamer' parts I've done before," he said, "of being the guy sitting on a 'hot dime.' I'm fed up with emoting in heavy vein. It's nice to have a part where I don't have to slap someone across the face with an alligator. I've never been a wrong guy but I have been adolescent in behavior. O.K., so I was one-quarter sandpiper and three-quarters bamboozler. Well, now I've grown up. I'm not so quick with the squirt gun anymore. I've got a tuxedo now and I wear gabardine instead of denim. So what happens? People tell me I've gone Hollywood and I am a swell fellow. I've got a house, and I live like a normal human being, and I want to be considered that. I have to live down that 'slob' tag some writers hung on me."

Marlon persevered through daily singing and dancing lessons. But his voice never attained a lyrical quality. He described it himself as "the wail of a bagpipe oozing through a pile of wet tissue." A critic reviewing the musical in *The New Yorker* wrote that he sang "through a rather unyielding set of sinuses." Marlow vowed, "Never another musical."

Frank Sinatra, playing the role of Nathan Detroit to Marlon's Sky Masterson (and miffed with Marlon because of litigation over the *Waterfront* assignment), declined, on professional grounds, to appraise Marlon's singing. Privately, he was heard to mutter about "the mating call of a yak in heat" and stage-whispered that his costar was "the most overrated actor in the world." He became further annoyed with Marlon over the interminable retakes required by Marlon's inattentiveness, or "deliberate screwing around" as Sinatra phrased it. Throughout the production each actor vied to upstage the other before the cameras; most observers declared Marlon an easy victor. Marlon extended a peace pipe by a gesture of professional acknowledgment. "Frank," he said, "I'm new at this musical racket. So I'd appreciate it if we could rehearse together—whenever you'd like and at your convenience." Sinatra was not to be mollified by gestures. "Look, Brando," he snarled, "don't give me that Method-actor shit." The two men remained on cold terms thereafter.

After speaking with several members of the *Guys and Dolls* cast, I had brought my retrospective of Marlon Brando up to date. If I had truly expected to arrive at cohesive conclusions to explain his acting genius, his troubled mentality, or his arrant and antisocial public acts, I could not claim such an insight. The evidence was too scattered and too inconsistent. And there is a tendency for the anecdotal trees to obscure the essence of the forest. I despaired, even then, of ever fathoming a personality of such curved surfaces and psychedelic colors. I thought of Freud's study of Leonardo da Vinci. Having demonstrated that da Vinci's paintings sprang from his childhood fixations, Freud concluded that his genius, whatever the source, was so superior that before it one could only rejoice. Until our personal conflicts intervened, that was the attitude I strove for toward Marlon.

In 1955, as I was preparing for my first trip to America, Marlon formed his own film production company, Pennebaker Productions (after his mother's maiden name). Other superstars had shown that personally controlled corporations could command a greater percentage of a film's profits and also could benefit from tax regulations. Marlon installed his father as president and treasurer of Pennebaker and retained for himself the title of first vice-president.

As the motive force behind the company, Marlon took charge of planning and creating. The search for scripts, actors, and financing involved meetings with producers, writers, bankers, and studio executives. Pennebaker's offices were rented from the Paramount management. It was the promotion of Pennebaker's interests that brought Marlon to Paramount Studio one morning in October. It was there he encountered his leading lady from *On the Waterfront*, Eva Marie Saint, who was on the lot filming *That Certain Feeling*, and invited her to lunch in the commissary.

And it was there, while nibbling at her nape, that his eyes turned to a nearby table, and he mumbled, "Who is that good-looking broad in the red sari?"

# Three

**M**arlon arrived for our first date dressed as an ice-cream peddler: white polo shirt, white pants, white socks, and white sneakers. It was my first view of him beyond our brief encounter in the Paramount commissary, and my first opportunity to appraise him freely. With his broad shoulders and thick, sinewy arms, he might have been a middleweight prizefighter. He balanced a steatopygous form on squat, sturdy legs and moved with a lissome stride that conveyed a forceful yet feminine grace. He seemed to tower above his own height. The jutting forehead, broken nose, and softened jawline framed an entire gallery of faces. His features could—somehow—have belonged to anyone or to no one else; they were, at once, both unique and universal.

As chaperone, Marlon had chosen his friend and Pennebaker associate, George Englund; George was to become a producer of films (*The Ugly American; Shoes of the Fisherman*) and, with Cloris Leachman, four children. The three of us drove to a lobster restaurant whose dimly lit interior ensured the food from visual inspection. Only Marlon's canescent attire was distinguishable.

He questioned me about India. I questioned him about

America. George Englund communed with his lobster. Having yet no associations with the name Marlon Brando, I asked what professional interests he had. He told me he was well known as the author of "Twinkle, Twinkle, Little Star."

Our date ended early—I was pressed by an early call the next morning. On *The Mountain* set, Spencer Tracy asked if I had enjoyed myself the previous evening with Marlon Brando; he had read a notice of it in a Hollywood tabloid. Thus I learned that Marlon Brando was probably the most publicized actor in America, that he had starred in eight motion pictures and on the Broadway stage, and that anyone seen with him became an immediate candidate for notoriety.

I was so embarrassed by this discovery that I couldn't agree to have dinner with him again. When he called for dates, I was reduced to stammering refusals. Almost two months passed before our second date (the end of 1955). Marlon had flown to New York in an unavailing attempt to develop a Pennebaker property. When he called after returning, we began meeting for dinner and an occasional movie. Rather than feeling annoyed, Marlon was piqued by my unfamiliarity with his name. In his own devotion to nonconformity, he is drawn to anyone who turns at a different angle.

I went to bed with Marlon mostly out of curiosity. His seduction technique showed all the subtlety of a guillotine. We were watching television one evening in my apartment; abruptly, he picked me up and carried me into the bedroom. When I asked if he had rape in mind, he answered, "Rape is just assault with a friendly weapon."

Marlon's pattern of lovemaking resembled a well-rehearsed, polished performance. He imparts a selfish type of sex, wanting warmth and naturalness. His scale of emotions lacks the grace notes. Physically, Marlon is not well appointed. He screens that deficiency by undue devotion to his sex organ. "My noble tool," he characterizes it with some puffery.

I had been forewarned that Marlon had engaged in "all kinds of sex with all kinds of people." Marlon himself had told me, "I'll try anything twice." I was unaware at that time—my naïveté was impressive—that intercourse was conducted in other than the "missionary" position. A few weeks after we became lovers, Marlon asked if I had an aversion to any "offbeat" sexual practices. Without a clue for guidance, I acquiesced blankly; the desire to please a lover could not, I felt, be an errant trait. But the tantalizing premise of this scenario had no climax. Having raised the specter of rituals known only to the Kinsey researchers, Marlon never pursued its exorcism. With me, at least, his sexual appetites ran to unseasoned fare.

Once begun, the self-momentum of our affair carried it forward. I couldn't escape a sense of insecurity both in our intimacies and our secular activities. Marlon never phoned in advance of materializing on my doorstep, often at three o'clock in the morning. He rarely acknowledged the prefatory niceties of courtship (candy, flowers). After making love he could vanish without a word. That mysterious affluvium that envelops two lovers never thickened beyond a thin mist.

Appearing in public with Marlon Brando subjects one to the whimsies of the faithful Brandoloters. Some wanted to "touch the girl who touches Marlon." Others, more aggressive, stole gloves and handkerchiefs as souvenirs. One middle-aged matron from the Midwest shadowed me into the ladies' room in pursuit of my autograph. While I was seated, *flagrante delicto*, she nonchalantly passed her book and pencil under the cubicle door.

In Marlon's presence, I noted, many ordinary people frequently behaved with an extravagance quite foreign to their basic natures. Some swooned, some acted silly, embarrassed, tongue-tied, or—worse—determined to demonstrate their equality by accosting him rudely. It illustrates, I suppose, the "movie-star" syndrome. Perhaps the phenomenon began when the word "star" was coined. Who has not wished upon a star?

After finishing *The Mountain*, I was signed for *Battle Hymn* in January 1956 opposite Rock Hudson, on an MGM loan-out to Universal..This opportunity came at a propitious moment since I was remaining in the United States under the suspended sword of a temporary work permit.

Rock Hudson evinced an unassuming—almost diffident—demeanor. He accepted direction with grace, was prompt, prepared, and cooperative on the set. Away from the cameras, he was courteous but reserved. When I learned of his confused personal problems, I felt a sense of pathos, as if he were burdened with that cross unwillingly.

I met his wife Phyllis when she visited the *Battle Hymn* set; a small, quiet woman whose mannerisms seemed a mirror-image of her husband's, Phyllis Hudson was also in the throes of a personal crisis. We became friendly in short span, and she confided that she was consulting a psychologist regarding the stunted turn of her marital life. When Rock was filming *A Farewell to Arms,* I was a guest at their beach home in Santa Monica. Phyllis at that time suspected and accused her husband of peculiar infidelities; the marriage was close to dissolution. They were divorced shortly thereafter.

The story line of *Battle Hymn* centered on a group of Korean orphans who were to be rescued from enemy bombardment. One of the youngsters, who had been sent from an orphanage in Korea to Nogales, Arizona, the picture's location, was a sad-faced, introverted boy named Kwan Yung. Although a bright child, he was slow to respond, never smiled, and remained aloof from the other children. I fell in love with him at our first contact. By the completion of the filming I had broken through his psychological curtain to the vulnerable seven-year-old behind it. If American laws had then permitted it, I would have adopted him as my legal son.

After the picture Kwan Yung and the other orphans were sent back to Korea. There, he escaped from his guardians and attempted to board a plane for America where he believed I was waiting for him. He was found after three days and returned to the orphanage.

What proficiency I had acquired as an actress was largely creditable to Spencer Tracy. It was not so much the wisdom of his advice ("Just learn your lines and try not to bump into the furniture") but his willingness to perform as father-confessor and his exhortations whenever he felt I was succumbing to lower standards that bolstered me professionally and personally. Spence's three maxims for the successful actor were one: "Listen and relate to your fellow actors; don't worry about emoting—listening is more important"; two: "Be professional; never relax and forget your professionalism"; and three: "Never go to a studio doctor."

A violation of rule three, Spencer insisted, was responsible for much of Judy Garland's misfortune. A studio doctor, more concerned with film schedules than his patient's mental balance, prescribed amphetamines for her and launched a long history of addiction.

I once transgressed rule two by arriving late and unrepentant on the set. I had been lunching with Pearl Bailey and had forgotten a one o'clock call. "The trick is to put them on the defensive," was Pearl's prescription. "Always be furious before they can be furious—especially when you're wrong." I returned to the set raging and deceived everyone except Spence. He administered a verbal and physical spanking; that ended my apprenticeship as a prima donna.

(Years later, I visited Spencer while he was working on a picture opposite an actor who, mimicking the Marlon Brando-Stanislavski style of acting, was haranguing the director about his role. "What is my motivation for walking through that door?" the man asked. Spencer's Irish bile bubbled over: "Because you're fucking well getting paid for it—that's why!" he bellowed.)

While I was engaged with *Battle Hymn*, Marlon left for Japan where, in February, he began his role of Sakini, the Oriental houseboy, in *The Teahouse of the August Moon*. Producer Jack Cummings, a nephew of Louie B. Mayer, had signed Marlon by promising a "message" film and the right to select his director. Marlon had become intrigued with Oriental culture, and the picture's theme—the futility of attempted Americanization of occupied lands—posed a telling allure. As director he designated fellow MCA client Daniel Mann (*Come Back Little Sheba; The Rose Tattoo*).

Sakini was conceived as a fey, whimsical character, and that conception—portrayed by David Wayne on Broadway—had gained the play a Pulitzer Prize. In the motion-picture version, Marlon played him, as Bosley Crowther wrote in the *New York Times*, "too elaborate, too consciously cute. His Sakini is less a charming rascal than a calculated clown." Physically overwhelming for the part, Marlon immediately plunged into "Dr. Brando's liquid diet" (two straight Martinis for dinner, one for lunch, and a pimentoless olive for breakfast) and soon shed thirty-five pounds from his normal 175-pound weight. He also plunged into an intensive course covering both the Japanese language and "Japlish," the Japanese-filtered English that has almost gained the status of a dialect. Production was delayed until he had achieved a linguistic proficiency that satisfied his standards. As ever, Marlon's accommodation was not to management but to his own artistic integrity.

Between takes on the picture, Marlon isolated himself from other cast members. He remained in his hotel room in Nara (a small town of shrines and temples that furnished most of the location sites for *Teahouse*) reading Buddha, Confucius, and Lao-tzu; he continued reading during the one-and-one-half-hour makeup sessions (taped eyelids, rubber tear ducts, brown contact lenses over his blue-gray eyes, and a black straw wig) required each morning to transmogrify a Nebraska cosmopolite into an Okinawan villager. He left his hotel room and the set only to discourse on economics, Asian power politics, and Japanese sovereignty to groups of appropriately inscrutable Japanese businessmen assembled by a press agent. Marlon told me he lectured in Japanese. I'm not sure I believed it. I wonder if his audience believed it. But his simulated Japanese-accented English persisted for several months beyond its occupational necessity. "Rots of ruck" became his conversational sign off.

Marlon invited his sister Tiddy and his great-aunt June Beach to visit Japan at his expense. Aunt June, a freewheeling spirit then seventy-two years old, had never traveled outside the United States, and Marlon considerately undertook to broaden her theatre. Tiddy was enlisted as traveling companion and aunt-keeper.

Aunt June needed a keeper. She took umbrage at the male-oriented traditions she observed in Japan and resolved, like Carrie Nation, to hack a path to freedom. Japanese bathing customs became her special target. The *Toroku Ofuro*, a combination Turkish bath and (often sexual) massage parlor catering, of course, only to men, in 1956 rarely knew a *gaijin* to seek its pleasures. The presence of an elderly female Caucasian clamoring for admission unnerved many a Turkish-bath devotee as Aunt June launched nightly forays against the institution in which she could not participate. Police were summoned to remove the protesting Aunt June from sacrosanct premises, and bathhouse operators within range of her hotel organized a warning network to alert themselves to her approach.

Rebuffed on this front, Aunt June assaulted the custom of communal bathing. The rules for this practice are rigid: decorous behavior; disrobement in private; soaping and rinsing *before* immersing; and nonchalant acceptance of nudity (peripheral vision is called upon to observe anatomical structures of interest). Aunt June charged into the main bathing room, kicked and wriggled her way out of her clothes, and lathered herself in view of the other bathers who, with mounting apprehension, were finding difficulty in feigning nonchalance. Then, dripping soapsuds, with a shriek of "Geronimo," she hurled her seventy-two-year-old body into the steaming water.

In addition to the embarrassments of Aunt June, other troubles were besetting Marlon and the production schedule. Marlon and Glenn Ford discovered their common ground—a mutual detestation. They continually vied to upstage each other before the camera, thereby reducing their scenes to farce. "He was always stomping about in a huff," Marlon complained to me later, "he had a habit of waving his arms like a chicken wing." Director Mann was forced to admonish both actors for behaving like contentious children. The enmity between them continued; Glenn Ford yet resists a social or professional relationship with Marlon or anyone close to him.

Midway through May, Louie Calhern died. (His character, the bumbling American Colonel Purdy, was assumed by Paul Ford who had acted the part on Broadway.) Calhern's death was not unexpected; he had been drinking himself to oblivion. Marlon wrote: "Anna, I just learned that Louie Calhern died [he had played the title role of *Julius Caesar* to Marlon's Marc Antony]—I don't know what to think. Perhaps it's just as well; he was so unhappy. He went very quickly without any pain, in his sleep. His wife left him a short while ago and he had no family that he loved he was an alcoholic and terribly lonely. I don't think that he wanted to live I think he was half hoping that he would die. He was a very kindly man and we will miss him." At the funeral mass Marlon could hardly restrain himself from giggling. "I had the feeling that Louie was lying there enjoying it all," he said. "I half-expected him to sit up and drink a toast to the solemn-looking group around the casket."

Weather also hampered the production. The annual rainy season in Japan caught the film's executives unawares, and, after four months of frustrations and mishaps, the *Teahouse* set was transplanted to Hollywood early in June. Less than one-half the final footage had been realized.

Asia had left an indelible impression on Marlon's mind. America seemed to diminish by comparison. "Of all the countries in the world that suffer from backwardness and ignorance, America is first," he told a Japanese reporter. "[The Asians] don't strive for success the way we do," he said later. "They consider the moral development of the inner man equally important." He announced, upon leaving Japan, that he would return for a picture extolling the United Nations, one that would also explain Asia to his countrymen: "Americans don't even begin to understand the people of Asia. The average American couldn't tell you even three of the five main bodies of land that comprise Indonesia, what the capital is, what the native attitude to the Dutch is. . . . American prestige is dwindling among the free countries of Asia while the great masses of China and Russia are waiting to gobble them up. Our understanding of Asians will never improve until we get out of the habit of thinking of the people as short, spindly-legged, buck-teethed little people with strange customs."

While Marlon was in Japan, my social life was restricted to a few close friends. Spencer Tracy escorted me to dinners, to explorations of Los Angeles, on bicycle jaunts (he puffing and pedaling, I perched on the handlebars), and on long walks from his home in the West Hollywood hills (the previous residence of George Cukor). During our walks we discussed the nuances of Eastern and Western philosophies and exchanged metaphysical speculations. Spencer was a Roman Catholic—not an unquestioning votary but nonetheless devout. His father had urged him to the priesthood and predicted he would fail as an actor: "Can you imagine Spencer as a matinee idol?" Spence would usher me to Sunday morning mass where I bobbed up and down out of sync with the other parishioners. (My religious training at the Kurseong convent was both cursory and forgotten.) After mass Spencer would often repair to the Riviera Country Club for a chukker or two of polo, his favorite sport. He was quite perturbed when, after two near-injurious falls, the studio's protests relegated him to the sidelines.

I was surprised to discover that Spencer found life exceptionally difficult. That his son John was born deaf likely colored his vision. Some distant echo in his Irish ancestry survived to haunt his inner ear with leprechaunlike perversity. Perhaps to overcome this echo, he became an advocate of pure concentration in his approach to life and to his profession. "Concentrate, don't embroider," he would thunder at a costar he felt to be straying from the essence of his role.

Spencer was an actor's actor. Nominated for Best Actor nine times (the most ever), he won twice. He accepted his acting talents without pretensions and, consequently, counted more fans among actors than could any other film star. Yet he somehow felt uncomfortable with acting—as if he were fated for another calling. "It's not a responsible activity for a mature man," he told me during one stroll. In earlier years, he admitted, he had been thoroughly unprofessional. It was Katie Hepburn who had stoppered his drinking bouts and convinced him that acting was a serious profession, that through the character he played he could speak to the world. (I had met Miss Hepburn when she visited Spence on the set of *The Mountain*. She would arrange for the script girl to chaperone Spence lest he filch a few drops of alcohol.) Still, Spence maintained: "I'm only a middleman—a conductor—who takes the words and directions of others and translates them to film." This ingenuous manner often misled the imperceptive. Because he never used makeup for deception and never changed his accent, he was accused by critics of always playing himself. "Who the hell do they want me to play?" he complained.

Late in the spring I began preproduction work—wardrobe fittings, makeup tests, preliminary rehearsals—on *Ten Thousand Bedrooms* with Dean Martin, his first film after the breakup with Jerry Lewis; it was a disaster. (I never saw Mr. Martin at this time; his acting regimen excluded rehearsals.)

Because the film was scheduled for shooting in Italy, its participants were subjected to a medical examination by the insurance company. Abnormal signs were detected, and I entered Mount Sinai Hospital for a month of diagnostic tests. It was found that I was seriously infected by pulmonary tuberculosis.

Blood-specked sputum, coughing spells, and shortness of breath are the symptoms of "galloping consumption," as we called TB in India. In my mind I regarded it as a social disease; I felt shamed and remained out of communication with friends rather than admit my affliction. I confessed to Marlon only when I was removed to the City of Hope Hospital, a primarily terminal facility.

For the next three months I remained bedridden and over another four months I was permitted only weekend outings. Throughout this period Marlon grew more solicitous as my illness grew more serious. When I was on the critical list, his daily visits provided the succor, the emotional sustenance without which I would probably have succumbed. When I passed the critical phase, he arranged for a steady supply of books, flowers, candy, games, dolls, and amusements to lighten the weight of time. Marlon invaded the hospital. He set up a screen and projector and showed 16mm prints of old movies. (*Singing in the Rain* appeared to be his favorite.) He first badgered the nurses, then subverted them with ice cream, importuned the doctors, and commissioned himself as my personal quartermaster. Whatever might ease the pain, the fear, or the boredom materialized at his bidding. To the extent that our love mirrored an emotional bond, that love was planted, cultivated, and harvested during my confinement.

I loathe hospitals—the smell of disinfectant, the white-coated sentinels, the condescension, the smug and minatory prescriptions, the ambience of thanatosis. Even from the outside they depress me. I think of Pablo Neruda's line about being "pushed into hospitals where bones stick out the windows."

Seeking to shield its "celebrity patients" from observation, the hospital administration installed them in one wing of the surgical ward. This ward also accommodated long-term patients, many of whom had been haunting the corridors for twenty-five to thirty years. The sight of them, resigned, hopeless, hollow, pressed further on my despondency. Across from my room ran the special elevator to the basement morgue. When the elevator doors opened, I could see the shrouded bodies on their final descent.

A strange hierarchy of diseases governed social deportment in the surgical ward. Patients recuperating from lung surgery—with open drain flaps—were shunned as untouchables. Those with leukemia or carcinoma were the Brahmins of the ward, superior to those with less fatal afflictions, their class identified by striped flannel pajamas and monogrammed silk robes with tasseled cords. They would politely withdraw from the presence of a tubercular patient, disquieted over the possibility of contagion.

Visitors were infrequent. Friends and relatives accepted the judgment already passed on those who had had the ill grace to contract a distasteful disease. Were the patient as worthy as everyone else, would he have been fated for such an institution?

The prognostication, once the lethal course of the consumption had been thwarted, indicated an agonizing five-year convalescent process. That I was discharged after seven months, I credit Marlon's ministrations and the encouragement of a Negro named Charles who worked as a mortician in the hospital basement. Charles (I never learned his last name) had evolved a private philosophy that combined elements of Zen Buddhism, Norman Vincent Peale, and psychokinesis. Each day he would stop by my room to deliver discourses on conquering physiologic disease through mental energies. Strangely, his exhortations implanted an intangible animation within me that presaged recuperation. "Concentrate, concentrate," he would chant. "Mahaprajnaparamita! You can overcome. You can beat it, mon." I don't know if his effect was therapeutic or hypnotic but it helped in combating the potentially deadly depression.

I was particularly fortunate in having INH and PAS compounds available. (The City of Hope Hospital is in the forefront of tuberculosis research.) Prior to the discovery of these drugs in the mid-1950s, the incidence of death from TB was considerably higher.

The INH compound contains a monoaminoxidase inhibitor that, as a side effect, can stimulate sexual appetite. Other TB patients felt this stimulation, and some gratified it by inviting husbands, boyfriends, or attendants into their beds. Sex acts also took place in the supply rooms, the lavatories, and on the grounds. Hospital officials, aware of the situation, circulated a bulletin warning that sex in the sanatarium would bring down administrative wrath. As a prophylactic measure, a dense clump of camellia bushes near the wards was sheared. One patient thereupon posted a poem titled "Ode to Bush 13."

My few visitors were required to wear a surgical mask and gown when entering my room. Marlon offered no objection to this imposition on his freedom. Sometimes he would drive to the hospital direct from the *Teahouse* set, still in full makeup. (Shooting on *Teahouse* continued on the MGM lot through June and into July.) I was then confronted by the spectacle of an eastern Dr. Kildare as Marlon's Orientalized eyes squinted at me while he mumbled through the mask his "Japanese doctor" routine: "Herro, herro. I am Doctor Meshuggener Moto. Don't raff. I don't ordinariry make house cawrs." Any exertion was painful—and laughing exhausted me. But Marlon's efforts deserved appreciation, and I couldn't disappoint him. Even when he wiped off the makeup, he couldn't wipe off the part.

It was my illness, of course, that elicited Marlon's empathy. Yet, given that circumstance, the depth of his sensitivity was extraordinary. At parties I had heard him claim that "if I go into a room where there are a hundred people, and one of them doesn't like me, I'll know it, and I have to get out of there." I had never believed it, but there was no gainsaying his devotion.

Our sympathetic bond stimulated communion in other spheres. Marlon admitted to me his trepidations over critical moments in his career, his ambitions beyond acting, his ambivalent feelings toward women, his family conflicts and hatreds, his concept of pleasure without guilt. From my well of depression I couldn't command a full view of Marlon's philosophy but I remember the alternating advocacies of masochism and hedonism that startled Marlon himself as he listened to his own contrasting expressions. Although I was never so close to Marlon as when I was hospitalized, I never realized so starkly the pull of his internal conflicts. For dissimilar but dependent reasons, we had dismantled the psychological defenses between us.

Marlon's mind, I learned during our talks, is a museum of the miscellaneous, an uncataloged collection of captured, stuffed, and embalmed notions. Without a formal education and without a cohesive methodology, Marlon could never formulate a consistent channel for his life, his beliefs, his designs. Without a knowledge of fundamentals to moor his ideas, he lost them to every stirring breeze. His coupling to the natural world was philosophical rather than theological—as derived from René Dubois, Teilhard de Chardin, and others whom he had read without comprehension. Yet his approach to philosophy epitomized the antithesis of philosophy. Wittgenstein paralleled the philosopher's craft with the construction of a jigsaw puzzle: it requires artful rearrangement and manipulation of the pieces, not brute force. Marlon could blithely trim bits of knowledge to fit his conceived pattern; he could juxtapose two pieces of the puzzle that bore no relation to each other; he could treat each piece independently of its context.

My personal philosophical position has shifted with the various crises in my life. At this time, when tuberculosis had ravaged my physical and emotional strength, when it had eroded my grip on life, I found solace in the Buddhist reassurances of continuity—in samsara, the wheel of rebirth or reincarnation. In both major Buddhist schools of thought, the Theravada and the Mahayana, the wheel is central to the concept of rebirth and the journey toward Nirvana. I envisioned myself as a point on the wheel, rising and falling, tracing cycloids to the infinite end/beginning that releases me from the wheel. The most poetic imagery of rebirth that I have read occurs in the *Brihad-Aranyaka Upanishad*: "Even as the caterpillar, when coming to the end of a blade of grass, reaches out to another blade of grass and draws itself over to it, in the same way the Soul, leaving the body and unwisdom behind, reaches out to another body and draws itself over to it."

I could never persuade Marlon to a more than perfunctory study of Buddhist philosophy. His closest approximation came through his fancy for the Occidentalized Zen Buddhism promoted by Alan Watts and others. Marlon had attended Watts's lectures and purported to have attained a satorilike insight into the nature of his own being. With its more practical and personal emphasis, Zen is more suited to Marlon's personality. Where Buddhism reflects the analytic subtleties and dazzling imagery of the Indians, Zen presents the remnants of Buddhist thought filtered through the earthy, plodding Chinese psychology. For me, the vastly greater conceptual span of Buddhism warrants its exploration.

Philosophical differences between Marlon and me were not merely academic; they could erupt into veritable explosions. The Buddhism versus Zen Buddhism disagreement found its outlet on our marriage day when Marlon refused Buddhist rites, favoring the ritual affected by a local Zen cult. To avoid conflict, we had to forgo both ceremonies.

Another difference in our viewpoints concerned children. I had hoped that Marlon's influence could rescue Kwan Yung, the Korean orphan I had met on the *Battle Hymn* location, and could arrange, somehow, for an adoption. However, Marlon was opposed to adoption—"on principle," he said. He also objected to the boy's race. "A Korean kid with an Indian mother and a Caucasian father wouldn't know his ass from his aardvark" was Marlon's conclusion.

Oddly, in our wide-ranging hospital discourses, we rarely broached the subject of acting. I drew from him a brief comparison of his stage and screen performance. "True acting," he emphasized to me, "is like making love to the audience. You can do it on the stage. In front of the camera, it's like masturbation." In general he was reticent—even obstinate— about revealing his emotions toward the occupation that had enriched him and his audiences. The acting profession, for Marlon, was treated like an elderly aunt who had fashioned the family fortune with the proceeds from a chain of brothels.

Without formal training as an actress, I was unfamiliar—beyond casual reading—with the Method, as derived from Stanislavski's teachings and as generally applied to the Marlon Brando style of acting. All good actors have a method; I never understood what was gained by capitalizing the "m." Elia Kazan donated a sensible definition: "Oversimplified, it is a rational method to turn on the irrational. It is a way to give the actor a way to turn on his instincts."

My own career was forgotten. I had been replaced by Anna Maria Alberghetti in *Ten Thousand Bedrooms* although I remained on salary from MGM (a practical courtesy that Spencer had maneuvered through the studio). A role in *Ben Hur* was before the house. It was soon conferred on another actress. From a hospital bed the future loomed too murky to distinguish such concrete features as acting opportunities.

I was, in the event, unable to cope with the daily agonies that actors are prone to: the uncertainty of livelihood, the embarrassment and cruelty of personal rejection, the questionable qualities of most roles, the superficiality and ignorance of critical judgments, the physical and mental impairment from the acting process itself. I have only discouraged those aspirants to the profession who sought my advice. The person destined for success in this field needs no outside counsel. Marlon neither encouraged nor deprecated my career nor did he enlighten me in the offices of techniques of acting. The faintest breath of competition could unfurl the banner of his ego. Later, I came to perceive that actors hate and envy other actors. That's why they defend each other so passionately.

When competition was excluded, Marlon could be gracious. My physician, Dr. Toping, noting Marlon's frequent attendance, asked if I would prevail upon him to narrate a documentary dramatizing the medical progress at the City of Hope Hospital. Marlon was delighted to contribute his talents to those concerned with my welfare. He provided the narration and proffered artistic advice gratuitously.

When Marlon was away he would write often and would dispatch his friends to the hospital with books, art supplies, and cheerful words. Larry Durran, Marlon's stand-in, was an occasional visitor, as was Sam Gilman, a Broadway actor who played bit roles in many of Marlon's pictures (beginning with *The Wild One*). A discreet and loyal friend, Sam Gilman was Marlon's close companion for over twenty years.

Mostly, Marlon's letters were filled with reassurances. From New York, where he was pursuing another frustrated Pennebaker venture (a stillborn film project titled *Tiger on a Kite*), he wrote, "The last two times we have talked for me have been illuminating and rewarding. I'll have you blabbering so much I won't be able to stop you."

When the world withheld its cooperation, Marlon reacted with peevish pompousness. A missed flight from New York to Chicago evoked this typical response: "For some reason that at this moment is still incomprehensible to me, we miss our plane. It was probably the fault of that impertinent chauffer we hired, and [Great-Aunt] June's dawdling didn't help matters any. I spoke to the chief of the Airport and demanded that the plane return to the field immediately and he had the nerve to *refuse*—as I live this will cost him his position! I have never been subjected to such disrespect and I shall deal with this properly at another time."

Marlon's introspective nature would usually reassert itself after such outbursts. "My, how pompous I sound to myself sometimes," he wrote. His personality revealed, through the years, more dualities than I could record.

Aunt June had accompanied Marlon on his New York trip, continuing to extend her experiences at Marlon's encouragement and expense. Her antics in Japan, if not forgotten, had, with time, faded from their original vividness. Marlon remained concerned over her mental state. "I don't quite know what to do with June," he worried in one letter. "She's been drinking steadily since we left. On the way to the Airport she insisted upon taking drinks from a bottle she had in her handbag. At one point while trying to disuade her from further drinking she struck me several times. By the time we got to the hotel she was completely drunk and attacked a woman in the elevator and tore off her dress. I never see her act this way before. I went in her room to see how she was and she was in her corset and stockings and walking flirtatiously back and fourth in front of the windows. She had been trying to intice a man accross the court to come to her room. I don't know which is worse, her drinking or her peculiar sex drive. Do other 72 year old women behave like this?"

Since Aunt June lived in Los Angeles (in a one-bedroom apartment shared with a dozen cats), I couldn't avoid an occasional encounter with her as Marlon persisted in his attempts to enlighten his macaronic relative. I don't believe she ever settled into a conventional mold. I heard, unreliably, that she had been expelled from a nudist colony for invading the men's shower facilities. The last time I saw Aunt June was on my wedding day.

As my time in the hospital lengthened, Marlon's attentiveness grew yet more intense. He began bringing with him his mother's possessions—earrings, a broach, her Bible; on one visit he brought the pillow she had died on (two years earlier). These gifts were accompanied by remembrances of his mother—mostly somber, painful remembrances. It was at this time that he told me of urging Carlo Fiore, his friend from the Dramatic Workshop, to seduce his mother when they were living together in New York. He seemed to feel that by absorbing and preserving his sorrows, they could prove beneficial. "Pain makes man think," he said. "Thinking makes man wise. Wisdom makes life endurable." I learned later that the lines were Sakini's in *The Teahouse of the August Moon*.

As flattering as the gifts were Marlon's comparisons of his mother to me. We were both equally kind, gentle, nonaggressive, he declared. We were both filled with love—love to be given and love to be held and treasured. Seemingly forgotten were the episodes of rage, drunkenness, and neglect that littered his childhood. Dodie Brando had become canonized in her son's pantheon of memories.

The culmination of these mother-girl friend fantasies came toward the end of September. Marlon's plane from New York had just landed, and he had taken a taxi from the airport to the hospital. It was late at night, after visiting hours, when he walked into my room accompanied by Carlo Fiore. Marlon had not yet concluded his ice-cream-suit phase; his white clothes shone almost phosphorescently against the glossy hospital walls. He stood alongside my bed awkwardly, obviously

71

nervous, obviously struggling for a speech that had rung true in private rehearsal but now cracked false against the rocks of actuality. He had taken a drink at the airport lounge before riding to the hospital, and his face was flushed. I did not know what to expect. I glanced at Carlo Fiore. He too was apparently unaware of Marlon's intentions.

The words, when released, erupted in pulsating waves: "I wish my mother was alive. . . . I wish she was here to meet you. . . . I'm sure you'd both love each other. . . . You are so much alike." Then came the contradictions: "Yet—it's better that my mother is dead. If she had lived, I could never have loved you. She wouldn't have let me go." This last thought was from a letter by D. H. Lawrence to his wife, Frieda. It was probably part of the prepared speech. "No, I shouldn't say that," Marlon continued. "I loved her. . . . I think I really loved her. . . . I wish I had done more for her when she was alive. I wish she hadn't been an alcoholic all her life." Tears glistened on his cheeks. At first I imagined I was witness to a command performance and that Carlo Fiore was its choreographer. But the tears were genuine. And Carlo was clearly embarrassed.

While the theatrical spirit was certainly in attendance, it was not in absolute control. Abruptly, Marlon exhausted his reflections on his mother. For the first time since he entered the room, he looked at me directly. "I have something important to tell you," he blurted out. "You know my feelings about you. I'd like to marry you."

We had never discussed the subject of marriage. We had never exchanged pledges of commitment. Indeed, I had read in the gossip columns that Marlon and Rita Moreno were a "hot item singeing the skirts of the Hollywood Hills." I had no reason to believe Marlon was not enjoying the companionship of other women nor would I have expected him—or any man—to remain continent during the several months of my hospitalization. The proposal of marriage thus materialized as a sleight-of-hand marvel, more to be applauded than honored. It was delivered with a peculiar epicene detachment as if by a stand-in for the lead actor in a long shot where their features were indistinguishable. Yet it came as no surprise.

Marlon's character had simply taken another leap into the improbable.

I cannot remember my immediate response. I must have assented in some manner—I doubt if I managed more than a nod—for Marlon seemed pleased. He turned to Carlo Fiore and registered a smile of self-satisfaction. Carlo's presence, I realized later, reeked of hermaphroditic scent; the scene offered ample dark speculation for a Sophoclean tragedy. Evidently my role in the drama was that of a bit player whose lines served only to bridge the troughs between the star's orations. His speech ended, Marlon arose, hooked Carlo by the arm, and exited with him, their footsteps clacking down the corridor. I sank back, numbed, as the curtain descended.

In the *Surangama Sutra*, the Lord Buddha speaks unto Ananda: "Suppose there is no light and people are unable to see things, does that mean that they cannot see the darkness? If it is possible to see darkness when it is too dark to see things, it simply means there is no light; it does not mean they cannot see. Supposing, Ananda, they were in the light and could not see the darkness; does that mean, also, that they cannot see?"

Engagement to Marlon Brando signaled little change in our relationship. Marlon continued his visits to the hospital when feasible for him and wrote his ambivalent letters when out of town. He could confide elements of self-distaste: "I just can't stand my hands," he told me during one visit. (His hands are large and strong, masculine but not at all unattractive.) "They look like a cow tromped on them. Now your hands are long and tapering, not bony like most Americans. I admire your feet too." Yet he could speak no more of his love for me. Whenever I raised the matter of our engagement, he sidestepped onto another topic. Always there was a barrier that prevented even the most intimate observer from penetrating the inner sanctum of his mind.

To my annoyance, Marlon sometimes regarded our engagement as a license for a bantering and deprecatory attitude. With great (and childish) delight he would address me as "fat ass." In one letter he elaborated at length on this appellation: "Anna, I am informed that your behind has become gigantic.

Let me tell you how pleased this makes me. I know, because of your sensitive nature, you will find it difficult to allow me to push the wheelbarrow that your behind will rest on, but after a time you will get use to it. I am happily looking forward to the exercise. You know, as I look out across the sea I sometimes think that I see it just above the horizon. But of course that is impossible I'm sure." With equal childishness I retaliated by detailing the nature, dimensions, and properties of his "lard ass." This "game" persisted for years, and, during moments of anger, "fat ass" and "lard ass" epithets were hurled with sharp-edged vehemence.

Games of one fashion or another formed a dedicated if subconscious pastime for Marlon. The "detached observation" game was a particular favorite. He would say or do something designed to provoke a specific response. If that response were not forthcoming, he would figuratively remove himself to a distance and observe the situation through his metaphysical telescope. Consequently his involvement—with men or women—was never sustained, never on an equal footing, never developed beyond the initial impulse. When he sensed the shadow of an emotional yoke closing on him, he would withdraw to his own inner nucleus. I believe Marlon yearned to share himself with another person but that he could not and cannot.

By Thanksgiving Day I was released from the City of Hope Hospital, my tubercular pathology suppressed. It was my second Thanksgiving, a strictly American practice unfamiliar to me before the previous year, and while his story of the Pilgrims and their feast with the (American) Indians was remote to my culture, I had reason to be thankful and joined in the festivities. The occasion was celebrated at the home of Marlon's sister, Jocelyn (Tiddy), located in Pacific Palisades, an oceanside suburb of Los Angeles. Marlon felt concern over his sister's health and he would encourage me to audit her progress. "I wish you would call Tiddy once in a while," he wrote during a later trip out of the country. "I am worried about her and although there is really nothing to do but sit around and try to keep her warm with faith and love it means an awful lot." Tiddy was then pursuing, with sporadic success, the jackrabbit of an acting career. (She had performed in the 1948 Broadway production of *Mister Roberts,* starring Henry Fonda.)

Also present at the Thanksgiving dinner were Tiddy's husband, Elliot Asinov, her two sons, and a few family friends. Marlon was appointed as the turkey carver. I remember the stuffed turkey, borne in on a silver tray, a visual and pungent incitement to our salivary glands, staked down before Marlon's poised knife and fork, a Dravidian sacrifice by the high priest. I remember watching Marlon cutting into it as if performing a cesarean section. I remember overeating and Marlon's assurance that gluttony is an essential part of Thanksgiving. I remember feeling content.

One week later Marlon presented me with an engagement ring—four clusters of pearls on a platinum band, purchased from La Petite Maison in New York where he had gone to attend the *Teahouse* premiere at Radio City Music Hall. He slipped it onto my little finger after announcing an "important surprise" and asked me to wear it only on that finger and to keep secret the engagement from everyone outside his family—especially from reporters. With another man, such an act might overlay a lack of sincerity or a lack of pride in his fiancée. With Marlon, it was a matter of personal privacy.

I spent my first night free of the hospital at the home of Marlon's maternal aunt, Betty Lindermeyer. Mrs. Lindermeyer lent me a nightgown for the evening since I had discarded all my hospital apparel (and everything else associated with my stay there). I awoke the next morning, shaken by the still vivid recollection of a dream in which Marlon's mother appeared before me. I described her accurately to Mrs. Lindermeyer and learned that I had been sleeping in Dodie Brando's nightgown. It was the only extrasensory experience I ever sustained; it left me uneasy and a bit frightened.

For a short time I moved in with a friend, Ina Berneis, a free-lance photographer, until Marlon found an apartment for me less than a mile from his rented home in West Hollywood. He selected a spacious two-story flat that composed one part of a six-unit complex designed in the late-Rudolph Valentino architectural style popular in the mid-thirties: arched passageways, panduriform swimming pool, seragliolike trappings, and a central courtyard garden overplanted with menacing, exotic flora that may have been related to the Venus flytrap. I learned shortly that the flat across the courtyard was occupied by Marlon, Sr. Only once previously had I met Marlon's father; his rude mien and vinegary, bulldog countenance inhibited any possible friendship between us. Marlon often apologized to me for his father's churlish mannerisms.

Brando père and Brando fils were dissimilar in temperament, in appearance, and in their behavior patterns. Marlon, Sr., was taller and heavier than his son, with gray hair and a brooding scowl. The residue of a thousand debaucheries etched his face. From childhood, Marlon remembered his father's blatant woman-chasing and neglect of his wife. "I despise him for what he did to my mother," he told me. An actor who had met both Marlon and his father described them as "just like two bees in a hive—only one is the queen and the other is a drone."

Over the ten months we lived in the same complex, Marlon, Sr., and I probably spoke together no more than a dozen times. Occasionally I could hear his voice across the courtyard raging at Alice Marchak, a young MCA secretary introduced to him by Marlon. Miss Marchak raged back. Once I heard her loudly threatening suicide ("I'm going to slash my wrists"). Marlon rescued his father by engaging her as his personal secretary, a position she has maintained through two wives, innumerable affairs, and the assaults of business and social acquaintances.

During my first weeks back in the world, Marlon often escorted me to dinner and the movies—invariably driving his second car, a used Volkswagen strewn with beer cans, stained hamburger wrappers, and discarded newspaper sheets. Dressed in evening clothes or a silk sari, I never appreciated arriving at a fashionable restaurant or motion-picture premiere and alighting from a mobile garbage can. But Marlon was unperturbed at such scenes; his first car, a white Thunderbird convertible (a gift from Sam Goldwyn for his role in *Guys and Dolls*), was reserved for private occasions behind the public eye. (This two-car fetish is ingrained in Marlon. At present he alternates between a battered old station wagon and a white Mark IV Continental.)

When he was engaged in business out of town, he would solicitously telephone at least once each day. In one instance he called from New York where he was meeting with Stanley Kubrick for preliminary planning of a project that eventually materialized as *One-Eyed Jacks*. He insisted that I join him there, and I flew across the country—only to pace about for two hours at La Guardia airport waiting for him to appear. When we reached his suite at the Plaza Hotel, and he continued to ignore my anger, I grabbed at the nearest object, a bar of soap, and flung it at him (missing widely).

To mollify me, Marlon promised a tour of the remote sideshows of Manhattan. He then took me to Central Park. We hired a hansom cab and clip-clopped along for an hour while I watched the rear end of a horse, and Marlon called out the Latin names of the passing trees. "I'd rather explore the places you used to frequent," I suggested, thinking of his earlier adventures I had surveyed. "Those places are in the past," he said. "There's no way to get there from here."

In December Marlon signed for the role of Major Lloyd Gruver in the Warner Bros. production of *Sayonara*. For more than a month he had vacillated over the project with director Joshua Logan and producer William Goetz; he thought the Michener book frivolous and disparaging of the Japanese. The part was offered, for a time, to Rock Hudson. According to Mr. Logan, Marlon finally agreed to a contract because of his admiration for the director's sensitivity and taste in after-shave lotions. "I like you," Logan quoted Marlon as telling him. "I like the tender way you took the leaves off that plant while we were talking yesterday. I didn't know you were sensitive enough to care for flowers and I didn't know you wore a lemon scent." According to Marlon, he was unimpressed with Logan's achievements (including *South Pacific*, *Mister Roberts*, and *Fanny* on Broadway, *Picnic* and *Bus Stop* on film) but welcomed the opportunity to return to Japan for another "message film." (The James Michener novel *Sayonara* explores American racial prejudice toward the Japanese.) Marlon confided to me his opinion equating Josh Logan to an equine posterior but concluded that "he'll let me re-write the script and he won't give me any trouble on the set." I had met Mr. Logan once before, at Marlon's home, during contract negotiations for *Sayonara*. He had just recovered from a serious nervous breakdown. Although he acquits himself as a charming southern gentleman, a pool of temperament can be sensed below the surface. When it boils over, I understand, it can be as volcanic as that from any prima donna.

Further, Marlon was offered $300,000 plus a percentage of the film's gross revenues. The money was needed since Pennebaker Productions was proving a financial drain, not yet having produced a picture or even a satisfactory script from its hired writers and functionaries on salary.

Several days before Christmas Marlon left Los Angeles, presumably for Japan and the *Sayonara* set. On Christmas Day I attended a party at the home of Peter and Ina Berneis. Friends of Marlon were present and spoke of his being in Japan. While the party was in progress, Marlon telephoned for me. I heard the operator refer to the Coral Sands, a hotel in Honolulu.

"Marlon, what are you doing in Hawaii?"

"Mumble, stutter . . ."

"I don't understand this deception. Why are you in Hawaii?"

"Well . . . mumble, mumble . . . well, then . . . I suppose you might as well come over."

So I did. Marlon, Sr., drove me to the airport where a ticket had been reserved under the name of Joanne O'Callaghan. In Honolulu I squirmed for two hours in the airport lounge before Marlon arrived. I was furious. Beyond the wait, intuition or finely tuned subliminal receptors whispered that he had used the time to deceive me in some way (actually to rid his hotel room of evidence of the previous night's dalliance, so a mutual friend later confided). Driving with him to the Coral Sands Hotel, I sat in silence, fuming. Marlon couldn't ignore the silence: "Why don't you just get it out? You're angry over my being two hours late. Like in New York. Do something. Let it out." He was driving at 75 mph. I turned and slapped him, a fierce whack across his face. He nearly lost control of the car, then stopped it still on the highway. "What did you do that for?" "You asked me to," I said. It was the first time I had hit him (or anyone). It foreshadowed many fights to come.

One week into the new year—1957—Marlon went on to Japan, and I flew back to Los Angeles to fulfill an MGM motion-picture commitment. The picture, an unsophisticated comedy about Navy public relations titled *Don't Go Near the Water*, had me cast opposite Glenn Ford, a pairing that Mr. Ford deemed objectionable. His vendetta with Marlon, begun during the filming of *Teahouse* in Japan, apparently enveloped anyone close to Marlon. He flaunted his dislike for me early in the shooting schedule. In shots with his back to the camera, he would wave his hands in front of my face. In our closeup two-shots, he would whisper obscene limericks in my ear ("There was an old hermit named Dave, . . ."). He never passed up an opportunity to carp at me: "You're reading your lines all wrong. . . . You're making me turn my wrong side to the camera. . . . I warn you—I have casting approval."

A highly competent actor, Mr. Ford enjoyed an advantage over me of twenty years' experience. I drove up to Spencer Tracy's home for consultation and consolation, whichever I could elicit from him. Spencer's advice fixed on a professional level; he tendered little comfort for my bruised sensibilities, believing an emotional response to be the mark of a frivolous actor. He had once told me of meeting George M. Cohan who criticized his performance with "Spencer, you've got to do less." Now he urged, "Underplay! Make the throwaway lines gain by seemingly ignoring them. Underplay—the eye of the camera centers on stillness. Underplay, and you will be the magnet for that eye."

Our next scene together, the following day, found Mr. Ford again prancing about before the cameras. I stood in one spot staring at him. He stopped the shooting twice to shout, "You're spoiling my performance." With Spencer's spirit egging me on, I said, "Mr. Ford, why don't you underplay with me?" That proved the final stroke. "You're out," he screamed. "Out, out, out." He strode off the set. "She's out, I tell you, out, out." I was out. My part was given to Gia Scala, a green-eyed, tempestuous young lady who was to become a close friend.

In Japan Marlon was demonstrating more control over his circumstances than I over mine. At a press conference called upon his arrival in Tokyo, some sixty reporters observed his tongue wedged firmly in his cheek.

"I am so pleased to be back here in Japan because it gives me another opportunity to investigate the influence of Buddhism on Japanese thought, the determining cultural factor."

"Why did you choose to do *Sayonara*, Mr. Brando?"

"This picture strikes very precisely at prejudices that serve to limit our progress toward a peaceful world. Underneath the romance, it attacks prejudices that exist on the part of the Japanese as well as on our part."

"What is your opinion of Mr. Logan?"

"I welcome the invaluable opportunity of working with Joshua Logan, a man who can teach me what to do and what not to do."

These and other statements were featured prominently in the Japanese press, and "Herro, Marron" became the cry of the crowds surrounding his hotel (the Miyako Hotel in Kyoto) and the filming locations straining for a sight of the modern Lieutenant Pinkerton. The love affair was reciprocal. "They kill me," he declared to Truman Capote who had persuaded Marlon to an exclusive interview in his hotel suite. "They really kill me. The kids too. Don't you think they're wonderful, don't you love them—Japanese kids?"

Cho Cho San, in this opera veritable, was Miiko Taka, winner of Warner's "worldwide talent search" for the female lead opposite Marlon Brando. Several well-known actresses—Audrey Hepburn was Logan's nominee—were considered and either rejected or found to be uninterested. My name too was submitted for the part of Hana-ogi, the Japanese dancer; Marlon vetoed my nomination, claiming he wished a "pure" Japanese for the role. (He also vetoed my participation at any level.) Miiko Taka, a Nisei born, raised, and married in Los Angeles, was "pure" racially but thoroughly American by culture. (She had never traveled to Japan.) She was barren of previous acting experience, and Joshua Logan found her exasperating; producer Goetz, on the other hand, found her fascinating and installed her as the picture's costar. After *Sayonara* she performed in one other picture and then retired. (During lunch breaks from filming, she would remove the veneers fitted over her teeth to enhance her on-camera image. The veneers were swept away with the crumbs, thus requiring the technicians to strain through two cans of garbage to recover them.)

Mr. Logan's problems multiplied well beyond those with Miiko Taka's ineptitude. Japanese entrepreneurs and the Japanese government were not cooperating in providing the materials and locations he desired, nor was the U.S. Air Force, which evinced a sensitivity to the portrayal of miscegenation acts involving a U.S. serviceman. Denying the existence of racial bias, Air Force authorities ironically added credence to the theme of Michener's novel.

Mr. Logan's biggest problem on the *Sayonara* set was Marlon. First, Marlon insisted on reversing the planned ending. In the original version the American officer and the Japanese dancer cannot surmount the racial and cultural conflict stirred up by their liaison and soberly bid each other "sayonara." To show that such prejudice could be overcome, Marlon demanded that the lovers should, in conclusion, vow their matrimonial troth—thereby rendering both the title and the logical resolution of the story inoperative. Mr. Logan acquiesced to this questionable revision, whereupon Marlon proceeded to attack the entire script. In his interview with Truman Capote, Marlon complained that his writing efforts were passing unappreciated: "Back in California ... Logan said to me, 'We welcome any suggestions you have, Marlon. Any changes you want to make, you just make them. If there's anything you don't like—why, rewrite it, Marlon, write it your own way.' Rewrite, hell. I rewrote the whole damn script. And now they're going to use maybe eight lines."

For publication, Marlon told Capote: "I give up. I'm going to walk through the part, and that's that. Sometimes I think nobody knows the difference anyway. For the first few days on the set, I tried to act. But then I made an experiment. In this scene I tried.to do everything wrong I could think of. Grimaced and rolled my eyes, put in all kinds of gestures and expressions that had no relation to the part I'm supposed to be playing. What did Logan say? He just said, 'It's wonderful! Print it!' "

In his letters to me, Marlon vented his rage, contempt, and condescension toward Logan in terms he thought too scurrilous for Capote's ears and represented the picture as having "a lot of promise of being a resounding fart in the high winter winds."

The director remained oblivious to his star's feelings. The two men argued vehemently over dialogue, interpretations, and camera angles. But Logan believed that the arguments were conducted between gentlemen with a mutual respect. "Marlon's the most exciting person I've met since Garbo," he gushed. "A genius. But I don't know what he's like. I don't know anything about him."

Like other directors of Marlon's films, Logan missed the essence of the Brando impulse. A member of Marlon's retinue in Japan was drawn by Mr. Capote to disclose a more accurate appraisal: "Marlon always turns against whatever he's working on. Some element of it. Either the script or the director or somebody in the cast. Not always because of anything very rational—just because it seems to comfort him to be dissatisfied, let off steam about something. It's part of his pattern. Take *Sayonara*. A dollar gets you ten he'll develop a hoss on it somewhere along the line. . . . With Marlon you never know from one minute to the next."

Logan several times found himself the victim of a Brando prank. Once Marlon arrived on the set with his right arm in a sling. "I think it's broken," he announced. "The doctor said if I move it, I'll be crippled for life." Logan nearly experienced a coronary seizure. He was vainly attempting to adjust camera angles to hide the sling when Marlon called out, "Too bad I can't move it like this," as he raised his right arm and waved it at the camera. "One more picture with Brando and I'll be an old man," said the harried director.

Joshua Logan was then in the midst of a thirty-year struggle with manic-depression (successfully ended with lithium treatments after psychoanalysis and antidepressant drugs had failed). Yet even through pranks and an extended production schedule, his enthusiasm went undiminished. "I've never worked with such an inventive and creative actor," he persisted. "Whenever he came up with something new, I wanted those creative moments recorded. And a lot of them are in the picture." Marlon obviously thought otherwise. Virtually all his suggested changes were edited out of the final footage. His most effective scene—where as Major Gruver he discovers the bodies of Red Buttons and Miyoshi Umeki (after their double suicide)—was fashioned over his objections. Marlon believed the appropriate reaction should be a violent outburst, smashing the furniture and rending his hair in a display of angst. Mr. Logan wanted no Grand Guignol theatrics. He had Marlon push through a silent crowd of Japanese to behold the bodies of his friends, then stand silently for a moment as if the reality might dissolve with his suspended breathing, and murmur, "Oh, God!" Viewing the rushes, Marlon conceded the dramatic values of Logan's version.

Years afterward, even through the optics of hindsight, Joshua Logan still described his star as "the greatest natural talent of our time, a special sort of man with a special sort of possibilities. He can act anything. His complex is that he thinks everyone wants to put him down. He hates authority. He'll defy anyone with power—producers, directors, writers, politicians. He has only confidence in those who are poor and anonymous."

Off the set in Kyoto Marlon posed, for the most part, his usual anchoritic self. Cast and crew he again treated as part-time lepers. He secluded himself in his Miyako Hotel rooms, reading philosophy and writing scenes for a proposed Pennebaker production (then titled *A Burst of Vermilion*), emerging only for his on-camera chores or for occasional tours of Kyoto with his personal entourage. This group comprised Marlon's father, his aunt, Mrs. Betty Lindermeyer, his chum, Carlo Fiore, who was accorded a brief role (as an Army chaplain) in the film, a secretary, Cecelia Levin, and his personal makeup man, Philip Rhodes.

Marlon, Sr., and Mrs. Lindermeyer were invited to Japan in accordance with Marlon's policy of fostering his relatives' cultural growth, a policy that sometimes led to preposterous encounters—such as that of Aunt June and Japanese bathing rituals the previous year. Aunt June was excluded this time not from embarrassment but because Marlon rotated his family favors.

Marlon's letters reflected his pleasure in his relatives' reactions to Japan and his pleasure in finding harmony and tranquillity in the Japanese culture. Mostly, so he wrote, he remained alone in his hotel suite, preoccupied with his own musings, wandering off occasionally into the psychological underbrush, trying "very hard to demonstrate in daily action what I feel is true and too think and feel correctly," and pondering the pathways of his introspective search.

These thoughts brought to mind a fan letter that Marlon once received from a sixteen-year-old girl. In the final line the girl gushed out her feelings for her screen hero: "Oh, Marlon, I love you because you are so suffisticated." It was a serendipitous insight.

One evening Marlon broke his seclusion and submitted to the widely quoted interview by Truman Capote published in *The New Yorker*. To ensnare his quarry, Capote resorted to the only psychological finesse that could succeed: "I made up stories about what lushes my family were," he admitted, "and, believe me, I made them lurid, until he began to feel sorry for me and told me his to make me feel better. Fair exchange." It was the only substantive interview ever suffered by Marlon, and he regretted it. "I'll beat him to death with a wet noodle," he hollered to a friend. "He got me stoned out of my gourd," Marlon told me later, "straight vodka 'till two in the morning. It ruined my diet. And that pudgy little bastard's got a total recall. Every goddamn word he remembered." Whatever the caloric value of his vodka-laced interview, Marlon's diet had been abandoned with his arrival in Japan. (His extra twenty pounds were visible in the film despite the technical skills of the cameramen.) As for the psychological skin peeled back by the interviewer, Marlon grumbled for several weeks over what he deemed an "unconscionable invasion of privacy." "I told him too much—more than I wanted to." Some critics agreed and berated Capote for inflicting "a hatchet job" on his forthright, trusting, and unsuspecting interviewee (and for reporting but one side of the conversation). Still, I think of Marlon's last words as Capote was leaving: "Sayonara. . . . And listen! Don't pay too much attention to what I say. I don't always feel the same way."

As with others who had exposed a coil of Marlon's inner workings to public view, Truman Capote was placed on Marlon's blacklist—in indelible ink. Marlon wrote him a note accusing him of breaking their friendship, betraying personal confidences, and comparing him with Judas, Benedict Arnold, and Attila the Hun. Oddly, the lines in the note were separated by three-inch gaps, the significance of which is lost in Marlon's subconscious. Capote called it "the longest, most confused letter I ever received."

While Marlon was on location for *Sayonara*, the Hollywood gossip columns were replaying rumors about liaisons with various Oriental beauties (as they had during the *Teahouse* production). I knew most such gossip to be ethereal, and Marlon would never condescend to discuss it, but I was insecure enough to question him on the subject. "Don't believe a goddamn thing you ever read about me," he said later. "Except for occasional pee duty in the chill of the morning, my noble tool wasn't once out of my pants."

More worrisome than the vague hearsay were the tidings that Rita Moreno had flown to Japan in highly publicized pursuit of Marlon. Evidently she materialized at the Miyako Hotel under an escort of photographers. Pictures of her and Marlon were soon available to all news bureaus, she smiling radiantly, Marlon looking discomfited.

Perhaps to reassure me of his loyalty, Marlon dispatched a steady flow of letters and almost daily telephone calls. In one instance, while we were talking (late at night—the Japan-California time difference resulted in midnight conversations on my end), I heard a noise at my downstairs window. "Hang up," Marlon commanded. "I'll phone the police." From Kyoto he then telephoned the West Hollywood sheriff's station to send a squad car to my apartment. Thirty minutes later he was again on the telephone to assure himself of my safety. Only the police were disappointed that no prowler was found; it would have been their first international case.

Toward the end of his stay in Japan, Marlon's sentiment overflowed previous bounds. He wrote lengthy, rambling letters that were curiously childlike and mature at once. He wrote of love, of phantices (sic), of passion and suffering. He despised suffering, he maintained, but felt that he had learned to suffer creatively without trying to resist it. He quoted liberally from several books he had read between takes on the set, Radakrishnare's *Reflections East and West* and Fromm's *Psychology and Religion* among them, and from the very film he was engaged in. Obviously his mood was spiraling ever more inward: he wrote of his concern with "religeous and philosophical questions," of his interpretations of "faith, love, truth, and hatred," and of his need to "test the truth of intelectual hypotothises" (sic).

I had read somewhere that each letter is a model of its author's mind. From Marlon's letters, one image rose sharply into focus: he was floundering in a sea of impressions, reaching out seeking a human hand. I resolved not to let him drown.

*Sayonara* proved to be Marlon's most popular and profitable film until *The Godfather*, grossing well in excess of $10 million. It was nominated for nine Academy Awards—including those for best picture, best screenplay, best actor (Marlon's third nomination), and best director—winning four. Red Buttons and Miyoshi Umeki garnered Oscars for best supporting actor and actress; cinematography and art direction added the other two. Many critics disagreed with the public and the academy members. *Time* magazine dismissed the picture as "a modern version of Madame Butterfly which has gained in social significance but lost its wings—Puccini's music." Marlon Brando "is supposed to be a Southerner—his accent sounds as though it had been strained through Stravinsky's moustache." His acting was "Brandoperatic declamation . . . he seems to find it unsatisfying to have to scratch himself through a kimono."

Marlon, in these years, still regarded the Oscar as an honored tribute. Special evening attire was ordered for his attendance and possible stage appearance for the formal Academy Award presentations. He refused to let me accompany him (I was eight months pregnant) and drove off to the RKO Pantages Theater with George Englund. After the ceremonies he encountered Anthony Quinn in the parking lot. Both had lost the Best Actor award to Alec Guinness (for *Bridge on the River Kwai*). The two men gazed ruefully at one another. "I'll read you my acceptance speech if you read me yours," offered Marlon.

With his return to Los Angeles Marlon had imported elements of Oriental culture along with his physical baggage. He insisted that evenings at his home were to be passed in "the Japanese way." By Marlon's definition, "the Japanese way" meant I was to don the kimonos, *geta*, and other apparel of the traditional geisha that Marlon had brought from Japan and then to mince about the house (mincing affords the best means of locomotion when wearing a long skirt and high-heeled wooden clogs) bowing, tittering behind a fluttering fan, and serving him a *koppu* of sake while kneeling demurely on a tatami mat. My other geisha-type duties included mopping his brow with a damp cloth, laughing at his witticisms, and letting him peek up my kimono to see if I was wearing underclothes. Japanese-style bathing was also instituted; I was the *jochusan*, in charge of soaping, rinsing, immersing, and massaging operations. Our evenings ended after fifteen minutes of yoga exercises—Marlon, naked from the tub, balanced on his head (with the help of a wall), his legs crossed like a pretzel, his flaccid stomach oozed over his chest. Air hissed back and forth through his teeth. His face took on the hue of an overripe pumpkin. He then staggered into bed and collapsed. Fortunately for my sensibilities, Marlon's yoga and geisha fetishes soon subsided. His passion for the Japanesque, however, continued unabated, surpassing in its fulfillment Proust's taste for chinoiserie. Unquestionably, his sojourns in Japan had a climacteric effect on Marlon's mind, furnishing him an important part of his personal mythology.

Despite these affectations, despite the sentiment, despite the intimacies, within a few weeks of his return emotional constipation had set in. I could sense his affection for me shriveling. It became impossible to approach him without triggering an invisible but sentient turbulence. Like the sound of one hand clapping related in the haiku poem, the view of Marlon's emotions was a bit thin. Perhaps another seven-month term in a hospital was needed to sustain his fervor.

The first of our several premarital disengagements occurred less than a month after Marlon's return to his home in West Hollywood. He had taken me to his house for the evening, and after dinner we had worked our way into the bedroom. I was half undressed when I noticed a heavy black wig draped over an endpost of the headboard. It hung there, tresses streaming downward, like an obscene trophy mounted to commemorate a conquest. I stared at it, and wondered irrelevantly how the Amerinds displayed their collections of enemy scalps.

"Who does that belong to, Marlon?" was the logical if bland question.

"Omigod," he stammered. "It's Rita's."

"Rita Moreno?"

Marlon nodded. No words coalesced from his stutterings. "For Christ's sake, Marlon," I told him, "this is terribly indiscreet. If you have any savoir faire, say something." But he didn't. He just became more flustered, his stuttering rate increasing with each attempt at speech.

Finally, I could only retreat to the cliché of the outraged female: "Take me home!" Restricted to one-sided speech, further communication was impossible. He drove me home in unbroken silence, having first maneuvered his number-one car, the white Thunderbird, from its shelter. (It was blocked by his decrepit Volkswagen; if I arrived in steerage, I departed in first class.) When he stopped the car, I flounced out and slammed the car door with enough force to crack the window and jam the latch. "Don't bottle it up," Marlon often coached me. I was learning the rudiments of throwing temper tantrums and was later to earn a black belt in that dubious diversion.

Early the following morning Marlon telephoned. He was sheepish in his opening inquiries into my health. Then he launched an apologetic explanation of the wig on the headboard, but the stuttering intervened whenever he attempted to mention the wig itself or its negligent owner. He gave up on the explanation and asked if I would meet him in a nearby restaurant for a cup of coffee.

Over coffee Marlon recovered some composure. We talked for three hours, mostly about him, about his goals, his compunctions, his sense of loyalty, his moral and artistic imperatives, and about his emotional reliance on me. He promised that no woman would ever again distract his devotion; he promised to be an ideal husband; he promised that never again would he give cause for dissension. It would be best if I could forget having seen the wig on the headboard, he said (once we see something, can we unsee it?). In the end we made up. I like to think that Sartre's brilliant aphorism had an influence on my feelings: "It is not important what is done to us; it is only important what we have done with what is done to us." And there was no questioning Marlon's sincerity. I have rarely known him to perpetrate a barefoot lie when under emotional strain. (In normal temper he can deceive and dissemble with equanimity and can dote on both harmless and pernicious pranks.) Rather, it was the capriciousness of his spirit that left me insecure—his inability, despite his own desires, to maintain the momentum of his initial enthusiasms. His stamina never matched his intentions.

Our renewed engagement lasted for less than a week. I have forgotten what event triggered the second brief hiatus in our prenuptial liaison—some of our breakups were occasioned by other women, some by senseless arguments, the causes of which were forgotten long before the fever of the arguments cooled, and some by newspaper or magazine articles that accused Marlon of promiscuity, depravity, or some vague splenetic form of antisocial behavior. "Never believe a goddamn thing you read in the papers," Marlon declaimed. "They're figment factories—roaring rivers of endless lies. Screw 'em all."

Shortly after the Rita Moreno wig-on-the-headboard episode, Marlon flew to Europe for the preproduction tasks of a Twentieth Century-Fox film, *The Young Lions*. He did not depart on a note of tranquillity in our relationship. The specter of Rita Moreno still ruffled my feathers despite Marlon's efforts to expunge it. "It was my own fault—I shouldn't have gotten involved," he said. I was still angry enough to spin the needle back at him: "No, Marlon, it's my fault—my fault to be involved with you. You're a sick person." The words virtually followed him onto the plane.

While Marlon was away, my anger abated. (He telephoned as soon as his plane reached Paris.) I resumed a leisurely schedule of reading, painting, and dining with friends. I rarely dated another man; from across the courtyard, Marlon, Sr., was scouting my movements, doubtless ready to report any suspicious actions to his son (who would have excoriated his father for his efforts). Often in the afternoons I would sit in the MGM screening room watching films I had missed through my childhood. Greta Garbo movies were particular favorites among the MGM classics as were those of John Barrymore. I regretted that my years in the Kurseong convent had deprived me of these pleasures.

In June MGM arranged a loan-out of my services to Columbia Pictures for a film titled *Cowboy*, costarring Jack Lemmon and Glenn Ford. Reading the screenplay—a period piece about a young man (Lemmon) who learns the cowboy trade from an experienced practitioner (Ford) in order to win the crinoline-clad daughter (me) of a patrician Spanish hidalgo—I learned that my scenes were to be played mostly opposite Jack Lemmon; not a single two-shot with Glenn Ford was required. At a meeting with the producer, Julie Blaustein, I nonetheless thought it discreet to inform him of the antagonism that Mr. Ford felt for me and my consequent ejection from *Don't Go Near the Water*. "Perhaps you would be better advised to use an actress more congenial with Mr. Ford," I told Julie. "After all, he has casting approval." "Not at this studio, he doesn't," declared Mr. Blaustein. "If you want the part, you've got it."

I rang up Spencer Tracy and poured out the problem to him. As always, Spencer favored the offense: "Do it, Anna. Do the picture. It's poetic irony—that he's got you again after kicking you out of *Water*. Too bad you don't have any scenes together; I'd come watch that myself."

A week before the picture began its shooting schedule, Mr. Ford called me at home:

"Are you well enough to be in the picture, Miss Kashfi?"

"I am perfectly all right, Mr. Ford. Your concern is touching."

"I was only trying to be considerate—for you and for the picture."

He was so considerate that when he learned he was sharing a makeup man with me (and Jack Lemmon), he became infuriated and demanded, on threat of withdrawal, a separate makeup man assigned exclusively to himself. On the set he avoided me and, for years, whenever we happened to frequent the same cocktail party, he would glare at me, then self-consciously follow a routine of milling about, sipping Martinis, and snapping up canapés. On location—just outside Santa Fe, New Mexico—he would often pass the evening at a local tavern, staggering back to our hotel at four o'clock in the morning, waking the staff and guests with raucous cowboy yells. He did, however, make one conquest. He was required, in a scene demonstrating his cowboy skills, to rope and subdue a ferocious bull. The particular taurine specimen cast for this scene would have been more suitable in a Ferdinand-the-Bull role. The animal was introduced to Mr. Ford, and it was love at first scent. According to the script, the bull snorts, paws at the ground, bellows its rage at its opponent, then charges murderously. A squad of bull-handlers stood by, armed with guns, whips, and prods to encourage the bull to follow the script and to protect Mr. Ford. Everyone on the set was warned about the savagery of this bull. "Ferdinand" glanced sweetly and coyly at Glenn Ford, turned sideways and sidestepped toward its would-be lover, as if too shy for a direct approach. It stood there, mooning its infatuation. Whips and prods were to no avail. Its acting career was finished; another bull took its place and performed in accordance with the script.

Other animals enlisted for the picture also proved uncooperative. For no apparent reason one afternoon, the two thousand cattle rented by the production company chose to stampede, devastating sets, landscaping, and a few of their number as well. For several days following, cast and crew were invited to feast on beef barbecues. I was still a vegetarian at this time (not from Hindu scruples), so did not partake of the unexpected bounty. On another occasion I was seated on a magnificent white stallion, waving good-bye to my lover, Jack Lemmon (a polymorphic actor who works well with everyone—his fellow actors describe him as a "pussycat"; our love scenes were so realistic that Jack's wife, Felicia Farr, watching from behind the cameras, raised a fuss whenever the director called for retakes). An assistant director yelled, "Action!" The horse reacted literally and galloped away, ignoring my protesting pulls at the reins. I fell off and bounced about thirty feet, ending with cuts, abrasions, and bruised ribs that required uncomfortable quantities of tape.

A deeper touch of misfortune visited the location when a wall of the bullfighting arena collapsed on two young children, crushing them to death. The wall was constructed as part of the film set and without the strength of a permanent structure.

Throughout the shooting of *Cowboy* a faithful succession of letters and telephone calls from Marlon buoyed our relationship over its disruptive waves. He wrote from Copenhagen, asking what types of Danish cookware he should send me. He wrote from Paris, where he revived an old and close liaison with Christian Marquand, an actor who was later to direct him in *Candy:* "Christian is a man now for the most part and he has grown enormously in character and in other parts. He is one of my dearest dearest friends and has an extraordinary capacity for intuitive understanding of people, and besides that I laugh with him till I am sick, and I haven't laughed like that for a long time. We do everything together—and enjoy it all."

In one phone call from Paris he told me that he was in his hotel room at the Prince de Galles changing his pants, after having spilt a cup of hot tea onto his lap. I gave him the "headline" for the incident (which he repeated to a Hollywood columnist): "Brando Scalds Balls At Prince de Galles."

Much of the preproduction planning and shooting for *The Young Lions* was organized from a Paris base (the Hotel Rafael). Marlon had made numerous trips to Paris and considered the city his second home. In this instance, however, a jaded sense of depression seemed to curb his enjoyment: "Its very rainy here in Paris and I am afraid that Paris has lost that special feeling. I dont miss California so much, I'm even glad to get away, but I've missed you and wish that you could be here I have had absoulty no intrest in running around here in Paris. Ive managed to avoid all the hectic social tangles that can afflict one in Paris and have spent most of the time in my room reading and thinking and working." For me, Paris was ever an exhilarating experience. I wondered if Marlon, at the age of thirty-three, was becoming surfeited with life.

Irwin Shaw's epic best-selling novel provided World War II as a canvas for painting the lives of its four participants: an American Jew (Montgomery Clift), a Broadway entertainer/playboy (Dean Martin), an ultra-Nazi (Maximilian Schell), and an opportunistic quasi-Nazi (Marlon). As adapted to the screen by Edward Anhalt and directed by Eddie Dmytryk, the story line afforded a penetrating look at the personal maelstroms within the currents of war. It appealed immediately to Marlon; he was seeking a role distinct from those of his previous pictures and felt that the character of Christian Diestl offered that distinction. He accepted the first proposal from Twentieth Century-Fox and contracted for the film.

In Paris Marlon visited Shaw to discuss their respective concepts of Naziism. Marlon asked if Shaw, now twelve years after the war, would have written his book differently. Mr. Shaw expressed his low opinion of the human race and doubted that any change was justified. Marlon responded that, "If we continue to say that all Germans are bad, we would add to the Nazi's argument that all Jews are bad."

Marlon's next self-assigned task for the picture was to revise the screenplay. One particular aspect of the story he considered anathema to his own image: the portrayal of the Nazi, Diestl, as the ultimate villain. At the end of Shaw's novel, Diestl shoots the Jew, Noah Ackerman, and in turn is hunted down and killed by the American playboy. Marlon could not tolerate such a characterization. The film ends with Diestl lowering his rifle sights from Ackerman's head; he is then shot casually by Dean Martin. According to *Time* magazine, Marlon wished to die, after being shot, outstretched on a barbed-wire fence—an opportunity to flaunt his metaphysical crown of thorns. It wasn't true. Nor was it true that Montgomery Clift adamantly objected to Marlon's proposed figurative crucifixion and told Dmytryk, "If you let Marlon die like that, I'll walk off the picture." Such reports are the dross of film productions and, in accordance with Gresham's law, tend to obscure the significant events.

(In the death scene as shot, Marlon tumbles down a hill and ends, face down, in a pool of water. Dmytryk instructed him, "Now when you fall in the water, stay there as long as you can because I have to give the cameras time to move away." The scene was shot. The cameras moved away. Still Marlon lay face down in the murky water. Alarmed, crew members rushed over and pulled him out. He jumped up laughing: "You know, I could always hold my breath longer than any other kid on the block.")

Whatever his purported motives for transforming the rather doctrinaire villainous nature of Christian Diestl, Marlon's concept (as initially suggested by Eddie Dmytryk and Edward Anhalt) sprang from his intuitive dramatic approach to character. In its original shape, Diestl's character was one-dimensional, monotonous. Rehewn by Marlon, it acquired a color, a substance, and a focus that animated the entire picture. Marlon may be whimsical in his announcements and his posturings, but he is never whimsical in his zeal for vivid, vital material.

Rumors spread that Marlon and Monty Clift were feuding on the set of *The Young Lions*. While a rivalry did exist on a professional level, it was not, at first, reflected on a personal plane. Marlon, when he spoke to me of Mr. Clift in calls from Paris, praised his costar for his acting, his intellectual resources, and his cooperation on the set. Clift, in turn, had long admired Marlon. When both were first nominated for Oscars, Marlon for *Streetcar* and Clift for *A Place in the Sun*, Clift swore that he voted for Marlon: "I thought he was so damn good, I'd have voted for him over me, over my own mother, or over John Barrymore." Both men had been students at the Actors Studio in the late forties; their acting styles were often compared by film and theatre critics. I never credited the comparison—Clift's acting suggests a restrained intelligence, Marlon's a fount of raw energy; both men were idolized by millions of zealous fans.

Monty Clift, even to the most imperceptive eye, was a troubled individual. He and Marlon were introduced by Eddie Dmytryk (who had directed Clift and Elizabeth Taylor in *Raintree County*) at a small dinner gathering in Paris. Marlon contributed his usual prescription: "You ought to see a psychiatrist." Neither James Dean nor the other recipients of such advice were appreciative of it. Clift was particularly offended since his experiences with psychoanalysis had been traumatic and unrewarding. Relations between them proceeded at a lower temperature; fortunately for the picture they shared no scenes.

A year before the shooting of *The Young Lions*, Monty Clift had left a dinner party given by his close friend, Elizabeth Taylor, at her Beverly Hills home and, presumably in a drunken stupor, had driven into a telephone pole. Plastic surgery repaired his lacerated face to a degree, and makeup hid the residual scars from the camera, but his features never regained their mobility, and his public following declined steadily to his death from a coronary collapse at the age of forty-five in July 1966. It was reported that he failed to appear on schedule for *The Young Lions* and was unearthed by the producers of the film in a third-class bordello in the south of Italy, stupefied with alcohol.

As the film production advanced, Clift managed a sober professionalism, and Marlon expressed pleasure with its progress. He described his hopes for the picture in several letters, describing his working relationship with Dmytryk as "the best since I've worked with Gadge Kazan." Rare praise, indeed.

"We had a test of strength at the beginning," Eddie Dmytryk recounted to me subsequently, expressing his view of the relationship. "But I've had tests of strength with others, including Bogie, and the director has to win or he's in trouble; if a director doesn't have a strong hand, he shouldn't be a director. After that, Marlon was charming. He got the idea it was a good serious picture and buckled down. I was printing take three or four toward the end of the picture. . . . And I knew that by reputation he would do thirty or forty takes of a scene and then act up."

Carlo Fiore, Sam Gilman, and makeup man Philip Rhodes accompanied Marlon to the Paris filming location. If Marlon's relatives—especially Aunt June—distressed him on their trips abroad, his friends could claim their own neuroses. On weekends Marlon hid from everyone connected with the picture, including his friends. He was particularly worried about Carlo Fiore, lamenting his ardent woman-chasing and the failure of his marriage. (Carlo had been married for three months at this time—to Marcia Hunt, a fashion coordinator. At the wedding ceremony Marlon had served as best man and I as bridesmaid.) Sam Gilman was more capable of maintaining his psychological balance. His taste for ladies sans lipstick bothered Marlon. "Sam," Marlon told me, "always collected girls who looked like depraved nuns."

Late in August the European scenes for *The Young Lions*

were finished; the production company was transplanted to Borrego Springs, California, to complete the shooting schedule. I had finished all but a few night sequences on *Cowboy*, so I was able to move into Marlon's hotel in Borrego Springs. Marlon was looking more trim and handsome than at any time throughout my recollection. His hair was cut short and dyed blond (for his film role). He had abandoned his white-clothes phase for a season of stripes—mostly dark blue stripes on a light blue background. We had an ardent reunion and a quick sexual gratification, the consequences of which were nine months in the development.

A change had overtaken Marlon—he was mellower, more resilient, more communicative. We went on lengthy walks together through the countryside, exchanging reflections on the meaning and purpose of life, death, love, religion—the spectrum of intangible concepts. Marlon's theological creed continued its pragmatic course. "One's religion is whatever he is most interested in," I remember him saying, proving that he had read James Barrie while in Paris. That he felt a need for giving was evident, as was his lack of knowing what or how to give. Marlon never accepted himself as a self-actualizing person—that is, as someone whose tendency is to become actualized in what he is potentially—although I envisioned him in such terms. His desire for self-fulfillment, I thought, was obvious to everyone; however, Marlon rejected this description when I tried to pin it on him. Elements of self-criticism, of self-disaffection—possibly elements of self-deception—were still—always—parts of Marlon's consciousness, but these elements now showed in a softer, less damaging light. "I want to do something with my life—something worthwhile, something better than I'm doing now," he told me repeatedly. "I don't know what. I wish I could know what. But however much you squint, you cannot see the future." This theme, in various forms, has been with Marlon since his early years and continues and likely will continue to plague him. Robert Graves put it more profoundly: "To evoke posterity is to weep on your own grave."

Love was a subject uppermost in Marlon's musings. Like the other abstract subjects we discussed at the time, love, I believe, can only be weighed and defined in the loneliness of one's own existential doubt. Marlon generally agreed that personal abstractions were not amenable to external scrutiny, indeed that they might suffer from exposure. Yet in certain moods—emotional or alcoholic—he turned volubly introspective. "You've got to have love," he had told Truman Capote when in the latter mood. "There's no other reason for living. Men are no different from mice. They're born to perform the same function. Procreate.... What other reason is there for living? Except love? That has been my main trouble. My inability to love anyone.... I can't. Love anyone. I can't trust anyone enough to give myself to them. But I'm ready. I want it. And I may, I'm almost on the point, I've really got to.... Because—well, what else is there? That's all it's all about. To love somebody."

In an emotional mood, stretched out on the grass beneath a scorching California summer sun, Marlon continued in the same channel. "Do you know what love is, Anna? Have you ever felt it before? Can I trust you with it? Have you read Heinrich Heine, Anna? He asked, 'What is love? Has no one fathomed its nature? Has no one solved the riddle? Perhaps the answer would bring greater misery than the question itself, and one's frightened heart stands still before it in horror, as at the sight of the Medusa.' Have you read that, Anna? What do you think of that? What do you think of love?"

I never tried to answer these questions. Marlon didn't want an answer, and any attempt would have splintered his mood. He expanded on his ideas of love. He spoke to me of erotic love, selfish, genital love, agapean love, distant, idealized love, psychological love. "Love is the absence of anxiety, the absence of personal defenses," he said. "It is spontaneous. Above all, it is honest." In much of this groping for a definition of love, it seemed that Marlon was continually trying to square the circle. My concern was whether or not he had space in his life and in his person for love. As for definitions, the Hindu poet Tagore wrote the final word: "Love is an endless mystery/for it has nothing to explain it." Beyond that lies futility.

"What was Marlon trying to say to me?" I asked myself during the days in Borrego Springs. "Was his the final *cri de coeur* of a man who had lost himself?" He was patently searching for resources within himself. He was patently compelled by need to pursue that search. He seemed forever stranded between his previous values and a code still in evolution. I had long since resolved that Marlon's Superman image held no greater depth than the blue leotards of the original. He had been labeled a "Don Juan," but the characterization was accurate only in the sense of his doubts of his own virility, in his loveless childhood, and in his search for a mother as well as a lover. (In quantity of loves Marlon probably exceeds Don Juan's Spanish mille e tre.) Marlon is neither a saint masquerading as a sinner nor a sinner masquerading as a saint; he is a kaleidoscope whose image depends on the angle presented to the viewer. If he sometimes wears a halo, a close look will reveal the horns peeping through it.

Whether there were hidden facets within Marlon that I could never see or understand or whether he was mostly illusion, I could not, in the end, determine. I did determine that I loved him; further abstractions beyond that love seemed pointless. Where Sancho Panza sees only windmills, Don Quixote sees wicked giants. I never saw the giants but who is to say they didn't exist?

The filming at Borrego Springs accorded me an opportunity, for the first time, to watch Marlon perform before the cameras. I was impressed at the facility with which he slipped out of his skin and into that of his film persona, zipping it up for a wrinkle-free fit. His unease within his own frame undoubtedly helped him to such an adroit transformation. If he did not know who he was when off-camera, he assuredly knew when on-camera. And the director knew—and allowed him the latitude to express the characterization. And the production crew and his fellow actors knew. They regarded Marlon's talents—and Marlon himself—in a special light. They ceded to him a respect I have never seen since from professionals in the motion-picture or theatrical industries. (Eddie Dmytryk had directed my first picture, *The Mountain;* I could compare his actions on that picture with the greater intensity he invested in *The Young Lions.* Eddie might well regard me with circumspection, for I nearly drowned him when jocularly interfering with a water-polo game he was playing against Max Schell in the motel's swimming pool. "Don't let her get away with that," Marlon yelled out to him. "Grab her by the short hairs and pull her under.")

Observing Marlon while he is engaged in the fragmentary acting required by the film-making process offers an insight into the man. The creative impulse for an actor is—like a love affair—as private and personal as his red corpuscles. Seeing that impulse build into a screen portrayal is as revealing as taking his blood count. Marlon, being a superb actor and a complex individual, has—or did have—the driving need to release through the prism of his own complexity whatever spontaneous and intimate impulses form within him. With talented people this need is generative, not an affectation; the artistic integrity shines through every performance. Critics who accuse Marlon of affectation misunderstand this internal drive. If Marlon professes disrespect for his profession, it is because he responds in complex ways to a combination of people and situations, and some of these responses can be destructive. Thus he can indulge in pranks on the set, in misrepresentations to the press, and in capriciousness with his friends and acquaintances. What he says is not always what he means.

Before Marlon began his film career, no major actor had discovered the courage to battle the "Hollywood establishment." "First you get wooed, then used, then seduced, and then pissed on," Marlon told me. "Screw 'em all. If they want me, they'll have to take me for what I am." Because he was a first-magnitude star, Marlon could adhere to his principles— and he did. Harry Cohn, Columbia Pictures' mogul, sighed, "There's nothing we can do about these stars. If Marlon Brando will make a deal with me tomorrow for fifty percent of the picture and the right to piss all over the set, I'd kiss his ass."

I wished only that Marlon were not so profligate with his talent. I believe a gifted artist should be as responsible with his genius as an inheritor of great wealth with his fortune. The artist carries the absolute responsibility to unveil for us the essence of human capabilities—not always the good, not always the bad, but the truth as he sees it. That Marlon has sometimes squandered his genius is probably the most telling criticism that can be leveled at him.

In retrospect, the brief time I passed with Marlon in Borrego Springs was, outside of the seven-month interval of my hospitalization for tuberculosis, the most tranquil and perceptive period of our relationship. It is likely that our affair and, indeed, our marriage proceeded from the momentum generated between us at that time.

Back in Los Angeles in mid-September, after production work on *The Young Lions* was concluded, we reestablished our previous patterns. Few pressing matters arose to engage my time, which was occupied consequently with viewing old MGM movies, practicing painting and furniture crafting, and other similar pursuits. Marlon frequently consumed much of each day in the offices of Pennebaker Productions on the Paramount Studio lot. He concerned himself with financial and administrative problems and sporadically revised the Western screenplay (retitled *Ride, Commanchero!*) he had been writing during breaks from the *Sayonara* set. (In the event Pennebaker's first production, *Shake Hands with the Devil*, a drama about the 1920 Irish insurrection starring James Cagney, was issued without Marlon's participation.) He was receiving a flood of unsolicited scripts and film proposals from studios and producers. Nothing emerged to claim his fancy. Worse, his interest in the Western project languished, and he took to moping about his house, his energies concentrated on pounding bongo drums. There was to be a two-year hiatus between the release of *The Young Lions* and that of his next completed film, *The Fugitive Kind*.

News of our liaison had filtered to the press, although no publication reported our engagement; Marlon's passion for secrecy in this matter was absolute. I was importuned by columnists seeking an entryway to the Brando sanctum but managed to deflect most inquiries. I felt most columnists were chasing sensationalism rather than truth. In one newspaper I read of myself quoted as saying, "Dating Marlon Brando is the most exciting thing that's happened in my life. He's very charming, intelligent, and has a nice sense of humor. And he's easy to be with." It may have been an accurate quote—that was the type of pablum I learned to feed to reporters. It is a defense mechanism adopted by everyone shielding their private lives.

Marlon, of course, had erected a barrier between himself and the press, a barrier he buttressed further after the Truman Capote interview. "Reporters are all scum," he thundered at me. "Hired buffoons. Scribblers. Assassins with poisoned typewriters. The dregs of society. They rank on the same level as used-car salesmen, publicity hacks, and the shitheads who write the movie reviews." Producers and the financial figures who controlled film production he treated with equal disdain. He was fond of quoting Sidney Perelman's assessment of Hollywood: "A dreary industrial town controlled by hoodlums of enormous wealth, the ethereal sense of a pack of jackals, and taste so degraded that it befouled everything it touched." "Winchell was right," he said. "In this town, they shoot too many pictures and not enough actors. You can add producers, directors, and editors to that list."

This sort of fulmination was typical of Marlon when he was restless, without a project demanding his thoughts and energies; in other moods he has expressed the opposite opinions, especially for his fellow actors whom he generally held in esteem. No one familiar with his polar moods credited his tirades in a permanent ledger. If consistency is the hobgoblin of little minds, Marlon's surely qualifies as gargantuan.

Marlon was readily distracted at this time. When we dined at one of the many Japanese restaurants in Los Angeles (Chinese and Japanese cuisines are Marlon's favorites; "otherwise," he says, "I'm a meat-and-potatoes man"), it was not unusual for him to forget his shoes when leaving; he could drive home, walk across the yard into his house, and not notice his stockinged feet until he sat on the bed to remove his shoes. Once he left a Japanese restaurant wearing an unfamiliar pair of shoes. He never became aware of the switch—I later exchanged the shoes without disturbing him. On another occasion he occupied the drive to the restaurant by lecturing me on Japanese mores: "You must understand, Anna, the nature of the Japanese and not get jealous when a man is paid much more attention than a woman. It is their custom, and a woman shouldn't show her feelings. I don't want you to resist it." I do admit to a feeling of irritation over this theme since

Marlon had been praising the superiority of Japanese culture to me since he returned from filming *Sayonara*. In the restaurant we were attended by a strikingly beautiful Japanese girl. She allotted Marlon and the couple we were dining with her cursory attention and devoted herself to my service. She knelt in a corner, springing up to fill my sake cup after each sip. It was more embarrassing than humorous when she stroked my hair, told me I was beautiful, and asked if she could visit me at home. Although the girl was obviously a Lesbian, I enjoyed watching Marlon fume at her attentions to me. He was infuriated and wrenched us from the room at the last bite of his sukiyaki. The girl added to his rage by racing over to help me with my shoes while he struggled alone with his. I cannot remember that Marlon ever again escorted me to a Japanese restaurant.

An evening later I learned that my father had died. My half brother, Bosco, called from New Delhi to notify me. According to Bosco, he had been fatally shot; the body was cremated a few hours later without an autopsy. If Bosco knew more of the mystery, he wouldn't tell me. I never learned further details of my father's death. He was forty-nine years old. We had been close in spirit although separated by distance. He had telephone me a month previous to advise against marrying Marlon: "He's a bum. I don't care if he is famous, he's still a bum." I had slammed the phone down on him for his impertinence. Now I couldn't reason with him. He was beyond regrets. I felt giddy, with a sensation of falling in space.

Marlon heard the news and immediately drove over to my home. He insisted that I take half a Miltown. For the first time in my life I resorted to a pill for consolation, and it nearly knocked me out. But after I had managed an hour's fitful sleep, Marlon decided that the best prescription was a public outing. He literally dragged me with him to the Coconut Grove where I found myself dancing in his arms as Freddie Martin's music throbbed in my head. We had never danced together before nor were we to do so again. Marlon detested what he called the "artificial ritual" of ballroom dancing. Afterward, I fell into bed and slept for twelve hours.

Pressures continued to build up in succeeding days. My governess from India telephoned to offer condolences; she ended by supporting my father's judgment of Marlon. Then my ex-fiancé, Rico Mandiaco, appeared on my doorstep after a year's silence. He too urged me to forgo marriage with Marlon. "It would be the greatest mistake of your life," he repeated over and over. Instead of crushing his skull with a skillet, I took another sleeping pill and retreated to bed.

At the end of the week a row with Marlon flared up, puncturing the euphoria gained in Borrego Springs. We were lying in bed together—at his house—when we heard a commotion at the front door, downstairs. Between banging and pounding noises, a woman's voice screamed out, "It's me, Rita! R-I-T-A!! Rita! Let me in! Goddamn it, let me in!" Marlon didn't appear startled. "I'd better go down and see what she wants," he said. "After all, I can't offend her feelings." I suppose it was his calm tone as much as the presence of Miss Moreno that incensed me. "What about my feelings? Get her out. It's her or me," I screamed at him. "Make a choice—right now!" Marlon went downstairs where I could hear muffled bits of conversation over the next twenty minutes as he persuaded the lady to depart without violence. I dressed and crossed Marlon on the stairs as he was coming back to the bedroom. "I'm leaving, my dear Rico," I screeched, knowing his vulnerable points. "All right, my dear Rita, go!" he hollered back. We stood on the stairway for five minutes, calling each other Rico and Rita until I burst out laughing at the ridiculous scenario we were playing out. His face purpled; he choked and began to stammer. Laughing at him is, for Marlon, the ultimate indignity. I stomped from the house, slamming the front door with a crack that rang into the night like a rifle shot.

When Marlon telephoned the next day, I told him, "I don't want to get involved with a sick person like you," and hung up. I returned his mother's earrings and other personal gifts from him. He brought them back a day later. We talked. We huffed and puffed. And, as usual, we ended with mutual pledges of devotion. Further, in this instance, we set a date for our marriage—within the following two weeks.

Fixing a wedding date did not preclude further quarrels between us. Perhaps we were both apprehensive about the forthcoming event—we argued over Marlon's house (I was fearful of living in the place with its many stairways and slippery floors), we argued over other women, and when I discovered that I was pregnant, we argued over the probable color of the baby.

"What is yours is half mine and what is mine is half yours," Marlon said, paraphrasing a line from *Sayonara*. He appeared delighted with the prospect of fatherhood—he had always been fond of children—but fretted that the baby might have a dark color. He bought and read several books on the mechanism of genetic inheritance in his anxiety about the baby's racial traits. "Are you familiar with Mendel's law?" he asked, and proceeded into a discourse on genes, chromosomes, ova, spermatozoa, and the peas and pods in Mendel's garden. It gave Marlon visible pleasure to survey this field; from his reactions one might have thought him personally credited for the genetic engineering involved.

Premarital pregnancy in 1957 America was still viewed as the great middle-class tragedy. I was not affected by this attitude, however, since the stratum of Indian society in which I was raised did not label an illegitimate child as a social pariah. We were family-oriented without being preoccupied with legalisms. Nor did Marlon consider uncertified conception to be a stigma. Despite accusations to the contrary, I never believed that my pregnancy bore the least responsibility for the eventuality of our marriage.

Several days before the wedding, Marlon and I drove to Riverside, California, for a license and the mandatory blood tests—Riverside was chosen to preserve secrecy; our impending marriage remained, for Marlon, at this late date, an appointment *in pectore*. We were escorted by two of Marlon's business associates from Pennebaker Productions, George Glass, a veteran motion-picture publicist previously associated with Stanley Kramer (Marlon had met him during filming of *The Men*), and Walter Seltzer, an ex-publicist for Hal Wallis. (Marlon had replaced George Englund with Glass and Seltzer as Pennebaker's executive producers. He was especially impressed with Glass's integrity, he told me, and often quoted his definition of an actor: "The kind of guy who if you aren't talking about him ain't listening.") Both men circled around Marlon protectively, like destroyers conveying a richly laden merchant ship. They shielded him from passersby, intervened with clerks, and stood at ready-alert as the nurse withdrew a blood sample. I felt like a piece of flotsam bobbing in their wake.

Our final premarital argument centered on the type of ceremony we should engage to consecrate our nuptials. My long-held desire was for a Buddhist ceremony. I admire the simplicity and symbolism of the Buddhist rites: the incense offering, the exchange of beads, the meditation and chanting of a sutra. Its peaceful setting contrasts with the hectic gaiety of the Christian sacrament. Marlon contended that no Buddhist monk could be located in Los Angeles and that he would therefore arrange for a Zen ceremony. Zen, I felt to be ill-suited to my temperament. We compromised with a Presbyterian minister reading the conventional marriage vows.

I floated about in a cloud of nerves my last few days of spinsterhood. I suppose most brides develop self-doubts, questioning the wisdom of the marriage, questioning the character of the bridegroom, but my doubts seemed deeper than a bride should experience. Were we truly in love? Was Marlon capable of more than pinchbeck sentimentality? He was obviously an exceptional man but with a corkscrew personality that bore into my raw center. He was more a taker than a giver, more an egoist than a lover. He was a man who substituted art for living. Yet I loved him, and these questions sank beneath the sugar-coated human delusions that attend love. I could sense his creative vitality when he was near. His was an organic temperament evolving throughout his life like a product of nature. I believed him in *Waterfront* when he turned to Rod Steiger and said, "I coulda had class. I coulda been a contender. I coulda been somebody."

On our wedding eve I retired early to a fitful sleep. Previously throughout my life, whatever sexual fantasies occupied my dreams were neither imaginatively rewarding nor psychologically profound. (The most droll fantasy featured an Agnilike god with four heads and seven limbs enticed by an enigmatic, multiarmed, multibreasted Diana goddess.) Now I found myself at the Colosseum in Rome some two thousand years ago. I stood in the wings wearing my red sari from the Paramount commissary, waiting to enter the arena. The preceding act—the MGM lion casually devouring a few Christians—had left the audience impatient for my entrance. I heard the fanfare, and then the announcer appeared in the center of the arena before a microphone stand. Murmurs of excitement rumbled through the crowd. "It's Marlonius Brando," I heard them say. I walked out to the microphone where Marlonius introduced me: "I take grrreat pleasure in presenting Miss Anna Kashfi!" He ripped the sari from my body. I was completely naked. I looked up into the rows of benches where fifty thousand men stared back, all in identical white togas with short skirts. I bowed and pirouetted around the arena. Fifty thousand Roman citizens alternately applauded and masturbated in unison. "Illa aget annon aget?" Marlonius yelled. "Adripita sum in capistrum meum Virgoforma somnavi," I whispered. A gladiator, Rico Mandiaco, strode from the wings, covered my naked body with the latest Dior fashion, and raised his broadsword against Marlonius Brando. Marlonius drew his own sword and slew Rico. Then he slew the MGM lion, then the Christians, and, finally, dispatched all fifty thousand masturbating Romans. He turned back to me and called out, "Ave Anna, farewell," as he ascended slowly at first, then with increasing speed like a rocket from its launch pad. Higher and higher he rose until he became a small speck in the distance and vanished into the Roman skies.

## Four

**O**ctober 11, 1957, was an unusually warm day, even for a southern California autumn. A Santana wind flowing in through the desert passes heated the air by compression and threw a clear blanket of complacency over the Los Angeles basin. The morning newspaper told of important events in the world for that date. Jimmy Hoffa had just been elected president of the International Brotherhood of Teamsters in Miami Beach. The Soviet Union had successfully launched its first Sputnik into orbit, and President Eisenhower issued a statement expressing concern that the United States was not further ahead in the production of intercontinental ballistic missiles. In the seventh and final game of the World Series of baseball, the Milwaukee Braves defeated the New York Yankees, 5 to 0. I had been in America for two years and had not gleaned the flimsiest notion as to what motivated men clothed in flannel knickers to dash about after a little white ball.

Marlon had insisted on a small setting for the ceremony, the wedding party to be limited to close friends and family. Present were Marlon's aunt, Mrs. Betty Lindermeyer, his sister

Tiddy, Great-Aunt June, Peter Berneis (best man) and Ina Berneis (matron of honor), and two friends, Mr. and Mrs. Louie L'Amour. Neither Sam Gilman nor Carlo Fiore were invited, nor was Marlon, Sr. ("I'll bury him first," Marlon had fumed.) Several of my friends were also pointedly excluded. Pearl Bailey was my first choice for matron of honor, but Marlon vetoed her presence—"I'll not have that black broad at my wedding."

Midmorning Marlon drove to a jewelry store in Pasadena to purchase a wedding band. He was attired in his nuptial costume—a billowing black cape over a dark blue suit (with necktie), a cane, and a black homburg settled squarely on his head. I suppose only Marlon would qualify the outfit as inconspicuous. It fitted in with his idea of secrecy. (The previous day a photographer from Paramount Studio had appeared at Marlon's home to pose us in formal dress; the photographs were later released as "official wedding pictures.")

The ceremony was scheduled for early afternoon at the Eagle Rock home of Marlon's aunt. I dressed in a pale sea-green sari embroidered in gold, and was driven to Eagle Rock (a subdivision of Los Angeles north of the central business district) by my friends, Kathy and Louie L'Amour. En route, I asked Louie to stop the car. "I have a premonition—an eerie feeling—that I shouldn't be doing this," I told him. "You can still back out," Louie said, "there's sixty minutes left." That statement struck me as so ludicrous—"It's sixty minutes to doomsday; all those who do not wish to attend, please move to the rear"—that I rejected my feelings as nervous tension, and we continued.

When we arrived at Betty Lindermeyer's house, I had not appreciably recovered. Great-Aunt June greeted me with a worked lace handkerchief: "It's for something old. It's been in our family for generations—more than two hundred years." I tucked it into my sari, and provoked her wrath: "You dare take a family heirloom and put it in your undies!" Then Marlon showed up, his cloak trailing over chairs, lamps, and potted plants. "For Chrissake, Marlon," I snapped at him, "take off that damn cape." "My God," I thought, "that man has a gift for the absurd."

It struck me suddenly that I couldn't be married in a Christian ritual without a nosegay—Madonna lilies—as a symbol (a symbol of what I can't remember). Someone made telephone calls. The lilies had to be flown in from San Francisco, occasioning a two-hour delay in the proceedings. We opened the champagne bottles. By the time the lilies arrived, I was tipsy enough to have said "I do" to a baboon.

Officiating was the Reverend J. Walter Fiscus of North Hollywood's nondenominational Little Brown Church of the Valley; a large, florid-faced man with protruding incisors, he managed a nasty grin throughout the service. "Do you, Anna Kashfi, take this man, Marlon Brando . . ." We were joined in wedlock.

Marlon had neglected to plan for our honeymoon. As we drove from Mrs. Lindermeyer's home, he asked, "What would you like to do now?" I said, "I don't know, Marlon, what do you have in mind?" We rode around Los Angeles for an hour, then called Marlon's agent, Jay Kanter. Mr. Kanter graciously offered his Beverly Hills home for the evening, moving to Arthur Lowe's house so that Marlon and I could enjoy his in private. Our wedding night was not distinguishable from most of the other nights we had stayed together. Marlon evidenced none of the gallantry, the fervor, or the uxoriousness of the typical bridegroom. And I was feeling resentful that our marriage had not been launched with a Pacific cruise or a whirlwind circuit of the European capitals. My disappointment showed. It was not a night to remember.

The following morning I telephoned Kathy and Louie L'Amour and wangled an invitation for us to join them at their ranch house in Palm Desert (about a hundred miles east of Los Angeles). We remained there a week, lounging about, watching television, and strolling in the desert. Louie L'Amour had researched and written Western novels whose sales surpassed those of Zane Grey. (His output totals several hundred short stories and seventy books, including *Hondo*, *Stranger on Horseback*, and *How the West Was Won*.) He could entertain us with a wealth of frontier lore. Marlon and Louie passed several hours each day shooting at tin cans with a .38 revolver. Kathy and I cooked and cleaned the house. The four of us combined to pick oranges from an orchard adjoining the ranch. I wanted to explore the Amerindian relics in the mountains surrounding Palm Desert, but Marlon remained in a sulky mood throughout the week and refused to stir himself to any distance. At breakfast he entertained us by extinguishing cigarettes on the back of his hand. Of such events were made the soil of our honeymoon.

As news of our marriage surfaced, reporters set out on our trail. After tracking us to the Palm Desert ranch, they spied on us with binoculars or phoned the house with the usual silly questions: "What were we eating?" "Were we holding hands?" "Did we share the same toothbrush?" Louie answered the telephone, supplied innocuous bulletins on our activities, and shielded us from the more aggressive members of the press.

Meanwhile, other reporters were probing my background. They located my mother and stepfather, William Patrick O'Callaghan, living in Wales. Mr. O'Callaghan allegedly claimed to be my father, and, according to the same sources, my mother did not dispute this claim. "Why Has Our Daughter Disowned Us?" "Come Back, Joanne, We Still Love You!" headlined the British tabloids, propounding the theme of the hometown girl who went to Hollywood, changed her name, her race and nationality, renounced her parents and her heritage, and married the world's most famous and fascinating actor—"A story which itself could have come from inside the Hollywood fairy-tale factory!" By the time Marlon and I returned to Los Angeles from Palm Desert, the local press was printing leaders such as "Who Is Anna Kashfi?" "Who Is Joanne O'Callaghan?" "Was Marlon Brando Taken In By A Ringer?" We were besieged by a crush of reporters ("a pack of hyenas," Marlon called them) camped on our doorstep.

I had always thought my appearance to be typically Indian—black hair, high cheekbones, sepia skin, and copper-penny eyes. If there are native Welsh who match that description, I have yet to discover them. I had used the name of Joanne O'Callaghan on my passport to circumvent the quota on Indian admissions to the United States. I had used the name while hospitalized, and Marlon had addressed letters to me and arranged for plane reservations in that name. Subsequently, the U.S. Immigration and Naturalization Service checked and confirmed my Indian origin as attested to on our marriage license application. I was still traveling abroad with the green card issued to foreigners. I had applied for permanent resident status but was not granted that designation until the birth of our son.

With the furor over my name and nationality building to a crest, Marlon disappeared. His two public-relations men from Pennebaker, George Glass and Walter Seltzer, burst in to resolve the controversy by inquisition. "Where were you born?" "Produce your birth certificate!" "Who are your parents?" "Why does your mother speak with an accent?" "What is your religion?" "What schools did you attend?" "Do you drink coffee or tea?" "Do you intend to become a U.S. citizen?" "Are you anti-American?" "Did you marry Marlon for his money?" They stood over me on either hand, alternating questions so that I was forced to respond by swinging my head from side to side. I was reeling on the brink of hysteria before they relented. Their verdict was reached in private consultation and, I presume, presented to Marlon. I was half-expecting an auto-da-fé to be proclaimed for the following dawn.

Evidently the verdict was for acquittal or, at least, for *nolle prosequi*. Marlon reappeared the next day without mentioning the subject or alluding to the Glass and Seltzer interrogation. That evening we dined out (an Italian restaurant) with Carlo Fiore and his wife, Marcia (then braving another brief reconciliation). Over lasagna, I asked Marlon if he believed I had lied to him or to his associates. "All I want from you," I told him, "is that you accept me as a woman." Marlon dismissed the incident as inconsequential. "It's just some garbage rooted out by a flock of vultures," he said. "When it blows over, and the truth comes out, we'll sit down and have a good laugh about it together." Still, I could sense that he was reserving his final judgment. Later I found letters sent in his name to private investigators in England, France, and India. What, if anything, was exhumed from the past, I never learned.

When the hackles raised by the Joanne O'Callaghan affair had smoothed themselves out, we were able to resume a normal relationship—normal, that is, for Mr. and Mrs. Brando. Even in his rejection of convention, Marlon is not a textbook nonconformist (à la hippies, yippies, beatniks, and other antiestablishment stereotypes). Normality for us was redefined with each sunrise, with each turn of the hourglass.

As Mrs. Brando I was transformed into an instant Hollywood celebrity—"Take Anna Kashfi, add alcohol, a strip of 35mm film, a slice of southern California dementia vita, garnish with Marlon Brando éclat; shake and stir; let marinate at home in the Hollywood Hills; presto!" A germ of the Hollywood celebrity exists in all of us. In a favorable environment, such as the Hollywood of the fifties where the power, sex, and money myths held greater sway than they do now, the germ can multiply itself like a cancer culture fed with sucrose. We bring to the environment our own flaws of character, twisted motivations, and moral cowardices. If we end as neurotic, confused, status-conscious, guilt-ridden, pretentious remnants, we blame the setting rather than the defects of the stone. People in Hollywood are like people elsewhere, only more so.

This knowledge, of course, is retrospective. In the events and with the immaturity of fewer years, I was incapable of rising above the tide. Even had I been gifted with unclouded foresight, I doubt that I could have stayed the momentum of the moment.

When Mr. and Mrs. Brando hosted parties or attended them, the parties included the famous, the talented, and the merely notorious. I remember the thrill of meeting and speaking with people whose names were common coin. And I also remember how quickly the thrill waned with the realization that fame was not necessarily synonymous with a charming or fascinating personality. Sadly, most of the surviving memories are of shabby, niggling conduct: a buxom actress, veteran of a thousand beds, falling half-naked into a swimming pool; a well-known producer imitating Tarzan yells while swinging from a chandelier; Clifford Odets disparaging his fellow professionals, slapping Marlon on the back, and addressing him as "Marlon, old boy." I remember dining with Marlon at Humphrey Bogart's home. Mr. Bogart closed the evening by chewing on pieces of his Martini glass. After swallowing the shards, he turned to his guests and announced, "My, this is hard liquor, isn't it?" (Bogie was a heavy drinker, and alcohol intensified the pugnacious, arrogant flank of his character. I had met him my first months in Los Angeles while lunching with Spencer Tracy at Romanov's. "And what do you do for a living, Mr. Bogart?" I had asked him as Spencer kicked my leg under the table.) These occasions were not numerous; Marlon detested the pro forma Hollywood soiree, and he never felt obligated to reciprocate dinner invitations. Nor was he the tuning fork to others at a gathering. He often stood apart from the clusters of partygoers in morose and vacant silences, uncomfortable in their company, preferring to relate his impressions on an individual basis.

As our marriage continued, I saw less and less of Marlon. We had been together more often when he was fiancé instead of husband. The change appeared to beget an alienation in our union. While we had previously argued and reconciled, we now had fewer arguments but less communication. It seemed that the ink was barely dry on our marriage contract before the gilt was off the gingerbread. Home for Marlon became "a place to hang his T-shirt" (in the words of one observer) between nocturnal wanderings. In rare domestic moods he would escort me to a neighborhood movie or a round of the local beatnik hangouts. More often he would decamp to a friend's apartment (usually that of Sam Gilman, George Englund, or Peter Berneis), and I would not see or hear from him for several days running.

When Marlon did remain at home, he would typically sleep until 1:00 P.M.–having hammered on his bongo drums until the previous dawn. (Why are humans not equipped with earlids?) He would then rise, brew a cup of coffee, and drive away to return in time for the next bongo session. Since I was enrolled in a 9:00 A.M. dance class, it was a rarity when we encountered each other.

Sporadically, I attempted to discharge my housewifely duties. I was not an accomplished cook, and my efforts in that department went unsampled. Marlon did not appreciate ornately prepared foods; like many Americans, he could swallow a meal while in motion or in his car at a drive-in eatery. (My first experience with American dining habits occurred in an elegant restaurant in Paris where an American at the next table ordered hamburger and loudly called after the waiter,

"Don't forget to bring the ketchup." It is an unfair generalization but Europeans refer to American tastes in cuisine as "the ketchup complex.") I also tried to mend his dressing habits. I ordered.suits for him and laid out his clothes. Left to his own initiatives, Marlon frequently went about with unmatched socks.

By default, I inherited the household management chore—a part-time maid and a gardener were our sole employees. "Have Pop open up a joint account for you at the bank," Marlon said, "so you can handle whatever we need." Marlon, Sr., was then acting as his son's business manager. He showed up at our house to supervise my conduct with the joint account. I was asked to produce the sales slips from the grocery markets, which he then audited with the scrupulousness of a bank examiner. "Aha," he said at one point, "it's evident you don't know much about shopping. You paid thirty-one cents for this roll of toilet paper! You married my son for his money. In this state there is a community property law—that's why you married him." I didn't know the meaning of community property, and he explained that the law conferred on me 50 percent of Marlon's income and equal voting rights for its control. "In that case," I said, "I herewith exercise my 50 percent. You're fired!" Marlon supported my decree, and Sr. was replaced by a Los Angeles management firm. I was learning to manipulate the sinews of power.

In December *Sayonara* was scheduled for its Los Angeles premiere. Alice Marchak, Marlon's secretary, rang from the Pennebaker offices to advise me on ticket arrangements and the proper evening dress. However, I couldn't bring myself to attend the opening in the glare of publicity. I knew that Marlon had inserted several incidents from our courtship—in one scene he presents his Japanese girl friend with a gift wrapped in a silk scarf, exactly as he had done with me in the City of Hope Hospital. Later we viewed a public screening of the film at a nearby Beverly Hills theatre. The sight of fragments from my private life amplified on the screen triggered a rage against Marlon. I erupted with a temper tantrum and refused to speak with him for several days.

Fissures in the foundations of our marriage were widening into chasms. Marlon expressed his view to a Hollywood columnist: "I can't really talk to Anna. She is so emotional, so immature." That he would descend to any public comment betrayed his discomposure. I called the same columnist and struck back: "As a romancer, Marlon leaves a lot to be desired. He's just plain clumsy, and that's the truth. If he were not a film star, I doubt whether he'd get to first base with women." In another interview titled "Anna Kashfi admits she is a spoiled little girl," I added credence to Marlon's brief: "I haven't had too many romances but in the other romances I did have I got my way in everything. It was always what I wanted to do. When you live with a person it's different. Suddenly you are living with a man and you have to be very tolerant. . . . I can't stand most of Marlon's friends—they're leeches—and I can't hide my feelings about them. Sometimes I would sort of entertain them but I was never at ease and I resented them terribly. And, of course, they resented me too because I was in the way."

Various commentaries on our tribulations occupied the Hollywood press. Typical was the gushing from Hedda Hopper: "When Anna Kashfi married Marlon Brando, I thought how wonderful and hoped that some of her gentleness would rub off on him. He's always been a non-conformist and plays more at being a character than being Marlon Brando. I've liked Anna ever since I met her and got to know her quite well. I was never able to know him. He was always so rude, I didn't care to get close to him. When Anna telephoned to tell me she was going to have a baby, I thought it such good news and their happiness would be complete, but how wrong I was. Two months after their wedding Marlon just walks out and disappears for a couple of days, leaving Anna sitting in a hilltop house alone." I did not know Hedda Hopper "quite well"; I had met her two years previously at a farewell party for Grace Kelly. I never telephoned her for any purpose. In our one meeting I observed that her style of speaking matches her style of writing—unvarnished Hopperese. She was no more capable of understanding Marlon than was her prose deserving of the Pulitzer Prize.

Nor did I understand Marlon at any significant depth during our marriage. "You've got to shape up, Marlon; your antics are breaking us up," I told him on New Year's Eve

(1958) from my smug and bunkered vantage point. He only stared at me; Marlon considered such attacks unworthy of defense.

The renascent spirit of the new year did promote an effort to doctor our sickly marriage. We agreed that removing to a new house could prove salutary. Our maid and gardener had been fired when I caught them sexually coupled in the tool shed, and I was usually alone in the large house. I was continually tripping on the stairs, and feared I was subconsciously hoping to lose my baby. Fortunately, one of my intimate friends, Pier (Anna) Angeli, monitored my safety by telephoning several times each day. If the phone rang unanswered, she or her husband, Vic Damone, rushed over. Twice she found me lying at the foot of a staircase and moved me to a nearby hospital. Once, knocked out by a fall down the stairs, I regained consciousness in an ambulance just as it was passing Marlon's favorite Japanese restaurant on Sunset Boulevard. I swore that I saw Marlon emerging from the restaurant's parking lot with a dark-skinned girl clinging to his arm. Later, I couldn't convince myself that the sight was not a hallucination.

Marlon suggested that I look for a Japanese-style cottage— one with the privacy that fitted his description of his hotel suite in Kyoto during the filming of *Sayonara*. "And make sure," he instructed me, "that the house has no white rugs, no white drapes, and no swimming pool." After canvassing scores of homes in the Hollywood area (via numerous real-estate brokers), I found a single-level Japanese house on Mulholland Drive—the ridge dividing the western half of Los Angeles. It was a small place—two bedrooms, a maid's quarters, teakwood-floored living room, dining room, and kitchen (rental: $1,000 per month). It commanded a panoramic view of the San Fernando Valley to the north and the canyons to the south. It also had white carpets, white drapes, and a swimming pool. Marlon was enchanted with it. We settled ourselves and our possessions there within the week. Marlon hung out a sign on the gate: "Unless you have an appointment, under no circumstances disturb the occupant."

Secure behind the transcendent moat surrounding our hilltop *shiró*, far from the madding crowd, Marlon was able to concentrate on his business and film ventures. Associates were summoned to the mount rather than gathering at the Pennebaker offices on the Paramount lot. Marlon installed a four-foot, gold-filigreed Chinese gong in the living room and convened meetings by striking the gong with a massive leather-headed clapper. He also sounded the gong's thunderous clamor to gain the attention of his confreres when overlapping conversations threatened the conference. Throughout the house, dishes rattled in the cupboard, chandeliers swayed, and heads throbbed whenever the gong was detonated. It might have presaged the entrance of Genghis Khan or the beginning of a J. Arthur Rank movie.

Although Marlon was enjoying these activities, and that enjoyment was reflected for a time by a more placid demeanor, our marriage was not becoming noticeably stronger. I asked Marlon if I could consult with the psychiatrist he had engaged for sporadic sessions. With the consent of both Marlon and the psychiatrist, I attempted to ferret out the mainspring of the Marlon Brando clockworks.

Dr. Gerald Aronson was a young man, unobtrusive in appearance. I sat in his small office in Beverly Hills while for several minutes he fiddled with his pen and shuffled his papers. Then he looked up at my light blue dress and declared, "Blue doesn't look good on you." I explained to him that I was concerned over the deterioration of my relations with my husband and that I had come to him for an analysis of the situation. "What can I do to save the marriage?" He dropped a book from his desk top and picked it up. "What do you want to do to save it?" he asked. I had been told by another psychiatrist that Marlon needed a feeling of superiority to overcome a more deep-seated sense of inferiority and for that reason fancied dark-skinned women as his sexual partners. I asked Dr. Aronson if he could agree with that statement. "What do you think about it?" he asked. I had the feeling that if I were his patient, I would soon be lying on his couch with my face to the wall.

After that aborted venture, our marriage slipped another cog. Two nights later Marlon awakened me at two in the morning to offer a suggestion: "Why don't you move to Hawaii and live there?" He was just climbing into bed. "But, Marlon, my friends are here, my pediatrician is here. Why would I want to move to Hawaii?" "Well," he said, "there's so much prejudice here in America, it might be wiser to avoid it. Also, you being Indian and I American, we have to think of the baby—we don't know what color the baby will be when it is born, do we? Anna, we must consider the baby." I rolled out of bed and dragged the sheets and blankets into the spare bedroom. Weeks passed before we returned to sleeping together.

Prior to my visit to his psychiatrist, Marlon reversed his previous position and insisted that we hire a full-time cook. I thought a cook superfluous since I usually found myself the only person in the house at dinnertime. However, I rang Pier Angeli who was a virtual directory for domestic help; she recommended a buxom Italian woman known as Cook (in wealthy households, I am told, servants are addressed by their profession) who carried the aura of imperious culinary competence and who, indeed, demonstrated her worth by preparing imaginative and appetizing meals. For a month she evidently attended to her job without incident. Then her employment was abruptly terminated one evening. Marlon and I had gone to a movie, and when we returned, about midnight, I heard the washing machine chugging in the kitchen, rinsing a final load of dishes and glasses.

From the maid and others, I pieced together the story of Cook's enterprising ways. Whenever we went out for the evening, she would lay out the best china, the best crystal, the best silver, and the richest linen. She would then telephone a Sunset Boulevard bistro managed by her husband. He would relay invitations to all patrons present to drive up to our home for a guided tour of the Brando residence. Cook greeted these tourists at our front door, charging fifty cents per person. Coffee and hors d'oeuvres were available on the dining-room table. Also included was running commentary by Cook herself: "Marlon and his wife Anna sleep in this bed . . . . This bathroom is where Marlon goes potty." She was outraged when I fired her, evidently believing her sideshow concession to be a logical job perquisite. I couldn't decide whether to be annoyed by Cook's audacity or amused by the ludicrousness of her guided tours. "Fifty cents per person!" Marlon said, "I should think the traffic would bear a dollar."

A short time later we received a telephone call from Henry Fonda. Marlon answered and heard Mr. Fonda say, "Marlon, I'm in the process of hiring a cook here who's given your name as a reference. What do you think of her?" He looked at me and said, "We've got to do it to him." "Grab her, Hank," he said into the phone, "she's the greatest."

If nothing else, life with Marlon was never uneventful. He was a lightning rod for a range of people and events, and in turn he aroused a range of responses. Even among his friends, opinions oscillated from "a pure genius" and "the brilliant brat of the cinema" to "a Janus-faced shamster" and "a Balzacian character without charm." One actor who had shared a motion picture with him asserted that "Brando is a great actor; he should be kept caged until the director shouts 'Camera!' " Robert Mitchum, asked on a talk show if he had ever made a film with Marlon, replied that "Brando had never made a film *with* anyone." A director of one Brando picture said, "You must remember that Marlon, for all his intellectual pretensions, is really a child." A longtime friend from Broadway, invited to dinner but ignored while Marlon deserted us to address his bongo drums, confided to me that "Marlon's principal stimulation comes from listening to himself talk at great length on subjects he knows little about; he rarely shows an interest in other people's ideas but accepts his own conclusions without challenge."

Marlon's friends, at various times, included many well-known personalities. Dean Martin came to the house one evening to seek Marlon's coaching on the art of portraying a drunk. (He removed his shoes, as requested, to protect the teakwood flooring.) It was decided the technique could be analyzed only under operational conditions. Two bottles of Scotch were opened, and the two men sat across a coffee table commenting on each other's behavior as they became increasingly inebriated. Miyoshi (Nancy) Umeki came by for a four-day visit at Marlon's invitation, seeking sympathy. Marlon suggested she consult a psychiatrist. A parade of personalities with a variety of problems passed through our lives and received the same prescription.

Of those in the film industry, I thought Christian Marquand and Roger Vadim to be the queerest, the closest to Marlon in temperament. I first met the two men when I was about six months pregnant. They were guests at our home while on vacation from their activities in France. Both shared Marlon's philosophy of laissez-faire in human relations—no demands, no obligations, no judgments. Marquand and Marlon in particular displayed an affection toward each other that far overstepped the usual expressions of friendship. Marlon had related to me much of his feeling for Marquand and also had discussed with Marquand his sentiments for me. Thus, we were more than strangers when we met.

It was while driving Marquand and Roger Vadim to the airport that I heard the tale of the Parisian duck. The four of us were in Marlon's number-one car with Marlon driving. Marquand and Vadim were reminiscing about their escapades in the more bohemian sections of Paris. According to Vadim, who was telling the story with considerable animation, there was an establishment just off Montmartre named Le Canard Bleu (near the site of Le Sphinx, the famed World War II brothel whose slogan—"You can put what you want where you want it"—attracted thousands of American GIs). Le Canard Bleu specialized in supplying ducks for sexual intercourse, a particularly revolting practice, I thought—it must be the nadir of depravity—since the duck's sexual anatomy consists solely of a cloaca (the combination vagina and rectum). The duck was immobilized in stocks, its head in a guillotine, its rear exposed to the customer who then addressed the duck *en brochette*. Nearing a climax, the customer would call out, and an *aide de conduite* would release the guillotine blade and decapitate the duck. Presumably, the spasms from the headless fowl brought waves of ecstasy to its partner.

Marlon enjoyed listening to Roger Vadim recount the story, probably for the fiftieth time. Whether truth or hyperbole, his favorite expletive used to indicate mock anger was "Up your cloaca!"

I had ceased being shocked by such tales. I could never anticipate what Marlon might do, what he might say, or how he might react in a given circumstance. It was impossible to maintain a sense of balance when confronted by his neurotic alternations of mood and feeling, between manic rage and ferocity and striking generosity and tenderness, alternations that could reverse themselves irregularly without apparent stimulus. I couldn't fathom the spark that drove him so erratically, and Marlon wouldn't pause for a serious discussion. If he sometimes explored his psyche on the psychiatric couch, he refused to do so with me.

Marlon kept 16mm prints of his motion pictures at home and often watched himself on the screen despite his statements of disrespect for his craft ("Acting is something I turn off at 6:00 o'clock"). Those statements, I came to realize, are his means of saying he doesn't respect that part of him not under his control, the part he doesn't know intimately. He can watch his technicolored image with a schizophrenic detachment. He can dislike his own performance but will react to criticism with juvenile petulance. The proper study of mankind, he would seem to believe, is the study of his own films.

To that date Marlon's work comprised eleven films—from *The Men* to *The Young Lions*—of his total of thirty (ending with *Apocalypse Now*). Viewing them in sequence did not lead me to profound revelations. In the best of them one can observe—indelibly—the actor's art defined and invigorated; one can literally savor the multiple and paradoxical realities within a character. I was struck by the frequency of violence in most of them—Marlon is usually pummeled by fists or chains (*The Wild One*) or riddled by bullets into a bloody corpse (*Viva Zapata!*). Sometimes it seems that the violence becomes almost sensual, that Marlon as martyr weaves a patch quilt of masochism into his characterizations. Even in his less frenzied scenes, the inner climate of his mind seems roiled by a turbulent wind. I wondered if Marlon were the victim of feedback from his celluloid alter ego—trampled by a mechanical Moloch of his own creation. From an actor's viewpoint, I thought he occasionally overpowered his roles—I remember the elderly director who yelled at his young Method actor, "Don't just do something, stand there!"

121

One evening I was running *Desirée* (Marlon as Superman/Napoleon) on the screen in our living room. Marlon and a group of friends were also present watching the picture. I had my eyes closed, concentrating on the audio, probing the vocal nuances of Jean Simmons (the title role) and Michael Rennie, an articulate actor (we became neighbors several years later) who had studied and mastered the art of elocution. By comparison, Marlon's voice filtered through as a mumbling monotone. It occurred to me suddenly that the sound was not mumbling but an ingrained quality. "Marlon!" I said spontaneously, "you have a speech impediment. You lisp." With that, he stomped from the room. I didn't see him for over two weeks. It may have been a shallow judgment, but the reaction to it intimated the complex relationship between the solid Marlon and the Marlon of two dimensions.

Others had formed opinions of Marlon's diction. Frank Sinatra, not infrequently, mentioned "Mumbles Brando" to his audiences. Slapsie Maxie Rosenbloom (who subsequently played Big Julie in *Guys and Dolls*) was dispatched by Jack Warner to Max Reinhardt's acting school for voice lessons. "I met Marlon Brando dere," said Slapsie Maxie, "he talked just like me."

A natural question as my pregnancy advanced was whether the birth of our child could bridge our increasing emotional gulf. Marlon appeared to offer little if any concessions to my pregnancy, perhaps because I never ballooned up into prominence. He continued his peregrine habits, returning home unannounced to roost for unpredictable interludes and departing with an equal lack of ceremony.

As a young girl, I believed that the imminence of a child would bind husband and wife to a common design but I had also heard of cases where the pregnancy estranged them, the wife objecting to the distortions of her body, and the husband regarding the fetus as an interloper. In our case, neither feeling appertained. I was delighted and excited at the prospect of giving birth, increasingly so as the moment neared. If my feelings were selfish, unshared with my husband, they were nonetheless intense. If Marlon's apparent neutrality—he never commented positively or negatively on our forthcoming offspring—excluded him from an intimate emotional experience, I had grown inured to his indifference and thought little of it.

I was at this time—at age twenty-three—unfamiliar with the old wives' tales about the potential horrors and hazards of childbirth (breech babies, "poison" babies that infect their mothers' bloodstreams, women dying from the effort of parturition, etc.). On the other hand, none of my close friends had undergone the experience, and none could offer genuine reassurances. I was left to steer my own course.

From the moment I realized my pregnancy, I knew the baby would be a boy. Shopping for swaddling clothes with Pier Angeli and other friends, I bought only blue booties, blue panties, etc. The nursery was decorated in blue. The crib and rattle toys were blue. Had I been proven wrong, my face would have been blue.

I wasn't wrong. On May 11, Mother's Day, 1958, the uterine contractions increased their frequency beyond the critical threshold. I dressed and drove myself to the Cedars of Lebanon hospital in Los Angeles. At 7:30 P.M., virtually at sunset, Dr. Leon Krohn delivered a 7 pound 10 ounce boy. It was an easy birth—no pain, no complications, just a slight push as if overcoming constipation, and the baby emerged with a mild plaint of protest against the outside world. He was a beautiful child, brown-eyed, towheaded, exquisitely miniature fingers and toes, and smooth—not wrinkled like the shrunken version of Winston Churchill that many newborn babies resemble. He was not a stranger to me; we had established a relationship over the previous two months. I had spoken to him when swimming on my back or lying in bed at night, I had asked his preferences in food and drink when I dined, and I had admonished him whenever he kicked out rambunctiously. We had become intimate before he was born.

Marlon appeared at the hospital the following afternoon. He was not greeted with affection. I had carried my son for nine months without his support. I had given birth without his presence. "Well, Marlon, I hope he is the right color for you," I snapped at him. He didn't react but went to inspect the baby (temporarily held in a separate room to thwart photographers who had disguised themselves as doctors in attempts to locate the infant). When he returned he sat on the bed beside me, his eyes filming with tears. Never had I seen him so emotional. For some time we were silent. Then he said, "The baby's wonderful—beautiful. Thank God he looks more like you than me."

The next day Marlon again came to the hospital, this time with a reconciliation speech: "From now on, I'll be a perfect husband.... I'll love you.... I'll love the baby." I almost expected a soft-shoe dance while he sang "And baby makes three." We had not previously discussed the name of our child. Now Marlon proposed "Christian" for his given name, after his friend, Christian Marquand, who was designated our son's godfather. I resented and protested the association; I wished instead to perpetuate my father's name, "Devi." We compromised by entering "Christian Devi" on the birth certificate. Thereafter, Marlon invariably addressed our son as Christian or Chris, while I addressed him as Devi.

Hundreds of telegrams and baskets of flowers soon cluttered the hospital room. I saved those from personal friends— Spencer Tracy, Pearl Bailey, Pier Angeli, Ed Sullivan—and directed the others to the children's ward. It seemed that everyone in "show biz" wanted to acknowledge Marlon Brando's latest production.

Dr. Krohn raised the question of circumcision, the simple surgical procedure for excising the prepuce. I favor circumcision as beneficial to the child's hygiene and also because the incidence of uterine cancer is appreciably less in those women whose husbands are circumcised. Marlon, however, was adamantly opposed to the practice and was furious when he discovered the fait accompli (I had already given my permission to the doctor); a vehement quarrel ensued. "I've never been circumcised," he declaimed, "and my noble tool has performed its duties through thick and thin without fail." I suspect that Marlon considered the loss of the foreskin to be a loss in priapic stature—a psychological fear based on his own undistinguished pudendum. He also objected to the procedure as painful for the baby, despite the doctor's assurances that a three-day-old infant would not be traumatized by a brief pain. This concern, apparently, did not apply to girls, for Marlon had expounded on the desirability of female circumcision (a brutality advocated by some African tribes). Cutting or abrading the skin covering of the clitoris, he asserted, is painless, and it creates a greater degree of sensitivity.

I had decided upon breast-feeding my son and began to do so while still in the hospital (after being prepped by a special three-day diet). I continued to breast-feed him for four months, whereupon he suddenly rejected me, refusing further suckling. An examination disclosed that I had contracted a slight uremic poisoning that was souring my milk. Dr. Krohn prescribed a suction device to draw the residual milk. Once I poured some of the milk into a saucer and placed it out for our Siamese cat. After a tentative sniff, the cat rejected it.

Home behind the electric gates of our hilltop temple after four days in the hospital, we soon reverted to our previous footing. I concentrated on ministering to the baby, and Marlon pursued his role as a free-lance maniac. "Neither the baby nor the marriage is going to change my habits one bit," he swore. The statement was only half-true. He derived intense pleasure from the baby, tickling and cradling the boy, doting on him, and cooing to him in the idiotic, unself-conscious manner of the proud father. On the other hand, he continued—indeed had never ceased—fossicking about into a series of extramarital lodes. These affairs were conducted discreetly except when he felt the need to flaunt them at me.

Once, when the baby was several weeks old, Marlon walked into our home with France Nuyen on his arm. Miss Nuyen was dressed in tight pants, silk blouse, and bolero jacket, the epitome of glamour and sensuality. She was eighteen years old. I was draped in lounging pajamas, had just finished breast-feeding the baby, and was in the process of preparing my own dinner. Compared to her soigné demeanor, I probably looked like the old woman who lived in a shoe. She strutted into the kitchen, sniffed at the curry stewing on the stove, and exclaimed, "Curry! You're eating curry! You're eating curry while nursing a baby! Hmph!" Then she opened the refrigerator and took out the last mango (my favorite fruit, of which I usually kept a plentiful supply). Marlon had brought her home knowing that I knew of their relationship. Somehow, that act, by itself, seemed less outrageous until compounded by Miss Nuyen's tut-tutting my curry and filching my mango.

I ran into the bedroom, crying. Marlon followed me in to ask what upset me. "I'll give you thirty seconds to get her out of this house," I screamed at him. They left together.

Nor did the baby's presence diminish the parade of house guests invited by Marlon to occupy the spare bedroom. One guest, Maureen Stapleton (later to costar with Marlon in *The Fugitive Kind*), was recovering from a tubercular infection. Although obviously sympathetic to any TB patient, I couldn't countenance her proximity to my baby. "You're big and fat and can take care of yourself," I told her, and threw her out.

It was at this time, whether through self-pity or self-defense, that I first teetered onto the alphabetized descent into oblivion—alcohol ... barbiturates ... convulsions ...—that opened before me. I had known of Hollywood figures, several of them personal acquaintances, who followed such a trajectory to its lethal conclusion. Drinking, moderate at first, becomes an automatic resource for dulling emotional pain. Red jackets, yellow jackets (Seconal, Nembutal), and others in the sorority of dolls (as Jacqueline Susann called them) lift the anxieties of insecurity and paint a fuzzy glow over the sharp edges of daily conflicts. It was facile to impute my folly to Marlon's protean and malevolent idiosyncracies—"To live with Marlon Brando, I need something to avoid going berserk." Yet I managed to brake myself whenever the slide loomed too precipitously. Perhaps as a consequence of the struggle for self-preservation, I could be triggered—at the shift of a glance—into furious temper tantrums wherein I tore at Marlon's hair, threw dishes at him, and assaulted his ears with obscenities. Marlon was not at all cowed by such outbursts. IIe would thrust out his chest at me: "Go ahead, do whatever the hell you want." I usually answered his melodrama in kind: "Forget it! I wouldn't waste my time on you."

Striking out at Marlon was like hitting a ball tethered to a Maypole—no matter which way it is hit, it just wraps itself around the pole.

Between rages and chills of studied silence, between drinking and bouts of seeming madness, we continued a semblance of rational behavior. The intervals of tranquillity, however, were becoming fewer and shorter. Marlon's private space-time dimension—vanishing here and reappearing there—precluded any appreciable degree of marital stability.

In June Marlon, Sr., married. His bride, Mrs. Annska (Anna) Parramore, the widowed daughter of producer Eugene Frinks, was twenty-eight at the time, six years younger than his son. (She began signing her name as Anna Brando, thereby creating some considerable confusion in our mail, charge accounts, and social invitations). Senior called from New York to announce the marriage. I congratulated him, then forced the phone on Marlon who was dodging my efforts. "Hi, Pop, I hope you'll be happy," he said, and slammed down the phone. "That goddamn son of a bitch," he swore at me, "why the hell did you make me talk to him? I can't stand that man. The way he treated my mother.... And now this.... To hell with him."

Marlon's coldness toward his father was not an isolated example. He could show a lithic indifference to others' emotional stress. Earlier, we learned that Carlo Fiore's wife, Marcia, had died in an automobile accident near Palm Springs. She and I had become close friends when Marlon and Carlo were in Japan for the *Sayonara* filming. Carlo, although separated from her, was despondent. Marlon shrugged and changed the subject, unable to educe a word of sympathy.

I received the same callousness. During my breast-feeding phase I developed a painful postpartum ailment. Pleading with Marlon to drive me to the hospital was fruitless. He remained oblivious to my suffering until I rang Dr. Krohn who then prevailed upon him in hard-core, nonmedical language. Marlon's attitude is the more surprising since he ranks high on the scale of hypochondria. Innumerable times during our marriage, he would complain of sharp pains, persistent headaches, paralyzed limbs, or rare forms of cancer. These vague ailments invariably faded without trace to be succeeded by equally mysterious, equally evanescent complaints.

As well as passive coldness, Marlon was also capable of active assaults on my integrity. He had added a nurse to our already overstaffed household—which now included a cook, two gardeners, a chauffeur, and my private maid, Sako; with few demands to engage their attentions, they devoted considerable time to quarreling among themselves. When Devi was about two months old, I learned from the nurse that she was trained in psychiatry rather than pediatrics. Marlon had evidently hired her more to chaperone me than the baby. I fired her, I fired the gardener, I fired the cook, and I fired the chauffeur. I put Sako in charge of the house, picked up Devi, and booked the next plane to New York.

For three weeks I stayed in New York (living with friends in White Plains), not once writing to Marlon nor, as far as possible, thinking of him. I played tennis, went to movies and Broadway shows, and learned how to bathe and diaper my baby from an RN who lived with my friends. (I also learned from her how to distinguish the baby's cries of distress from those seeking recognition.) I visited several of Marlon's friends in the New York area, most notably, William Redfield, the Shakespearean actor. Mr. Redfield proved to be a man of independent spirit, a quality that ultimately skewered his friendship with Marlon. (In his book *Letters from an Actor,* he recounts some of his disagreements with Marlon and is not uniformly complimentary about either Marlon's acting or his integrity in guiding his career: "If Brando no longer functions as an actor, he can still do proper service as a spook.")

When I returned to our home on Mulholland Drive, Marlon took no more notice of it than he had of my departure. He asked no questions, never referred to my absence, and carried on as if I had been at home continuously. Nor did he appear to notice the reduction in the servant staff. "Though this be madness, yet there is method in't," said Polonius. He could have been speaking about Marlon as well as Hamlet.

In early summer Marlon again turned to his plan for a Western film, the screenplay for which now ran to several hundred pages; it was eventually released as *One-Eyed Jacks,* the title a reference to man's basic duplicity. A six-month preproduction period followed before the cameras began rolling in December. Meanwhile Marlon asked director Stanley Kubrick to remold the script and prepare the shooting schedule. Mr. Kubrick, a shy, taciturn, insecure young man had recently completed *Paths of Glory,* which with *The Killing* gained him a solid reputation. (*Dr. Strangelove* and *A Clockwork Orange* are among his later works.) He drove up to our house for almost daily meetings, as did producer Frank Rosenberg (who owned the rights to the source material, a Charles Neider novel, *The Authentic Death of Hendry Jones*, and who had initiated the project two years previous), George Glass and Walter Seltzer (executive producers for the Pennebaker production), a series of screenwriters (including an unknown cat lover named Sam Peckinpah), and Marlon's secretary, Alice Marchak. (I threw her out of the house each time she appeared.) All participants were requested to remove their shoes in deference to the teakwood floor. The Chinese gong was again heard throughout the neighborhood as Marlon used it to punctuate his authority.

I was tentatively assigned a role in the picture and thereby drew Mr. Kubrick as a watchdog. He followed me about for several days, taking notes on my actions and speech patterns. Only in the bathroom could I escape him. The shadowing, I presume, was part of his thoroughness in analyzing his actors. Marlon, of course, found nothing odd in such behavior.

To escape the gong, I took to swimming or lying out by the pool when the *One-Eyed Jacks* meetings were in progress. Once, lying parboiled under the summer sun, I was jolted by the unmistakable odor of horse manure wafting across the pool. In our front garden stood ten horses—candidates for the motion picture—that had been fetched up for Marlon's approval. (The equestrian coordinator, Bill Gohl, and his wife, Amapola del Vando, later testified in court regarding my aberrant behavior; their daughter, Lolly, was given a bit role in *One-Eyed Jacks*.) Then an entire street scene was set up on the front lawn so that Marlon and Mr. Kubrick could check camera angles. Members of the wardrobe department swarmed up from the studio to hold fittings in the dining room. As the summer progressed, our house became more and more indistinguishable from a movie set.

Despite the hectic activities, few solid accomplishments were scored that summer. Mr. Kubrick resigned from the project to direct *Spartacus* (replacing Anthony Mann). "We've been hacking at this script for months," he complained to Marlon, "and I still haven't the foggiest idea what the story is all about." "It's about the $350,000 we've already spent," said Marlon, displaying a rare awareness of the financial pressures that had been mounting from Paramount Studio. When production began Marlon installed himself as director of *One-Eyed Jacks*, his sole venture in that most difficult discipline ("I'd much rather not have to do the directing but I have no choice"). Kubrick asserted that it had always been Marlon's intent to direct himself. Knowing that the picture had become Marlon's second child, I had to agree. Further, Marlon had trespassed on the director's domain in previous pictures and had spoken to me of an abstract wish to direct his own film. Stanley Kubrick, at the time, was neither mature nor strong enough to dissuade him.

Late in August I received an offer from MGM to act in a film titled *Night of the Quarter Moon*. Several other acting opportunities had been rejected because of Marlon's opposition. "I won't have my wife working," he thundered like a pre-women's-lib Ibsen character. I had acceded to his wishes, but now with our marital ties stretched beyond restoration, I had no intention of remaining a rare vase locked up behind glass in his private collection. As soon as the offer was firm, I accepted and reported for work on the MGM lot.

My thespian juices had been stirred by several visits to the closed set of *Porgy and Bess* (the last Goldwyn picture on the Goldwyn lot) to which I was invited by Pearl Bailey; the sound stage had burned down months previously, and the film was once again in production. Observing competent actors such as Sammy Davis, Jr. (Sportin' Life) (a camera buff who bounded about snapping pictures of everyone who slowed to a nonblur), Diahann Carroll (playing the first major role of her career), Dorothy Dandridge (Bess), and Sidney Poitier (Porgy) could only inspire another actor to emulate their efforts. I became friendly with Sidney Poitier; we had taken singing lessons together at MGM and were both adjudged to be hopelessly incompetent. Sidney threw himself on Pearl Bailey for further instruction, but she too capitulated to his fundamental atonality and advised, "For Chrissakes, Sidney, why don't you just talk the song—like Rex Harrison does?" In the movie his singing was dubbed with another voice.

Otto Preminger directed the all-black cast of George Gershwin's American folk opera against the backdrop of Catfish Row. (*Time* magazine accused him of directing most of the picture "as though it were a Bayreuth production of Götterdämmerung.") His grand-operatic reputation as a tyrant seemed justified from his treatment of the actors, although he was quite charming to me. I witnessed several clashes between him and Pearl Bailey. Pearl's enduring bête noire is the American Negro stereotype as portrayed in films and onstage. She loathes the "yo'all" speech patterns and the classic tableau of the Southern mammy raising the white chillun' on the old plantation. Mr. Preminger insisted that she wear a bandanna in her movie role. "Ah ain't gwinna dew it," said Pearl, but she lost the argument. Subsequently, the director lashed out at her for thinning out the Southern accent he required. "Mr. Preminger," Pearl replied with dignity, "when you acquire an English elocution without dese, dem, and dose, then we can discuss accents in a rational manner."

Pearl was never caught far behind in the lists of one-upmanship. At her anniversary party she acquired a four-foot photographic blowup of Aunt Jemima with Otto Preminger's bandanna-wrapped features substituted in the portrait, and posted it in the hallway entrance of her home. When he arrived for the party Mr. Preminger could not avoid it. He accepted the checkmate with smiling grace.

The racial theme of *Night of the Quarter Moon* was avantgarde for 1958. A rich young man from San Francisco (John Barrymore, Jr.) meets a half-caste girl (Julie London) while in the islands. They fall in love and are married. Returning to San Francisco the girl is ostracized by her mother-in-law (Agnes Moorehead) who brings legal action to dissolve the marriage. In the climactic court scene, the girl's dress is ripped off so that her overall skin color can be ascertained.

My role was that of the girl's cousin, married to nightclub owner Nat King Cole. (In the original version I was to play the daughter to Louie Armstrong; but when he was replaced by Nat, I was elevated to the rank of wife.) I experienced some difficulty with the part because of a close identification with the racial theme. As before, Spencer Tracy's encouragement and instruction helped in repressing my personal reactions. "Don't fret about it," he said, "acting doesn't require much brainpower—look at your husband." Had I let that sentiment pass unchallenged, it would have admitted more disloyalty to

Marlon than I could then tolerate. Instead, and despite previous rejections, I again approached Marlon to plead for his advice in interpreting the role. "Goddamn it," yelled the foremost actor of our time, "I told you a thousand times—acting is like driving a trolley. It's boring. I don't want to talk about it. I don't want you doing it. If you have to work, go dig a well."

At the Cartagena Film Festival in 1961, I was given the Best Supporting Actress Award for my efforts in *Quarter Moon*.

A notable memory from the picture is that of producer Albert Zugsmith, who rushed about screaming, "We've got to have more sex in this film." He once barged into my dressing room, threatening to have me fired if I didn't insert rubber "falsies" over my breasts and derriere (although I was yet rather buxom at that time from breast-feeding the baby).

According to the gossip mongers, John Barrymore, Jr., and I were engaged in a serious affair throughout the filming. I never spoke of the rumor to John lest I seem to be encouraging it. John's wife, Cara Williams, evidently was more alarmed about the presumed liaison. She telephoned our home to discuss it. Marlon answered with two "No's" and a "Yes." As he repeated it to me, the conversation went:

Cara Williams: "Have you heard that your wife is having an affair with my husband?"

Marlon: "No."

"Do you care?"

"No."

"I think this is a useless conversation."

"Yes."

Halfway through the shooting schedule of *Night of the Quarter Moon*, Sako died. She had accompanied me to the MGM studios each day, carrying Devi and mothering him while I was working. On this day Nat Cole took sick with a rasping cough; since my remaining scenes were coupled to his, I was also dismissed for the day. At home we fed and bathed Devi and saw him to sleep. Sako asked permission to use the swimming pool—we were in the midst of a September heat wave. I cannot swim well, and possibly from fear of drowning I had decorated the pool with six or seven large rubber animals that functioned more as psychological lifeguards than as life preservers. I warned Sako to be careful and lay down for an hour's nap. In my mind, I believe I awakened with a premonition of direness—whether that feeling was authentic or whether it was reinforced by the actuality, I cannot analyze. In the event I went to Sako's room, where her clothes were arrayed on the bed. I looked into the shower, which was empty, and I ran out to the pool. She was lying face down at the deep end, on the bottom, directly below a smirking rubber elephant rocking unconcernedly on the surface.

I fled back to the house. I called the fire department, the police department, and Marlon's business manager. I called personal friends—Phyllis Hudson, others. A subjective eternity passed with no one coming to assist. I ran out to the pool, struggled into a pair of flippers, and lowered myself into the shallow end of the pool. I was working my way along the edge toward the deep end when a powerful arm reached down and pulled me from the pool. A gigantic fireman had appeared. He then jumped in and managed, with some difficulty, to lift Sako's body onto the pool deck. I saw the dark blue discoloration on her temple where she had evidently struck her head against the cement. The fireman knelt over her, pushing and releasing his weight against her chest. He continued the slow rhythm, pressure . . . release . . .

A police captain led me into the house. "Be calm," he said. "Don't let it affect you. . . . After all, perhaps it's for the best. We all know how unhappy Mrs. Brando was." The impact of his speech didn't penetrate my consciousness, but the words made me feel even sadder, and I began to cry, as if lamenting the unhappy Mrs. Brando, now relieved of her misery. I was wearing blue jeans, still dripping water, a shirt, no makeup, and my hair was unbraided. Evidently, our two identities had been interchanged in the minds of the police and firemen. "News" of my accident was broadcast on local radio stations. Helicopters whirred overhead. Reporters formed on the lawn and pounded on the front door. The noise drowned out all rational thought. I wondered why Sako's drowning attracted such attention.

Someone had telephoned Marlon. In the midst of the commotion, he walked into the house. He saw me, and stopped abruptly. I can recall reading the emotions on his face: shock, apprehension, disappointment. "Good God," he sputtered, "you're still alive."

For months before Sako's death, from the first moments our marriage had worn thin enough to let in the light of disillusionment, I had discussed with Marlon and with friends the possibility of divorce. I think we both recognized that divorce was inevitable, but Marlon shrugged it off. When I pointed out that his extramarital affairs could lead to only one outcome, he merely responded obliquely with the French aphorism that the bonds of matrimony are so heavy, it takes three to carry them. Publicists at MGM dissuaded me from any immediate action that might impair their interests, and Paramount executives also prevailed on me to postpone a possible divorce action that could risk their backing of Marlon in *One-Eyed Jacks*. So we dismissed the subject and avoided an irreversible confrontation.

That Marlon and I were irreconcilable opposites made no impression on him. He was a solipsist who saw the external world turning around himself. He was G. B. Shaw's "unreasonable man," vital to the outside world but impossible to those close to him. ("While the reasonable man adapts himself to the world, the unreasonable man persists in trying to adapt the world to himself, and all progress therefore depends on the unreasonable man.") For his part, he patently needed his own unbridled freedom—we had had fruitless debates on the psychological differences between freedom and license—and could not abide the confinements of marriage; he was compulsively armed against the perils of emotional attachment.

For my part, I could no longer suffer Marlon's contrapuntal patterns of living—at the risk of my sanity and my survival. From my view his world was flat, a whirling disc of relativistic contraction that left me dizzy. I had tried to find the trapdoor entrance to his mind. Indeed, I had left few stones unturned—beyond those of his family graves—in the search for a means to unlock and humanize him. I was not equal to the task, and my conscience told me that even a combination of Joan of Arc and Catherine de' Médici would have quailed before Marlon Brando.

In my reveries Marlon and I stood before a bewigged,

black-robed judge in the celestial court (whose earthly counterparts were to preside over us all too frequently). "I find you guilty," the judge addressed Marlon, "of having practiced assault and battery on the foundations of the laws of marriage and of having inflicted intolerable mental torment on your sweet, innocent, young wife (here the judge turned and leered at me broadly). You are hereby condemned to eternal devotion and repentance plus ten thousand years of serving breakfast to your wife in bed, diapering your baby, and forsaking your bongo drums and Chinese gong. Another fifty thousand years on probation with monogamous behavior is left to the discretion of this court." The judge slammed his gavel and scowled; two bailiffs chained Marlon and dragged him out through the swinging doors as his voice echoed back, "Please forgive me. . . . From now on, I'll be a good husband."

The daydreams, the hopes, the pleadings, the arguments, the fights, the infidelities, the paradoxes, the irrationalities, all had been intensifying throughout our marriage and before. No act by Marlon, however bizarre, could add more than yet another straw to the camel's load. It was the death of Sako that brought it all into focus. If life were so fragile that hers could be extinguished so casually, so randomly, so meaninglessly, I could not rationalize jeopardizing mine further in the company of an unbalanced intellect. One more day, one more hour, even one more minute of it, I thought, and I would go stark raving bonkers.

I jammed some clothes, toiletries, and personal papers into a few suitcases, called a taxi, tucked Devi under one arm, and fled the house on Mulholland Drive.

Marlon went into the bathroom, found a used Tampax in the waste bin, mounted it on a wooden plaque, nailed a frame around the plaque, and hung it on his bedroom wall.

## Five

**L**ife without Marlon was, for the first few days, a euphoric trance—as if I had gone from the oppression of a deep mine to the rarefied atmosphere of a mountain peak. Without the pressure, the enticement of alcohol and barbiturates dwindled to nought. I rented an Old English-style, dormer-windowed, two-level house in Coldwater Canyon; its huge cellar might have been modeled on an Elizabethan dungeon. From its Tudor ramparts, I could sally forth without fear of black knights or snorting dragons. I knew the feelings of the captive liberated from his captor.

To the press—the news of our separation had immediately been trumpeted by Louella Parsons—I coughed out these feelings: "I could never depend on him. I had to spend so much of my life alone. My decision is final and conclusive. I was stupid to have gone through it at all. I'm glad it finally is over."

The euphoria was tempered by Sako's funeral. Producer Albert Zugsmith grudgingly allowed me two hours leave from his set to attend the rites—obsequies held at a Buddhist burial plot in Los Angeles. Some of Sako's earlier employers— Betty Grable, Harry Ritz—attended.. Mrs. Lindermeyer and her husband, Oliver, also attended. Marlon appeared late—after the services had begun. He was attired in a dark blue conservative suit. He stood solemnly throughout the reading. An urn of incense was burned as the final respect for Sako—Mrs. Khasako Aizawa Milligan, age thirty-one.

Immediately afterward, I returned to MGM for a jolly, vivacious party scene before the cameras.

Six days after Sako's death I celebrated my twenty-fourth birthday. I invited the cast members of *Quarter Moon* to my new home. The occasion was treated by most as celebrating the separation from Marlon rather than as a birthday observance. It was true—behind every act, every thought, was the sense of emancipation.

It was difficult to believe that Marlon, for his part, experienced depression, retrospections, or regrets over our separation. Most of his actions suggested the contrary. But, with Marlon, at least one jarring exception must accompany every rule. Less than a month after leaving, I was home reading one afternoon when Jay Kanter, Marlon's agent, telephoned. In a panic, he blurted out his words in spurts: "Anna, it's awful. . . . I'm here at Marlon's. . . . He's in bad shape. . . . He's taken some kind of pills. . . . He's tied his hands together [How does one do that? I thought]. . . . He's out by the pool [Several beats passed here while Kantor gulped for air]. . . . He's about to throw himself in!"

"Grab him! Hold him! Don't let him do it!" I shouted into the phone. "I'll be right up there." I ran out of my house (forgetting to check if the nurse was guarding Devi), tumbled into my car, and streaked up the canyon road to Mulholland Drive. The gate was open. I slammed to a stop inside and galloped around a wing of the house to the pool. There was Marlon, teetering on the edge of the diving board. He was wearing tennis shoes and dungarees. Jay Kanter was on the board tugging at his arm.

"All right, I'm here," I said to Kanter, then turned to Marlon and shrieked, "Now, you son of a bitch! Now, jump!! I want to watch you drown!"

Marlon broke off his efforts to pull away from Jay Kanter. The two men stood, transfixed, as I patted my hairdo, turned around and walked back to my car, and drove off.

In retrospect, it was obvious that the "attempted suicide" was just another vaudeville act with Jay Kanter as MC. When the audience walked out, the act was given the hook.

Whatever few restraints our marriage had imposed on Marlon's behavior, the removal of those restraints accorded him more time in the horizontal position. First, he enrolled for a concentrated sequence of sessions on the psychiatric couch and he urged his friends to do likewise. ("That's the only reason I still act. . . . The principal benefit acting has afforded me is the money to pay for my psychoanalysis.") Second, he invited a procession of secretaries, salesgirls, housewives, and minor actresses to share his bed for an evening. ("I'm the only man on earth with three testicles—come on up and I'll show them to you.") Stories circulating from his lofty redoubt suggested that Marlon partook of this procession in various orgiastic combinations. He was evidently seeking fresh tastes for his jaded palate.

His two recreations were not unrelated. Marlon maintained that his success in sexual transactions depended on his performance on the analyst's couch.

Possibly it was some impulse of self-analysis that prompted him to install a video-tape camera at the foot of his bed. Thus, a small library of X-rated tapes was amassed. The scenes, I was informed, were more comical than erotic, as—without benefit of cameraman—parts of bodies heaved in and out of frame and focus. I doubt that Marlon ever reviewed the tapes, whether for entertainment or critical assessment. For him, it was enough to have scratched the itch.

Our personal contacts actually increased in number following our separation. Well before the birth of our child, I had spoken with my attorney, Seymour Bricker, about the details of a separation and a divorce action. Marlon's lawyers had prepared an encyclopedic file of data, charges, agreements, proposals, stipulations, and esoteric legalisms. One of these covenants awarded Marlon, upon our separation, thrice weekly visits for the purpose of expressing his paternal affection. Because of these visits plus the train of harassments from each of us to the other, I saw Marlon more frequently than I had when living in the same house.

Our enforced association (via our child) could irritate

Marlon. On one occasion his rage was vented against my front door—which splintered and gave way under his assault. I was conversing with my neighbor, Claire Lowe (wife of David Lowe, the theatre magnate), when the doorbell rang. It was about ten o'clock at night, and I was expecting no visitors. I knew instinctively it was Marlon and, squinting through the glass peephole, I could see the convex distortion of his face leering back at me. I was in no mood for another confrontation and went back to the living room where I had been sitting with Claire Lowe. A Frank Sinatra record was playing "I've Got You Under My Skin."

A week earlier I had attended a party (escorted by my attorney) for Samuel Goldwyn, Frank Sinatra, Shirley MacLaine, et al. The occasion was the premiere of a Goldwyn production, *Hole in the Head.* I had sat next to Mr. Sinatra at dinner, a proximity that infuriated Marlon when he learned of it. (His distaste for Sinatra persisted after their clash on the set of *Guys and Dolls.*) Now, hearing Sinatra's voice singing in my living room—added to the imagined treachery of the Goldwyn party—Marlon became incensed, dropped the reins on his temper, and battered at the door with his boot. Within seconds, he had broken the door, the lock, and the frame, and stormed into the house. He grabbed the Sinatra record from the Victrola and shattered it over his knee. "Don't you ever dare play that again," he bellowed at me (Claire Lowe sat frozen with fear) and stormed out.

With the precedent for violence now established, we were rarely far from the flash point of mutual mayhem. I was stricken with abdominal pains the first of February and taken to Cedars of Lebanon hospital (an ovarian cyst wanted excising). Marlon appeared at my bedside the same day. While commiserating with my condition, he detailed for me his renewed romance with Rita Moreno.

"Marlon, how can you do this to me? I'm in anguish."

"Anna, you just can't face reality. I've told you that over and over. Why can't you accept it?"

I pressed the button for a nurse. Marlon continued yammering at me about being psychiatrically deranged and denying reality. I began yelling at him, "Leave me alone! Get out!" No nurse answered the call. I screamed, picked up a flower vase, and threw it at him. It missed and broke against the wall, the water leaving an obscene explosion and drippings like a faded Rorschach blot. "She had no cause to do that," Marlon later asserted. "I was considerate enough to visit her in the hospital, and she threw a bedside water bottle and other objects at me, then grabbed me by the hair and tried to kick me in the groin." The conviction of Marlon's testimony even impressed me. There were times I doubted my memory if not my sanity.

In his professional life Marlon, as he had dreamt of doing through his last several pictures, settled himself into the director's chair. Assuming directorial control of *One-Eyed Jacks*, he issued a public explanation: "I've got no respect for acting. . . . It's the expression of a neurotic impulse. I've never in my life met an actor who wasn't neurotic. . . . The creative satisfaction I seek comes from creating—in films that means directing; that's where the action takes place. . . . The director is the emotional traffic cop who runs the whole works."

Most film makers agree substantially with Marlon's assessment of actors vs. directors. The film director can be likened to the conductor of a symphony orchestra. To the composer's (screenwriter's) framework he adds the flesh and injects the pulses that bring it to life. Each musician (actor) is effective only as integrated, by the conductor, into the overall composition. Musicians have a personal filter; they see the work through the eyes of their particular instrument. The conductor is forced to see it in its unity. A gifted conductor can produce a synergistic work whose effect transcends individual efforts. A weak conductor can obliterate the talents of his concertmeister.

Were I coining a pertinent aphorism, it would read, "Stage is for actors, film is for directors, and television is for residuals." Since he had decided to abandon the stage (like Charlie Castle in *The Big Knife*, Marlon talked of his return to Broadway, but the talk fell to a whisper over the years and died of anemia) and since he regarded television as "less than life," Marlon resolved to move into "the creative center of the film medium." ("In the theatre they expect you to freeze a performance and play it the same way night after night. I could never face that again.... The movies have a greater potential. They can be a factor for good. For moral development.")

As a director himself, albeit self-appointed, Marlon now felt qualified to pontificate on other directors: "John Ford—he directs from the director's point of view, not the actor's. He isn't interested in actors. He would never direct me in a picture.... Alfred Hitchcock—another antagonist of actors. He tells the same story over and over again, not from the human point of view but from the point of view of camera angles.... Elia Kazan—he understands actors and they understand him." What style would Marlon Brando follow in his directing, he was asked. "It would be a mistake to imitate anybody else," he said. "I'm going to follow my own intuition." I wish the reporter who interviewed Marlon could have elicited his remarks on the true ogres and megalomaniacs in the directorial ranks. How, for example, would Marlon have responded to Michelangelo Antonioni whose attitude toward actors was expressed in regally direct terms: "In the cinema an actor must make the effort to follow what the director tells him as a dog does his master. If you change your direction and take a different street from usual, your dog will raise his head and look at you in surprise. But at a sign he will come along behind you."

For a short time Sam Peckinpah was involved with the production and observed Marlon directing himself. "Strange man, Marlon," mused Mr. Peckinpah. "Always doing a number about his screen image, about how audiences would not accept him as a thief, only as a fallen sinner—someone they could love."

*One-Eyed Jacks* under Marlon's direction established several records in the motion-picture industry: overruns in shooting and preproduction, total footage exposed, greatest time required per scene, most takes per scene (106), and longest editing time, inter alia. In response to criticism for these records, Marlon majestically replied that he was shooting a movie, not a schedule.

Marlon examined every camera angle ten times. He kept cast and crew idle for days waiting for the wind to whip up the Pacific Ocean to his specifications. An Oriental girl he hired for a one-week role remained on the payroll for months. Producer Frank Rosenberg, driven to distraction by Marlon's style, declaimed, "This isn't a movie; it's a way of life." He assessed Marlon's performance with awe: "He pondered each camera setup while the 120 members of the company sprawled on the ground like battle-weary troops.... Every line every actor read as well as every button on every piece of wardrobe got Brando's concentrated attention until he was completely satisfied. It took six months to film *One-Eyed Jacks* instead of the sixty days for which we had planned. We finished shooting on June 2, 1959 [after a starting date of December 2, 1958]. And we took an additional one day— October 14, 1960—to film a new ending. Time and tide are costly in Hollywood, and Brando used both unstintingly in his efforts to get just what he wanted on the screen. He exposed more than a million feet of film, thereby hanging up a new world's record."

In an article for the *New York Times*, Rosenberg added, "Waiting for Brando to read a script to give you even a negative answer will age a man faster than trying to explain to Premier Khrushchev why he can't go to Disneyland.... Money was going out at a rate rivaled only by the current tapping of United States gold reserves.... Five days [after shooting began] I informed him that we were two weeks behind schedule—a mathematical incredibility that took its place among the legends but failed to impress Brando."

Marlon admitted that "the hardest part was in having to direct and act at the same time. When I could, I directed in such a way as to be looking at the others; when I couldn't, I printed five takes of a scene so I would be covered. Some actors can direct themselves, some can't—though both kinds have talent. I think all need direction, including myself; I think its invigoration very helpful. But the chances of finding directors that invigorating are very few."

The simple plot of *One-Eyed Jacks* revolves about two American outlaws—Rio (Marlon) and Dad Longworth (Karl Malden)—hiding in Mexico in the 1880s after robbing a bank. Rio is a womanizer; to seek new conquests he gives his most "precious" possession, his mother's necklace—"My mother gave it to me just before she died." (My God, I wondered if

Marlon's gifts to me of his mother's memorabilia had been equally counterfeit.) Dad abandons Rio to a posse; after five years in prison, Rio escapes and, seething with vengeance, tracks down his betrayer, now a border-town sheriff with a wife (Katy Jurado, one of Marlon's ex-girl friends) and a stepdaughter, Luisa (Pina Pellicer). For revenge, Rio seduces Luisa, only to fall in love with her. Sheriff Dad, upon learning of the seduction, binds Rio to a hitching post and horsewhips him. Subsequently, Rio is about to kill Dad when Luisa dissuades him. ("You think that to kill him will make you a man?") However, Dad shoots first and, in Old West tradition, is then shot and killed. In the original version Rio also dies. In the revision demanded by the Paramount distributors—for which additional shooting was required more than a year later—Rio rides off into the sunset, promising the pregnant Luisa that he will one day return to her side.

Why Marlon expended prodigious amounts of his talents, energies, time, and money on such horse-opera fare, I could not understand. Perhaps, in regarding the picture as his second child, he was unable to view it objectively; be it blind, lame, or retarded, it remained his child. Not until years later did he disown it. "It's very conventional," he said then. "I spent three years on it and became fond of it. It's like spending a long time building a chicken coop. When it's finished, one wants to feel it hasn't been a waste of time. But it turned out to be a potboiler. Whatya gonna do? My career as an actor is coming to an end." (Paramount executives were so furious at him for the "potboiler" remark that they would have happily ended his career.)

As usual, Marlon could seesaw from one pole to the other. He was overcritical; the picture offers superb photography— the panoramas of Death Valley and the California coast near Monterey (where Marlon stayed at the Tickled Pink Motel)— and a few dramatically effective action scenes. His direction drew creditable performances from the other actors, although a confused reaction to himself. Karl Malden (who had played opposite him in *Streetcar* and *On the Waterfront*) excused Marlon from responsibility for the picture's defects: "With *Jacks*, Paramount spoiled the one picture he produced and directed. [Mr. Malden was in error in his producing credit.] They changed the ending and one crucial scene. It would have been a classic, but due to studio interference the premise that situations and circumstances make a villain was lost. Brando's greatness as an actor showed in his direction; he could be one of the best."

In filming the most remembered scene of the movie—Rio being whipped by Dad—Marlon instructed Karl Malden how to flog him with a bullwhip. "Like this," said Marlon, and dislocated his shoulder. To the extras witnessing this scene in the movie, he offered a $300 bonus to the man whose face reflected the most horror. "Think of the horrible things in your own lives," he coached, "so the camera will photograph the horror in your face." (No one claimed the $300.) To film a drunk scene, he and Sam Gilman, who played a cowboy, provided realism with the aid of a bottle of bourbon. (He had evidently forgotten his analysis with Dean Martin.) After the first several takes of the two drunken actors, the cameraman sensibly followed their countless retakes without film in his camera.

Pina Pellicer, a twenty-year-old sloe-eyed "unknown" Mexican actress without a single motion-picture credit (her stage debut had been in the title role of *Diary of Anne Frank*), was Marlon's personal discovery. At first she was so nervous she developed a facial tic when the camera turned its eye on her. At her peak there was little danger—as with Anna Magnani in *The Fugitive Kind*—of her matching the star of the picture. Marlon coached her in acting, horseback riding, helped to teach her English, made love to her when the shooting schedule permitted, and dropped her when the picture was finished. She received the Best International Actress award at San Sebastián for her work in *One-Eyed Jacks*. She returned to Mexico City, engaged in two Mexican films, and committed suicide in December 1964.

Marlon traced wide cycles on his personality graph throughout the production. His personal secretary, Alice Marchak, followed him around the set through every cycle. "Some mornings he comes to work and is just brisk and businesslike as a banker," she said. "Other mornings he comes in muttering his lines over and over all different ways. . . . One day he dictated his business letters to me from horseback."

His idiosyncrasies extended beyond the set. For a meeting with one reporter, he rode into the interview room atop the back of an assistant production man. He delivered a few bland comments, then left as he had entered—pickaback.

Progress was not furthered by the director's absence over the weekends. Marlon had been flying to New York after each week's filming to rendezvous with France Nuyen, as their high-voltage romance arced across the continent.

Marlon, Sr., was employed by the company as part of the production staff. While filming on location in the desert, he and Marlon occupied the same motel room. It was the first time since Marlon's adolescence that the two had been in close proximity for more than a few moments. After a week, Marlon, Sr., changed to another room. "Bud kept the refrigerator stuffed with rotten fruit and garbage," he said. "I couldn't stand the stench."

From thirty-five hours of rushes, Marlon edited the footage to five hours. Each minute excised beyond that point was, to Marlon, cutting his own flesh. Paramount was forced to edit the final version to a length of two hours and twenty minutes, discarding entire subplots, when Marlon could not bear further surgery on his offspring. The initial budget of $2 million had grown to almost $6 million ($1,250,000 had been spent before production began), driving Pennebaker Productions into a deep financial pitfall. ("I'm not a businessman," Marlon asserted blandly, "I leave these matters to others.") When it was released in March 1961, the picture was generally dismissed as "an ego trip for Marlon Brando." It never came close to realizing a profit.

Dwight Macdonald, in *Esquire*, called it "an egregiously self-indulgent film." Other critics sneered at "Stanislavski in the saddle" and "the Method cowboy." It was apparent that in swinging for the head of the nail, Marlon had finished with a squashed thumb. Within two years, he claimed, he would retire from acting to devote full time to writing.

Halfway through the production of *One-Eyed Jacks*, I filed my divorce petition. It was a one-and-a-half-page complaint, one of the shortest ever filed in Santa Monica Superior Court. It charged Marlon with causing "grievous mental suffering, distress, and injury." A tentative property settlement had been reached February 28 between our attorneys. Marlon had shown no disposition toward being contentious. I anticipated no difficulties.

My sole witness in the default hearing was Kathy L'Amour. Her brief statement confirmed my frequent "abandonment" by Marlon: "Anna would call at one or two in the morning and say that she was afraid to be up there alone and that her husband wasn't home. We [including Louis L'Amour] would have to go up there and comfort her." Nothing further was needed.

In a syndicated interview I was anxious to justify my action and pinned the donkey tail of blame squarely on Marlon's nose: "During the time I was married to my husband, he would take off at all hours, day or night, without any explanation and sometimes would not return until 3:00 or 4:00 A.M. When I would ask him where he had been, he would tell me that it was none of my business where he had been and that he intended to lead the life that he had led before we were married. At that time we were living up on Mulholland Drive in an extremely isolated area. I was left alone very much and I was very lonely and afraid of being there alone. I did my best to create a social life together for us. I would arrange for small gatherings or parties, but he never attended them. This embarrassed me very much. I would ask him to take me away for a weekend, to go on vacations, to parties together, or to the theatre—but he never would. Sometimes discussions about this ended in very violent quarrels. I became very emotionally upset by this. I lost weight and I couldn't sleep."

Having relieved myself of that peroration, I flew to Hawaii with Devi (ten months old) for a holiday at the home of friends in Honolulu. Upon returning to California two weeks later, I found the divorce uncontested as per our agreement—an appearance, stipulation, and waiver were filed on behalf of Marlon on March 25 by his attorneys of record (O'Melvany and Meyers, a venerable show-business firm). On April 22 the interlocutory decree was granted by Superior Judge Merwyn A. Aggeler. It constituted my first exposure to legalese language. I was soon to become fluent in that arcane argot. The "Minute Order," as such a decree is known, read as follows:

"The cause is called for trial. Plaintiff present with her counsel, Cohen and Bricker. Anna Kashfi Brando and Katherine L'Amour are sworn and testified for the plaintiff. Plaintiff's Exhibit No. 1, Property Settlement Agreement, is received in evidence, approved and filed. The Interlocutory Decree of Divorce is awarded to the plaintiff. Custody of the minor child, Christian Devi, born May 11, 1958, is awarded as provided in the Property Settlement Agreement, and the parties are ordered to comply with the visitation rights of the agreement. Payments by each party are ordered performed by each party as provided in the Property Settlement Agreement. The Court further orders the Property Settlement Agreement by and the same incorporated and made a part of the Decree and the parties are ordered to perform the executory provisions of the agreement. The Decree is signed and filed. The Clerk is ordered to enter the Decree."

I can recite it from memory. The prose style is remarkably similar to that used for writing second mortgages.

In the property settlement Marlon was generous—at a time of increasing financial pressures from business and film enterprises. I received an immediate $60,000 plus $500,000 over the next ten years and $1,000 per month for child support until Devi attained his majority, plus medical and dental expenses over $500 per year. I could request additional support if unmarried after ten years. Further, outside of court, Marlon expressed a willingness to underwrite any financial emergency that might arise. I retained possession of an automobile, home furnishings, jewelry, and other personal effects. Marlon requested, as sentimental keepsakes, the handcrafted furniture I had fashioned before our marriage.

I received permanent custody of Devi, agreeing to confer with Marlon on "plans for the child's upbringing, education, and religious training." Marlon's visitation rights were delineated as one and one-half hours on alternate evenings plus Thanksgiving Day, Christmas Day, and Devi's birthday. Weekends and a summer month were to be added when the boy reached the age of five.

Salaries for nurses, governesses, and other servants, as well as traveling expenses, were to be paid from Marlon's pocket. An interminable list of "in the event"'s and "pursuant to"'s filled out the lengthy divorce document—mostly pertaining to substitute plans for missed visits, limitations on trips with Devi, and definitions of the city of Los Angeles.

More important—to me—was the clause, "Husband and wife agree that they will not say or do anything to or in the presence of the child or permit anyone else in his presence to say or do anything tending to prejudice, impair, lessen, or destroy the child's affection or respect for either parent." It proved to be an unenforceable injunction.

I had no plans to reorganize my life. Rather, I vaguely intended to rest for a year without a single thought beyond recovering from the ordeal of Marlon Brando and caring for my child. Marlon was not so aimless. "I intend to lead the life that I led before I was married," he reiterated at his first post-divorce public appearance (a Hollywood theatre charity performance by Betty Comden and Adolph Green). I soon discovered that I was still part of that life and would continue to be for another eighteen years.

Two weeks after our interlocutory decree came the first altercation. Although I had slapped and struck at Marlon before and during our married life, he had never retaliated. That gentlemanly record of forbearance—set in the face of not inconsiderable provocation—was broken shortly after our separation. Marlon was in my home visiting the baby in the upstairs nursery. I heard the child cry "Mama" and rushed into the room to comfort him. I found myself on my knees, trying to protect the baby's head. Believing I had interfered with his paternal prerogatives, Marlon had pummeled me to the floor. I fled downstairs to the kitchen. Marlon followed, berating me for not understanding him or his point of view. He grabbed a carving knife and put it into my hand. "Go ahead," he shouted, "use it—kill me!" I shrieked back at him, "You're not worth it." That rejection enraged him further. He battered me again, slamming me against the kitchen wall. Then he stomped from the house. I don't recall threatening to phone the police, although Marlon later claimed that I had.

Marlon's version of the incident differed in other respects as well.

"I was holding the baby," he told a court hearing later in the year, "when Miss Kashfi came in yelling, 'You don't deserve to hold the baby.' She snatched the baby from my arms. I grabbed her and she slipped and sat down with the baby. She went to the bedroom to call police. I asked her not to. She persisted, and I slapped her twice—once on the face and once on the shoulder, and I started to spank her. But the child began to cry, so I stopped. I started to leave the house via the kitchen. She grabbed a butcher knife and started to come at me. I pushed her away. She raised the knife. I told her to go ahead if it would make her happy. She threw the knife on the floor and came at me again, grabbing my hair. I freed myself and left."

For several weeks after that scuffle, I was careful to arrange for another person to be present whenever Marlon came to visit the baby. He confounded this arrangement by appearing on my doorstep at unscheduled and unreasonable hours. Two o'clock in the morning or two o'clock in the afternoon were indistinguishable to Marlon's unsynchronized time sense. We had never conformed strictly to the visiting hours set by the court, but now, in light of our recent violence, I felt it more discreet to deny him entrance. Unless I were in a benign mood, an increasingly infrequent state, I didn't allow him further liberties in the visitation schedule.

Marlon had just begun the gargantuan editing chores of *One-Eyed Jacks* when he signed with director Sidney Lumet (*Twelve Angry Men*) for the film role of Val Xavier in Tennessee Williams's *The Fugitive Kind*. He signed reluctantly. His investment in *One-Eyed Jacks*, his support and alimony payments to me, and his father's lack of business acumen (Marlon, Sr., had just sold the Penny Poke Ranch at a considerable loss after months of deficits) combined for a leeching financial drain. He was to receive $1 million for his acting efforts in the picture, the first time an actor had reached that figure, and the film was to be produced under the Pennebaker aegis (with a United Artists release). Previously, Marlon had given his verbal agreement to producer Sam Spiegel's offer for the title role in *Lawrence of Arabia*. But with the interminable delays in his shooting schedule on *One-Eyed Jacks*, Marlon never committed himself legally, and Mr. Spiegel, exasperated, conferred the part on Peter O'Toole. Marlon had no regrets: "Damned if I wanted to spend two years of my life out in the desert on some fucking camel."

Since *A Streetcar Named Desire* galvanized the Broadway theatre, Tennessee Williams had tried to lure Marlon back to the stage for the male lead in each of his succeeding plays. Marlon rejected each in turn. Williams persisted. In 1955 he revised one of his first plays, *Battle of Angels* (produced off-Broadway in 1942), specifically for Marlon and Anna Magnani as the principal characters. Retitled *Orpheus Descending*, it was rejected both by Marlon ("I don't understand it. . . . You can't play a void") and by Miss Magnani ("My Englize, she is not enouf for thees play"). It opened on Broadway with Cliff Robertson and Maureen Stapleton and closed to cold reviews after a two-month run. For the screen version the title was changed again—to *The Fugitive Kind*—and, in this medium, it received Miss Magnani's consent.

Before undertaking the assignment Marlon indulged himself in a Hawaiian vacation. He picked up three native Hawaiian girls in Honolulu, and the quartet caroused through a week in the outer islands. Other girls were appended as needed throughout the week. Marlon's contrails of discarded "loverettes" (one of the more respectable terms he used) were becoming visible across the globe.

Principal photography began in July (1959) in Milton, New York, a town eighty miles north of New York City. (Milton doubled for Marigold, Mississippi.) Joanne Woodward was added to the cast as was Maureen Stapleton in a supporting role. According to crew members, Marlon and Anna Magnani clashed daily over dressing-room facilities, upstaging positions, and listings in the credits. (Marlon's name came first in the U.S. release, Miss Magnani's in the Italian version.) The temperamental actress (she was known as "La Lupa"—the she-wolf) denied any disputes: "I'm really quite fond of Marlon. I admire him as an actor."

Through most of the production Marlon commuted between New York and Los Angeles (where, on weekends, he continued his editing of *One-Eyed Jacks*). "My average weekly velocity is fifty miles an hour," he said, "including right now when I'm standing still." On the brink of nervous collapse from the pace, he surrendered his Western epic to the Paramount editors—to their satisfaction and his chagrin.

Predictably, Marlon compared his own directorial techniques to those of Sidney Lumet: "Coming from six months on my own picture, on which I had spent considerable time trying to get this effect and that, I found Lumet's telegraphic rate of shooting quite different. We had about two weeks' rehearsal and eight filming. I admired Lumet's capacity to precut; he is an extremely intelligent and understanding fellow, but I'll never figure out how he could decide what angle was effective."

At the April 1960 premiere of *The Fugitive Kind*, the picture was booed by the audience, Marlon's characterization of the guitar-slinging, self-conscious antihero was booed, and Tennessee Williams was booed when he braved an appearance. The film recorded a poor showing at the box office. The public was clearly weary of Marlon's pseudopoetic knavery and also of Tennessee Williams's melodramatic Southern decadence. Williams himself was disenchanted with Marlon ("I just wish he didn't remember Kowalski so much") and accused him of disconcerting his costar with offbeat timing, slurred pronunciation, and improvised dialogue. I thought Marlon's performance was as perceptive as the material and direction allowed. Miss Magnani's acting radiated her usual strengths; I couldn't understand a word she spoke. Marlon was satisfied. As well as pocketing the million dollars, he was allowed to die, Christlike, arms outstretched, in a crescendo of soaring flames.

For these few restful months I had no direct contact with Marlon. I was able to regain a measure of equilibrium, to bolster myself against the seduction of drugs and alcohol. I was able to perceive that a challenging occupation was needed to focus my energies. Acting was the logical—and the sole feasible—calling I could aspire to; some proficiency, I hoped, might have seeped in if only through proximity to the country's foremost acting genius, and I resolved to pursue it more seriously than I had in the past.

In July, while Marlon was working in New York, I secured an acting role opposite Gardner McKay in the third of his weekly television series, *Adventures in Paradise*. (Paulette Goddard and Gloria Swanson filled the first and second programs.) The occasion was notable for Mr. McKay's first kiss before the cameras.

That television stint proved to be my last significant employment for years; the demand for my acting services became nonexistent. Producers and studio executives had consigned me to the leprosarium of untouchable actors. I lunched with a knowledgeable publicist from MGM and asked him if I were incompetent in the profession or if I had somehow transgressed the industry's moral code (neither offense having ever been regarded as a crime in Hollywood). He suggested the likelihood that the Hollywood moguls, trembling in their own anxieties and questionable projections, feared the least association with me would incur Marlon's displeasure, a displeasure that could undermine their positions in the pursuit of motion-picture making. Newspapers and magazines continued to print "Actress Anna Kashfi" as if the title were my given name. I find it sadly supererogatory; it engenders feelings of wistfulness and regrets.

With Marlon in New York little opportunity was at hand for further strife. In August, when he began commuting between the coasts for the editing of *One-Eyed Jacks*, we renewed the struggle. Again, the unscheduled, unannounced pounding on my door recurred, as he demanded that his allotted time with Devi, missed because of out-of-town filming, be compensated by midnight visitations. I resolved to seek a court order enforcing the specified hours or requiring advance arrangements. However, a few drinks after an argument with Marlon through my closed front door spurred me to more direct action. I drove up to his home to insist that he cease annoying me whenever his fancy dictated.

I don't remember fully the events that evening, although Marlon's recollection was apparently quite precise. Three months later he described my actions to the court: "Last August 15, at 2:00 A.M., while I was home in bed, [Anna] came in and flung herself on the bed and bit me three times and slapped me. I tried to restrain her and got her out of the house, but she went to get in her car and tried to run over me. I went back in my house and locked the doors. She threw a log through one of the windows and came back into the house through the window. I held her down on the bed and tied her up with the sash from my dressing robe. I then called the police. I told them I would not press charges and asked them to escort her home. She refused but the police persuaded her."

I remember the policemen who courteously drove me home and even retrieved my automobile. The other parts of the recital reflect Marlon's usual hyperbole. Four days afterward, the court ordered him to adhere to his established visiting times and to desist from molesting me at odd, unscheduled hours.

September passed without further trauma. Marlon completed his assignments on *The Fugitive Kind* and flew to Port-au-Prince, Haiti, for a vacation with France Nuyen. Two weeks' togetherness with Miss Nuyen may have curdled Marlon's romantic inclinations. Returning to the United States September 28, their plane landed at Miami airport where they were besieged by reporters. (Marlon had registered as Dr. Miles Graham of Omaha, Nebraska, to no avail.) Marlon ignored their questions, but France Nuyen, evidently in a furious state of mind, beat at them with her purse. In exchange, they printed unflattering pictures of her.

In October Marlon was back in Los Angeles, and we engaged in preliminary legal sparring in preparation for a major court encounter in mid-November. Marlon and his attorneys filed a contempt affidavit charging that I had failed to accord him reasonable visitation rights with Devi (now seventeen months old) and that I was hiding Devi from any contact with his father. I—and my new attorney, Paul Magasin—in turn accused Marlon of having beaten me, having ransacked my home, and of hiring detectives to follow and harass me.

An inflexible principle of law, I learned, is that for every charge, there must be a countercharge.

When we faced each other in the judicial ring, Marlon recounted the tales of slapping, biting, destruction, etc., and I contributed my version of those events. He claimed that I had kept Devi from him since the twentieth of June. He accused me of injuring his foot on one occasion when I—allegedly—slammed the door on it. (He was wearing sandals at the time.) Only a week before, he said, he had brought a tricycle and other presents for the child only to have me refuse him entrance and throw the presents back at him one by one. He denied employing detectives to follow me, denied that he had ransacked my personal effects, and denied telephone calls and attempted visits in the hours after midnight. "I sincerely regret any acts of physical violence that occurred between me and the plaintiff," Marlon concluded. "I believe that the facts show that the responsibility is not entirely mine." He was dressed in a dark blue suit with a conservative tie. He was quite persuasive.

Judge Aggeler continued the matter to mid-January and issued an interim order restraining Marlon's visiting hours with Devi and specifying his makeup privileges. I was to absent myself from the premises "for the duration of each visitation, including defendant's ingress and egress." Further, declared the judge, "said visitation shall be made in the nursery portion of plaintiff's house with the child's nurse provided by the plaintiff present at all times." In this order it was simple to identify myself as "plaintiff." In later cases the orders and counterorders became so complex that "plaintiff" and "defendant" (ugly words) became so interfused in my mind that I had difficulty remembering which was pinned on me at a given moment.

I was not saddling Marlon with total responsibility. To a reporter, shortly after the trial, I admitted, "It was difficult because we were both so moody that somebody's got to give. And I'm a pretty spoiled little girl."

I would not have believed it, but evidently the wording of the judge's order was as susceptible to interpretation—or misinterpretation—as were the violent affairs between Marlon and me. The routine of attempted visits, rejected visits, and unscheduled visits continued as if the trial had been nothing more than a ninety-minute television drama.

Separation and divorce were to relieve me of contending with Marlon. Yet we were still fencing, still thrashing at each other. It seemed that we were continually wrestling together, one turn from a precipice. To escape, I left with Devi for a two-week holiday in London—old friends, old sights, old remembrances would prove calming and reassuring. The trip did have value in these regards. Unfortunately, it was marred by my "parents" who, when news of my presence in London was heard, took the occasion to rehash the Joanne O'Callaghan allegations. Mr. Patrick O'Callaghan announced that all would be forgiven if only I were to call on him in Cardiff. He and my mother materialized at the Dorchester Hotel where I was staying, demanded admittance to my room, and proceeded to hold a press conference in the lobby. To protect myself against their charges, I was directed to Goodman and Goodman, solicitors. Although no legal action was filed, Goodie and Goodie—as they were known to their clients—took a personal interest in my situation and offered arrangements for me to reside permanently in London, well insulated against the harassments of an ex-husband. I was tempted but sincerely felt that to deprive Marlon of all communion with his son would be detrimental both to him and to Devi.

That sentiment proved ironic, as the next courtroom skirmish with Marlon demonstrated. His OSC (Order to Show Cause) read: "On December 8, 1959, Mr. Brando attempted to exercise visitation and was informed that Anna Kashfi was leaving for London, and that she was taking Christian Devi with her and she would not tell him when she would return to Los Angeles. Further, he states that on December 22, 1959, he was informed by [his business manager] Guy Gadboy that plaintiff had returned to Los Angeles, but that he was unable to exercise the visitation rights due to professional obligations." He also maintained that when he was admitted to his son's presence, the boy would run away from him; Devi was then nineteen months old. It was true—the child would toddle off whenever he saw his father approaching.

"On December 24," the OSC continued, "Mr. Brando gave notice that he intended to exercise his visitation rights on Friday, December 25, and he was informed by his attorneys, O'Melvany and Meyers, that the office of Guy Gadboy called to inform them that Anna Kashfi had said she would refuse to allow him to exercise visitation on Christmas Day."

No refusal could deter Marlon. Christmas morning found him determined to press his rights. According to his OSC statement, "On December 25, he went to [Anna Kashfi's] house with a companion and attempted to visit with his son.

When they drove up to the house, they parked on the street and a man came out of the house and looked at the car and went back into the house immediately, whereupon Anna Kashfi came out and told [Mr. Brando] to get off her property and that she would not let him see the child. . . . Anna Kashfi has willfully disregarded a court order of November 18 in denying, delaying, or interrupting visits"—and so forth for nine pages of close type.

Marlon amplified his description of the Christmas encounter when he testified during our January 7 trial: "Anna became emotionally disturbed when she saw me and my companion and heaped vilification upon us. She deprived me of the opportunity of seeing my son, and slammed the door against me. I put my Christmas gifts on the front porch and left. My efforts to see the boy the next day were also repulsed."

He had neglected to mention that his "companion" was a twenty-one-year-old half-Hungarian, half-Filipino actress named Barbara Luna. If I were "emotionally disturbed," it was over the thought of sharing my child with one of Marlon's "companions" on Christmas Day.

With these disputes, our behavior vis-à-vis one another barely touched the edge of civility. Yet I was not surprised to receive a telephone call from Marlon early one morning (about 2:00 A.M.). He was calling from Guadalajara, he said, where he had gone with France Nuyen to arrange for the birth of her child discreetly out of public view. A boy, Miko, had been delivered the previous day. "Would you like to adopt him?" asked Marlon in a reasonable tone. I was still groggy with sleep. "I'll see," I mumbled, "let me think it over." He hung up without leaving his number in Mexico. The matter was never raised again.

In mid-January we came together in court before Judge Allen Lynch. (An appreciable number of jurists presided over our years of legal battling.) Judge Lynch refused to accept for the record my "explosive charges" of Marlon's social misconduct. After at least six caucuses in his chambers with my attorney, Mr. Magasin, and Marlon's attorneys (he was here represented by Allyn Kreps, William Alsup, and Richard St.

Johns) and one private session with Marlon and me, he awarded Marlon sole possession of our son for two periods each week. The baby and his nurse were to be transported "from plaintiff's home to defendant's home" by Mr. Paul Gilbert, a private investigator. My suit was dismissed. I was admonished to be cooperative and told to secure a doctor's certificate in the event the baby was too ill to be driven to his father's home. "Throughout the hearing," reported the newspapers, "Anna Kashfi sat serenely while Marlon Brando huddled in a corner moodily chewing his fingernails." I too sensed that some other matter was weighing on Marlon's mind. At the conclusion I promised, "I'll do my part." Marlon was stern-faced: "The judge has decided for us."

Despite this victory to Marlon, he didn't request his rights to Devi for more than a week. He had flown to New York for a conference with France Nuyen and returned with her to Los Angeles where they were observed dining together in a "Little Tokyo" restaurant. (Marlon's choice of women may be fickle but his taste for Japanese food remains steadfast.) Newspapers played up the theme of "Brando's two loves"—France Nuyen and Barbara Luna. Miss Nuyen displayed her usual tantrums for the press, while Barbara Luna withdrew with grace. Asked her feelings for Marlon, she replied, "I'm not in love with him."

With Mr. Gilbert escorting Devi and his nurse to Marlon's house for visits, the number of personal contacts between Marlon and me again declined. OSCs, affidavits, and contempt charges continued at the rate of about two per month, but only our attorneys were called for hearings. Charges in each case centered about makeup privileges from missed visits, my trips (to Palm Springs) with Devi, and a plethora of technical legalisms. After each hearing I received a notice that invariably began, "Defendant's OSC and Affidavit in re Contempt dated — —, plaintiff's OSC and Affidavit in re Modification of Decree regarding visitation rights and Restraining Order dated — — came on for hearing in department — — of Santa Monica Branch of the above entitled court on — — 1960. The plaintiff was represented by . . ." Stipulations, citations, "pursuant to" 's, and "whereas" 's followed in abundance. This maddening language is designed, I suspect, to secure the position of legal esoteres as the exclusive group capable of its comprehension.

Toward the end of April my Final Judgment of Divorce was filed, entered, and signed. (The capital letters on the decree lend a greater weight of authority to the "Judgment.") This milestone in no way interrupted the flow of suits and countersuits. An event outside the court's jurisdiction wrought a temporary decline in our litigation, afforded me a summer of moderate tranquillity, and separated us for much of the next two years.

Marlon contracted to star in *Mutiny on the Bounty*, a picture that evolved into the mode, the mean, the median, and the fulcrum of his acting career and of his personal life. By comparison with the production storms of *Bounty*, those on *One-Eyed Jacks* would seem like ripples in a teacup.

**M**utiny on the Bounty—at a cost of $27 million—ranks as the second most expensive film in history. It is exceeded on this scale only by *Cleopatra*. It is exceeded by nothing in its inefficiency, its histrionics, its stupefying absurdities. The making of *Mutiny* could itself be a motion picture, an historical novel, or a daily soap opera serialized for years on afternoon television.

The course of the filming production ran for eleven months—after an initial thirteen months of preparation. During this time three members of the film company died, a Tahitian girl hired as an extra was fired for becoming pregnant, then rehired after her baby was born and weaned, and another Tahitian actress, the second female lead, married a French soldier and moved to Algeria, necessitating the excision of her contribution to the picture.

Before it was finished, *Mutiny on the Bounty* nearly impoverished MGM and, with *Cleopatra* and Elizabeth Taylor, wrought lasting changes in the Hollywood-star system and the unlimited-budget spectacular movie. It was generative in its influence; it was prologue to more than a decade of motion-picture history.

MGM's first version of *Mutiny on the Bounty* was produced in 1935, starring Clark Gable (Fletcher Christian), Charles Laughton (Captain Bligh), Franchot Tone, and Movita. Winner of the Best Picture Oscar plus seven other nominations, it remains a favored picture for many a moviegoer and a hallmark of nostalgia for most. The second version was conceived late in 1959 when director John Sturges was lunching with producer Aaron Rosenberg on the MGM lot. "If you're looking for a big budget flick," suggested Mr. Sturges, "why not redo *Bounty* with Marlon Brando as either Bligh or Fletcher Christian?" Aaron Rosenberg, a towering ex-All-American football tackle, embraced the idea as a long-sought gold mine. He commissioned a screenplay from Eric Ambler, the British mystery novelist, and requested Jay Kanter to elicit Marlon's reactions to the project.

Marlon expressed an interest—with the proviso that the picture concentrate on the latter portion of the Nordhoff and Hall trilogy where the mutineers contaminate their earthly paradise with human greed and hate. Rosenberg agreed. But after reading Ambler's script, Marlon decided it contained too much adventure and too little philosophy. Two additional writers, Borden Chase and William Briskill, were hired to inject philosophy, and Marlon was guaranteed script approval. He signed a contract providing for a $500,000 advance against 10 percent of the gross box-office return plus a further $5,000 per day for overtime (a clause that was to reward Marlon with over $1¼ million) and opted for the part of Fletcher Christian.

"Was he worried about superseding Clark Gable as Fletcher Christian?" he was asked. "Gable was marvelous in a lot of movies," said Marlon, "but he was just another fellow in a funny hat in *Mutiny*."

A $6 million budget was allotted. Sir Carol Reed (*Odd Man Out; The Third Man*) agreed to direct, costars Trevor Howard (Bligh) and Richard Harris (John Adams) were signed to contracts, and a starting date of October 1, 1960, was fixed for the filming in Tahiti.

Early in the summer Sir Carol Reed and Aaron Rosenberg

arrived at Marlon's home on Tower Road to confer with him regarding preproduction planning. By that time Marlon's focus on *Mutiny* had wandered. Instead, he proposed to his director and producer, they should supplant it with a film biography of Caryl Chessman, the convicted rapist and kidnapper who had been executed May 2 after a twelve-year, self-conducted legal battle. Rosenberg found the idea insane but listened to Marlon's prolonged exposition on the Chessman case. When he, at length, deflected Marlon's thrust back to the contracted plan, it was agreed that the three men should leave for Tahiti to supervise set construction and to interview candidates for the role of Maimiti, Fletcher Christian's native girl friend.

In Papeete Rosenberg and Reed scouted locations and organized the shooting processes while Marlon concentrated on examining the sixteen girls contending for the leading-lady part. One by one the young aspirants were admitted to Marlon's room where he crouched on the window ledge (of the second and top story of the Grand Hotel). "I'm ending it all," yelled Marlon as each girl entered. "I'm jumping out the window!" Each, in turn, broke out into uncertain giggles unaware that Marlon was studying her reaction to his threat of suicide. An eighteen-year-old waitress and dishwasher from a Papeete hotel, Tarita Teriipaia, was chosen; she had laughed the least.

During this period a 118-foot replica of the three-masted *Bounty* was under construction in a Nova Scotia shipyard at a cost of $750,000. Its authenticity, like that of sound-stage structures, was external. It was driven by diesel engines, contained modern navigational aids, and was outfitted with dressing rooms for a score of actors. It arrived in Tahiti two months behind schedule after a journey that nearly provoked another mutiny. Two fires broke out, fittings tore loose, and the ship's gyroscope couldn't compensate for the top-heavy rigging (for cameras and special equipment) in heavy seas. With forty-degree rolls, the entire crew of twenty-five suffered from seasickness. The original *Bounty* of nearly two centuries previous, with reeking holds and cramped, spartan quarters, posed no more of a trial to its men.

Meanwhile, the motion-picture company had invaded the

island of Tahiti. Virtually every tourist accommodation was commandeered. Neither transportation nor rooms remained available to the regular flow of visitors. Thousands of native Tahitians were employed as extras, bit players, or laborers. MGM requisitioned buildings, beaches, and warehouses; an influx of arc lights, cameras, sound equipment, costumes, props, and the other paraphernalia of film-making wanted unloading and housing. The island's economy inflated severalfold as the demand for its goods and labor multiplied, driving up wages and prices. Tahitian businessmen and politicians fought the Polyphemus from Hollywood that was devouring their people. In a losing struggle they picketed the Grand Hotel bearing signs that read "MGM, Go Home."

Waiting—on full salary—for the *Bounty* to sail into Papeete harbor, eighty-nine cast and crew members disrupted the island's social structure as well as its economy. Numerous and shifting liaisons between the American interlopers on the one hand and complaisant Tahitians on the other aroused storms of indignation and/or jealousy among the native males, both heterosexual and homosexual. Marlon, after dallying with the various handmaidens assigned for his comforts, fell in love with Tarita. Her displaced boyfriend, a Danish cook, was mollified with a job as MGM chef on location.

An unlettered, unsophisticated, "zoftig" example of Tahitian womanhood, Tarita never grasped the reality of Marlon Brando (which doubtless enhanced her appeal in his eyes) or the significance of her movie role. When the production phase was completed, the studio presented her with a new bicycle (an equivalent actress in Hollywood would have received a silver-chromed Rolls Royce). She was overwhelmed with blitheful emotions. Her affair with Marlon was one of the few achievements (beyond a number of illegitimate offspring, at least one of which carries the Brando consanguinity) that outlasted the production schedule. It endures today, cemented by two children, a private island retreat, and a South Seas laissez-faire attitude on the part of Tarita that allows Marlon to renew or ignore the relationship according to his fancy.

At the time he was cohabiting with Tarita, Marlon was secretly married to Movita and was still wearing the band I had presented to him on our wedding day. (He wore it through the filming of *Mutiny on the Bounty*.) I met Tarita but once, three and a half years later, in the summer of 1963. I was vacationing in Tahiti (at Marlon's suggestion and expense) and drove into Papeete for shopping. Several of Marlon's friends had enjoined me to be courteous to Tarita should I encounter her as she was a shy person with limited command of English. In one of the shops a young girl approached me and said, "We rather ought to get together, the two of us." Not recognizing her, I said, "Why should we?" "Our children have the same father," she answered. (Her son Tehotu was then a few weeks old.) My character couldn't muster the strength for courtesy; I only managed to refrain from slapping her. "A pity your child wasn't born in wedlock," I sneered at her, and walked away.

Shooting began the first week in December, and with it the first delays and the first contentions between Marlon and Carol Reed. A new script had been crafted by Charles Lederer (who received the screen credit), but Marlon was unsatisfied with the results. While script revisions were in progress, Reed daily reshuffled his sequence of scenes to accommodate the changes. Each time Marlon began a rehearsal, he would find fault with the lines (which had, in the event, been left unmemorized). Then he decided that the role of Fletcher Christian was ill-suited to his talents. Instead, he envisioned himself as John Adams, the sole survivor of the mutiny. Further shooting was delayed until a cable from MGM executives in California expressed their view of such a change in the choicest words Western Union would accept. (Some years later Eddie Dmytryk offered me his opinion that "when Marlon takes over, you can write off the picture. He has wonderful notions but doesn't have the trace of an organized mind. You have to prove to him he's wrong—or accept what he says. He doesn't know when to stop. Look at *Mutiny:* he had a great idea but overdid it.")

Marlon was accused by Reed of being frivolous, of being lazy, and of allowing his extracurricular activities to interfere with his professional duties. Indeed, Marlon had "gone native," running about barefoot in native garb, eating native food, and pounding out native rhythms on his bongo drums in long nightly sessions to admiring circles of Tahitians.

After several weeks of tortoiselike movement, the rainy season, which could be scheduled by the calendar, descended on Tahiti. Fifteen days of unceasing downpour convinced Rosenberg that a meteorological miracle was not in the offing, and the producer ordered the cast and crew back to Hollywood for interior filming—at an added cost of $2 million—with a scheduled return to Tahiti two months later. Carol Reed was either dismissed (MGM's version) or withdrew because of gallstone problems (Reed's version). When the press insinuated that he was responsible for Reed's ouster, Marlon denied it and called a meeting of the cast and crew to express his neutrality.

At the recommendation of Charles Lederer and with Marlon's approval, director Lewis Milestone (*All Quiet on the Western Front; Of Mice and Men*) was designated to replace Carol Reed. Mr. Milestone ("Milly" to his friends), a strict professional whose style in directing is inimical to Marlon's style in acting, accepted the assignment with some misgivings. The pacifist spirit of his films had impressed Marlon (they had met briefly before in Paris but were not close acquaintances), and for over a week he listened to his director with respect. Beyond that point the contempt of familiarity overtook Marlon—as it did so often in his professional and intimate associations. He began his parade of antics by cueing the cameraman behind the director's back. Mr. Milestone was too dignified to protest. He withdrew to a corner of the set, opened a newspaper, and sat reading while the cameras were shooting. Aaron Rosenberg came onto the set and asked why Milestone was not watching the scene. "Why should I watch it in pieces?" said the director. "When it comes out, I can go into a theatre, pay my dime, and see it uninterrupted in full." It was a vignette in a larger canvas but it presaged the barrier that was to arise between Marlon and Mr. Milestone.

"The picture should have been called the 'Mutiny of Marlon Brando,'" said Milestone in an interview in the *Saturday Evening Post*. "He cost the production at least $6 million and months of extra work. I've been in this business for forty years and I've never seen anything like it. Did you ever hear of an actor who put plugs in his ears so he couldn't listen to the director or the other actors? That's what Brando did. Whenever I'd try to direct him in a scene, he'd say, 'Are you telling me or are you asking my advice?' "

During the next weeks Milestone attempted several times to walk off the set. Once he was stopped by Marlon, who pleaded with him to continue directing: "I promise you I'll behave. I'll never do it again. You won't have any trouble from me." Milestone stared at him: "Marlon, as an actor you know the value of an exit. If I leave now I'll have a dramatic exit—but I can only do it once. The second time it becomes farcical, so don't make me do it twice. If you say you'll behave, I'll come back. But the next time you act like a maniac, I'll disappear. I can't make a second exit." Speaking of the incident years later, Milestone recalled, "His period of good behavior lasted the entire afternoon. The next day we were back in the same old soup."

With this frame of mind modulating the processes of filmmaking, the production continued. Sets constructed in Papeete were duplicated in Hollywood. Two separate mock-ups of the *Bounty*, one for interiors and another—a Brobdingnagian contraption set on rollers—for exteriors, were erected on the MGM lot. Expenditures rocketed through financial ceilings. Milestone advised Rosenberg and the top MGM echelon to "abandon ship before it sinks with everyone aboard." An investment newsletter counseled, "Stockholders, man the lifeboats! The *Bounty* has sprung a dozen leaks" as MGM stock sank with every setback. But, like Pyrrhus hurling his armies against the Romans, MGM committed its full resources to the ultimate victory.

In the spring the caravan of actors, technicians, managers, and its tons of filmic apparatus migrated back to Tahiti. Marlon took up residence in a rambling villa bordering the black sand beach, replete with Polynesian retainers, and resumed his liaison with Tarita and with the Tahitian life-style. "He played the bongo drums and danced bare-assed with the local gals all night," said one of the crew members. "He'd then arrive on the set bleary-eyed and unprepared for the day's shooting. Often he would fumble his way through thirty takes of a single scene."

Marlon's retention span seemed to be shortening. In direct over-the-shoulder two-shots, he would paste scraps of paper imprinted with his dialogue on the other actor's chest. If he forgot a line or objected to some aspect of the scene, he would simply freeze, glassy-eyed while the other actors moved through their parts uncertainly. He again plugged his ears with cotton (an artifice no longer original or humorous). "I have an ear infection I'm trying to cure," he explained to Milestone. He could haggle over a single line for hours while the entire crew stood idle. Arguments should be resolved, Marlon proposed, by democratic poll. Marlon was accorded one vote, Rosenberg and Lederer a half vote each. Milestone was excluded. "It wasn't a movie production," he said, "it was a debating society."

According to Milestone, "The arguments continued interminably until His Highness had won over either Rosenberg or Lederer. Usually I would take a nap until they informed me His Highness was ready to submit to my camera. It was harrowing but, in terms of the extra sleep I got, quite restful."

Marlon ballooned from 170 pounds to 210, necessitating special lighting, special makeup, and special camera angles so that "he wouldn't look like Stan Laurel at the beginning of the picture and Oliver Hardy at the end." Weight control poses a chronic problem for Marlon, aggravated in this instance by the appeal of Polynesian food. ("When I open a refrigerator door, nothing is safe, not even the pipes.") Now, the more his weight increased, the more he threw it around with spontaneity. At whim he would sulk in his villa or desert the set in mid-scene. "When he did show up," Milestone swore, "he would discuss it for four hours, then we'd shoot for an hour to get a two-minute scene because he'd be mumbling or blowing his lines."

At one point Marlon issued an ultimatum that he would be unable to work unless his personal physician, Dr. Robert J. Kositchek, were flown in from Beverly Hills to prescribe for his upset stomach. "No Dr. Kositchek, no Marlon Brando," he threatened. Dr. Kositchek, with a busy practice, demurred. MGM then persuaded him to fly to Tahiti over a weekend. He examined Marlon, pronounced him overweight, prescribed a diet, and flew back to Beverly Hills. He presented MGM with a bill for $10,000.

Marlon's relations with the other actors soon deteriorated, particularly with the British contingent (perhaps because of the generally hostile atmosphere on the set, the cast divided into American and British camps). Trevor Howard (Captain Bligh) could symbolize the "unflappable Englishman" image; in his professional career he hadn't once been disconcerted, hadn't once been moved to unpremeditated acts. Marlon dented but couldn't pierce his armor. "With Marlon changing his lines gratuitously, I never knew whether or not he'd finished a line," Howard declared from the bridge of his nose. "More often than not, I'd be standing there with egg on my face. In one scene there was a discussion on the set over one word—one word!—whether Brando would say 'why' or 'where'—that went on for hours. The man is unprofessional and absolutely ridiculous. He could drive a saint to hell on a dogsled."

With the more volatile Irish actor, Richard Harris, then playing his first major screen role, the confrontation went beyond the verbal stage. In the scene where Harris sets the *Bounty* afire, Marlon is obliged to respond with a vicious backhanded blow to his head. Instead, he delivered a gentle love tap to Harris's cheek.

"No, no," said Milestone, "you're supposed to backhand him—and strongly."

"I can't," said Marlon, "I threw my shoulder out of joint. It hurts when I do that."

"Well, then, use your other arm," Milestone offered, ever considerate.

"I can't. I threw that shoulder out too."

Milestone's temper control was impressive. "In that case, why don't you just go home, Marlon?"

Marlon sauntered off while Milestone suggested to Harris, "If he does that again, why don't you just kiss him?" Harris was amenable to any ploy for improving his performance. At the next take Marlon again flicked him lightly; Harris embraced Marlon and awarded him a resounding kiss on the cheek. Marlon was unperturbed. "I'll do it again," Harris threatened, "I'll kiss you on the mouth. I'll dance with you. I'll jump on your back." He then walked off the set for a temper-cooling period of three days.

"You shouldn't have done that, Dick," Marlon reprimanded him when shooting resumed. "You should know that I'm the star of this picture, and you're opposing me. Remember, the star should have the best scenes." He then refused further work until one of Harris's better scenes (dying in the blazing ship) was cut.

Harris found the experience too traumatic for more than a few words: "The whole picture was just a large dreadful nightmare for me, and Brando was just a large dreadful nightmare for me, and I'd prefer to forget both as soon as my nerves recover from the ordeal."

Marlon denied all charges. Harris, Trevor, and the other actors were mistaken in their recollection of their conversations, he maintained. "The film managed to get screwed up without me.... Everybody in it gave up in disgust.... It's not true I couldn't remember my lines—there were twenty-seven scripts for the movie. It was impossible to memorize all of them."

As the months passed, more of the production members emulated Marlon in "going native." Barefoot revels through the night became common as did the throbbings of dozens of amateur bongo-drum players. Most of the men acquired one or more Tahitian mistresses, a circumstance fraught with two hazards: rotten teeth and venereal disease. Both problems were virtually epidemic throughout Tahiti, particularly the latter. "Anyone over the age of puberty is suspect," declared one film technician. "The only way to find a girl that's even safe to contemplate is to wait in front of the local grade school and pick out the girl with thick glasses and pigtails who's carrying an armful of books." Emergency shipments of penicillin, if not eradicating VD, kept it under control.

A cooperative effort was initiated to solve the rotten-teeth problem. Those men who were repelled by their mistresses' decayed teeth paid for the services of a dentist who was flown in from the States. The dentist, appalled at the state of dental deterioration among his new clientele (rock candy constitutes the principal diet of many Tahitian girls), announced that every mouth he had examined was a hopeless case. For each, he decreed total extractions followed by a full set of dentures. When additional finances had been negotiated, he imported more than fifty sets of dentures to be measured, cast, and fitted. The girls were delighted with their artificial teeth, and their benefactors found relief from the winds of halitosis.

Unfortunately for the production schedule, the girls now spent their days clacking their new dentures before friends and relatives in the interior rather than reporting for work as extras in the film. Nor were the men responsible for bringing the dentist to Tahiti pleased with the unavailability of their sex partners. A practical solution was arrived at by retrieving the dentures and locking them in a file cabinet on the set, each with a name tag attached. To be issued her dentures, a girl was required to appear at seven o'clock in the morning and surrender her ID card (needed to receive her daily pay). She then performed both her dramatic and concubinary functions. At day's end she could regain her ID card only by returning the dentures, which were locked up overnight in the file cabinet.

A naval officer from the French fleet anchored off Papeete was asked if the French administration knew of the debaucheries of the MGM personnel. "Of course, M'sieu," he said. "Then why do you tolerate it?" "Because, M'sieu, they're doing it in one spot. If we disturbed the situation, they'd soon be doing it all over the island."

Through the torpid summer months the production staggered on. Director Milestone retired to his bungalow. "You feel you know more about everything than anyone else," he told Marlon, "so you obviously don't need a director." Charles Lederer left for the United States (where his aunt, Marion Davies, was dying of cancer). Marlon and Rosenberg cavorted about the locations, erratically providing what little direction they could. Day scenes were shot at night. Shipboard scenes were shot on land. Scenes depicting winter events were being filmed in sweltering tropical heat. The actors were suffocating under heavy wool uniforms waiting for the cameras to roll. The cameras were waiting for Marlon to appear. Marlon was in his dressing room immersed in a washtub of ice cubes. When he walked out to confront the sun and the cameras, he could well simulate the winter chill. Harris and Trevor subsequently refused to appear on the set before Marlon announced his readiness. The production had reached the point of an English stage farce.

Milestone described Marlon's general attitude: "Instead of boarding the *Bounty* at the dock in Tahiti with the rest of us every morning, Brando insisted on a speedboat to take him out to the ship while we were at sea. Three weeks before we were to leave Tahiti, he decided to move from the house we had rented for him to an abandoned villa nearly fifty kilometers away. It cost us more than $6,000 to make it habitable for him for the week or two he lived in it. That's the way it was for the many months we were shooting."

With everyone involved on the picture nearly prostrate from the heat, the temper tantrums, the absurdities, and the interminable delays, the company returned to Hollywood for the final pickup scenes. Milestone, lunching with MGM production head Sol Siegel, again advised that scrapping the picture would ultimately minimize the losses. "You'll save millions," he prophesied. "You have a lead actor who doesn't want to do the picture properly and there's no way you can make him do it." Mr. Siegel spurned this economic wisdom and persuaded Milestone to remain as director pro forma. Milestone's judgment was to prove the sounder.

Viewing the rushes, producer Rosenberg despaired of assembling a cohesive motion picture. Without an alternative, he edited the footage into a rough cut. From this evidence, it seemed unlikely that the picture was fit for public release. Then Marlon came to the screening room to see the film. "You know, that's a damn good picture—only the ending is lousy," he said, and offered to forgo his overtime salary for two weeks of shooting a new ending.

Charles Lederer had crafted a dozen rewrites of the Pitcairn Island sequences ending the picture. Bronislav Kaper, responsible for the musical score, composed different versions for each finale according to its mood. (He flew to Tahiti to record a chorus of three hundred Tahitian singers.) None of these satisfied Marlon. Since he had been granted control, Marlon was not about to relinquish the opportunity to broadcast a message to mankind. Finally, Lederer—and his friend, Ben

Hecht—found a formula that encompassed philosophy, entertainment, and the obligatory Messiah-complex scene. New sets were built. Two additional weeks of shooting were enacted, and Marlon flew in from Thailand (where he was already filming *The Ugly American*) to contribute his part. George Seaton was persuaded to act as director *sans façon*. His condition: absolute secrecy.

This final chapter in the production was described by Mr. Milestone as "like a ship in a storm without a pilot or a compass." Milestone had promised Sol Siegel he would not add further to the gales of deleterious publicity buffeting the studio. "I showed up on the set each morning promptly at nine o'clock—or whatever time the call was for—and sat in a dressing room until I left at a decent hour. There was no point in being anywhere else. Why should I stand near the cameras and watch a clown? I was just there so the press couldn't report I had walked off the job. With Carol Reed out, two directors quitting would have hung an albatross on the picture."

The press was airing a steady flow of *Bounty* stories even without the directorial controversy. In the spring of 1962 President Kennedy asked writer-director Billy Wilder to dinner at the White House. Prepared for a discussion of politics or foreign affairs, Mr. Wilder was not prepared for President Kennedy's first question: "When in the world are they going to finish *Mutiny on the Bounty?*"

*Mutiny* premiered in November 1962. Reviews were devastating. *Time* magazine sneered that "the *Bounty* wanders through the hoarse platitudes of witless optimism until at last it is swamped with sentimental bilge." Arthur Knight, in *Saturday Review*, wrote, "Brando makes of Christian a fop, a dandy." His insight into the workings of the motion-picture business proved unclouded: "*Bounty* and *Cleopatra* are the auguries by which the entire industry will chart its future course." British reviewers scoffed at Marlon's accent. Eric Shorter, in the *Telegraph*, wrote, "Marlon Brando sounds as if his part had been dubbed by a subaltern at Sandhurst." Cecil Wilson opined, "He done it by stiffening his jaw, mincing through his teeth, and addressing the villain as Cept'n Blah." Unaccountably, the film received Academy Award nominations in seven categories, including that of best picture. It ultimately earned a box-office return of about $10 million, one-third the break-even sum.

Responsibility for the debacle was kicked about as if it were a soccer ball. Marlon, of course, presented the largest target, and virtually no one connected with the picture could refrain from flinging a stone or arrow in his direction. Director Milestone summarized his sentiments: "I can only say that the movie industry has come to a sorry state when a thing like this can happen, but maybe this experience will bring our executives to their senses. They deserve what they get when they give a ham actor, a petulant child, complete control of an expensive picture." Marlon later accosted Milestone to demand "why you treated me so badly and fed such awful slop to the press." "I didn't treat you badly," Milestone replied. "You behaved badly. And if you sue anyone and I'm called to testify, I'll stand by everything I said. It's the truth." Speaking with him many years afterward, I found his criticism diluted a modicum: "Marlon was promised a character to play—he was right in that. He wanted to play not Fletcher Christian—who was a leading man—but John Adams. The studio wasn't up to that. Marlon was the star, and he had to play a major name. So they promised him—to keep him quiet—that they'd combine the two stories into one. And that was a fatal mistake because the crack between the two stories couldn't be cemented over. Pitcairn Island was a whole new story. They built all those beautiful and expensive sets for Pitcairn Island, and never used them." Milestone never saw the film: "Why should I waste my time with it? For the same money I can go see a good film."

Trevor Howard indulged himself in a rare comment to the *Daily Mail:* "The only thing I could feel for the fellow was pity. Yes, I really think Brando is to be pitied. He hasn't a friend in the world. He never speaks to anyone unless it's someone smaller or younger. . . . I saw him try a ju-jitsu trick one day on a young Tahitian. But the Tahitian turned the trick on him, and Brando sulked for the rest of the day."

Writer Charles Lederer was unequivocal in his assessment of liability. "It would be difficult to find someone more culpable than Marlon Brando," he told me. "He was unscrupulous, conscienceless, detestable, and was at the ready with a quick-draw tantrum whenever he didn't get his own way."

Producer Aaron Rosenberg acquitted Marlon of first-degree guilt: "Milestone conducted himself badly. . . . You have to understand Marlon. You have to appreciate him as an actor. . . . You must allow him to make his contribution to the script and direction. Otherwise, he can't work."

Marlon was infuriated with the criticism and defended himself: "If I do something stupid, I expect to get rapped for it. If I give a lousy performance, I expect to get bum reviews. But I don't expect to get blamed for something I haven't done. I have searched my conscience to see if I could have been responsible for the chaotic history of this picture. I cannot see that I have." To a *Variety* reporter, he added: "If you would send a multimillion dollar production to a place where, according to the precipitation records, it is the worst time of the year, and when you sent it without a script, it seems there is some kind of primitive mistake. The reason for all of the big failures is the same—no script. Then the actors become the obvious target of executives trying to cover their own tracks. . . . It's all so simple. If an actor was working for me and got out of line, I'd get the Screen Actors Guild on the phone. They have the authority to punish actors. They've done it before." (Regarding this last sentiment, a producer friend of mine asked: "Would the Actors Guild punish Marlon Brando? Sure. Would the football commissioner cancel the Superbowl? Would the government cancel Fort Knox?")

Marlon also threatened legal action against MGM unless the studio ceased implicating him for *Bounty*'s astronomical loss. He filed a $5 million libel suit against the *Saturday Evening Post* for printing Milestone's remarks (the suit was subsequently withdrawn). Still, a majority of the press, the public, and the motion-picture industry convicted Marlon on all charges. Guilty or innocent, he was to serve the sentence pronounced: a ten-year reputation as mischief-maker, nihilist, and high-insurance risk.

The final scene of *Mutiny on the Bounty* was all too symbolic: the *Bounty* sinks in flames, Marlon's charred body trapped in its hold. Some observers swore that a close-up would have revealed the MGM lion strapped to the masthead.

# Seven

Our legal warfare had been subdued without a formal truce throughout Marlon's tribulations with the *Bounty* filming. Two major engagements (plus a number of skirmishes fought by our representatives) were recorded before cameras rolled in Tahiti. In each instance the outcome was inconclusive.

In mid-1960, I had filed a brief against Marlon, charging that his public antics adversely affected our son: "Defendant father, in blind zeal to obtain specious rights and makeup visitation privileges, has misjudged the best interests and welfare of the child. . . . Further, defendant has shown a blatant disregard of his promise to conduct himself properly with due regard to public conventions and morals . . . [and] has done and committed acts and things that have tended to degrade himself and his family in society and has brought upon himself and his family public contempt, scorn and ridicule. . . . [Such conduct] could encourage the child to follow in improper footsteps of his father so far as morals are concerned."

Marlon replied through his attorneys that "the alleged objectionable conduct was none of plaintiff's business."

In court I was called to testify first—while Marlon leered at me. His attorney, Mr. Kreps, was questioning if I had employed a private detective, Paul Gilbert, to spy on Marlon during his visitation periods. Since the court had approved Mr. Gilbert, I felt the examination to be persecutory and balked at some of the more insidious interrogation. Judge Lynch then growled at me that he would decide which questions were proper. I flared up: "Isn't that too bad! I thought this was supposed to be a democracy." I leaped from the witness stand and stalked out of the courtroom.

I fled into the ladies' room. The bailiff, immobilized at first by this unprecedented escape of a witness, was then balked by that feminine sanctuary. He could only knock politely and plead with me to open the door. When I emerged he escorted me back to the courtroom where I issued a public apology for leaving the witness stand, blaming the sudden onset of *le malédiction feminin*. Judge Lynch decreed a ten-minute recess.

In the corridor I orated to a cluster of reporters that Judge Lynch and Marlon Brando had conspired against me. "They killed Chessman, and this guy lives," I concluded with no particular logic. When I become furious, logic flees the scene.

When we resumed, I told Judge Lynch that "I feel Mr. Brando is an immoral man and I don't intend my child to grow up in that environment. . . . If I did not feel that way, I would not only allow him makeup privileges but I think I would still be married to him."

Marlon complained in his rebuttal that since the first of the year I had refused eight times to let him see Devi and that on five other occasions he was working out of town and unable to exercise his privileges.

I re-rebutted: "I have received threatening phone calls from someone who sounded like Mr. Brando. . . . I have heard early morning knocks at my door which moved me to call the police and my attorney."

Marlon re-re-rebutted by denying "having telephoned or approached Miss Kashfi's home."

Then a nurse, Mrs. Sydney Crecy, who had accompanied me to London the year before, was summoned to the stand to laud Marlon's paternal behavior: "His conduct was that of a loving father. The baby's crazy about him, and he seems to be crazy about the baby. They are very close."

After two days of such testimony, Judge Lynch ordered that the private investigator be discharged, that Marlon's visitation rights be recognized by all parties, and that he would not be entitled to additional rights because of his work outside Los Angeles.

Our last memorable court battle of 1960 took place in October, immediately prior to Marlon's departure for Tahiti. His attorneys filed an OSC re Contempt on the grounds that I was guilty of willfully disobeying the Court Order of the previous June. I countercharged that I required assurances that the people in the defendant's house at the time of the child's visits conduct themselves with appropriate decorum since the child had—in the defendant's home—acquired such phrases as "Go to hell" and "Fuck you." (Devi was two and a half years at this time.)

When all the redundant testimony about visits denied, excuses, and counterexcuses had been heard, Judge Benjamin Landis (a new entry in our judicial marathon) asked Marlon and me to stand before him. "You both might have a sick child on your hands," he said, "if you don't stop your feuding over him. . . . This boy is likely to develop allergies unless you mind your ways and be reasonable about visitation rights. . . . You are this child's parents and you must not allow the conflict between you to warp his life. . . . It is necessary for a child to grow up feeling love and respect for both parents. In the case of divorce, it is doubly important to guard against letting the bitterness between parents rub off on their son."

Then, addressing Marlon alone, he said, "Mr. Brando, you are an artist and you have a certain right to your eccentricities but the child has rights too. They should be observed." Marlon stiffened, and asked that these "eccentricities" be defined "so that I may eradicate them if they do exist." Replied the judge: "That matter is not before us."

Judge Landis then denied Marlon's contempt charge.

Publicity from our trials spread with the trade winds. When

Marlon arrived in Tahiti, he angrily brushed off reporters who would question him on his feelings toward his son and ex-wife. In Paris, where he was supervising the Pennebaker productions *Paris Blues* (Paul Newman, Joanne Woodward, Sidney Poitier) and *Naked Edge* (Deborah Kerr, Gary Cooper), Marlon, Sr., told the press soliciting his view of the case, "The one thing I regret is giving Marlon Brando my name."

Most of 1961 passed without direct confrontations between us. For the first three months of the year we neither spoke with nor saw each other. At the beginning of April Marlon telephoned from Tahiti. He told me he had married Movita the previous summer and that he wanted their son, Miko, to be a brother to Devi. (Had he forgotten France Nuyen and the phone call from Guadalajara?) He suggested that I and Devi should move to Tahiti to live. "It would be better for Christian as well," he said, "I don't like the racial prejudice in the States, and Christian will experience that prejudice because of your Indian blood."

During a courtroom scene the end of June Marlon admitted telephoning me about his marriage. "Was Miss Kashfi upset at the news?" he was asked. "Yes, she was jealous of the woman to whom I am married—Maria Castenada (Movita). I told Anna about the marriage," he said, "because I wanted her to hear it from me. I knew it would be found out sooner or later and I thought it would be fair, honest, and considerate of me to tell her rather than for her to find it out through gossip.... Then we discussed the relationship of the little boy I have by the other woman, and Christian. But she [Anna] screamed, railed, and raved at me."

Marlon then explained that Miko was Movita's son and that she was pregnant at the time of their marriage. "But I've never lived with her since," he swore, "and I've had no sexual relations with her since the baby was conceived." (Nonetheless, a second child, Rebecca, appeared some years later.) He insisted that they had been married in Mexico, with the presiding justice of the peace pledged to secrecy. The marriage certificate, he said, had been hidden away in a box rather than filed in a registrar's office.

Movita was present in the court when Marlon was testifying

to these events—in addition to an entourage of PR men and agents that surrounded the star. Subsequently, while I sat in the witness chair, she proceeded to smirk and distort her face at me. The judge banged his gavel and threatened her: "If you don't stop that nonsense this minute, I'll have you removed from the courtroom. You're distracting the witness."

For this trial Marlon had flown in from Tahiti, remained for thirty hours, much of it in the courthouse, and then flown back. His cause for complaint was that he had been deprived of his regular visitation rights without reason during a brief visit to Los Angeles in mid-April. My new attorney, Mr. Paul Caruso, counterfiled, accusing Marlon of "repeatedly harassing and abusing plaintiff via the telephone so that plaintiff has had to have her number changed on the average of once a month for the past year."

Changing telephone numbers merely obliged Marlon to send telegrams. One such was detailed in my brief: "On April 16, 1961, defendant sent plaintiff an urgent telegram at 11:30 P.M. asking her to call him. Plaintiff did so immediately, and defendant kept her on the phone until 1:15 A.M. There were no urgent matters to discuss; defendant told plaintiff that she should leave the country. Plaintiff became ill and hysterical, and her physician was called [and determined] that she required a sedative."

After all legal documents and testimony had been presented at the trial, Judge pro tem Erich Auerbach dismissed both OSCs. "You should minimize this turmoil and work out a solution," he lectured us, "because this case is becoming a vendetta, and the child is becoming an instrument of vengeance." Marlon sat glowering throughout the lecture, his hair pulled back into an eighteenth-century queue. I thought he resembled Captain Bligh more than Mr. Christian.

It was during Marlon's April hiatus from *Mutiny on the Bounty* that Rita Moreno attempted suicide at his home on Mulholland Drive. Although the incident was germane to my legal counterattack on Marlon as a "morally unfit father," I omitted it from my Declaration. It would have been gratuitously cruel at that time to publicize it further. I heard of the attempted suicide as I was preparing Devi for a visit to his father. Harrison Carroll, the columnist, phoned to say, "Don't send your son up to Marlon's. Rita Moreno's there, and she's taken an OD of sleeping pills. An ambulance and a doctor are there now. They're pumping out her stomach."

To protect Marlon, the "official" story placed the attempted suicide at the home of Marlon's secretary, Alice Marchak (who, in actuality, was at Marlon's house and called for the ambulance).

Miss Moreno recovered. She remained friendly with Marlon, shared a motion picture with him (*The Night of the Following Day*), married a New York psychiatrist, and became involved in the genesis of the Third World Cinema Corporation (1971), a group promoting racial minorities in films. More recently, she has resumed her acting career with a number of successful TV ventures. I have yet to conclude whether I resented her more for her claims to Marlon's affections or for her ability to solicit his interest in honing her acting skills. "What you do," Marlon told her when she asked his approach to accents (a specialty where he excels), "is speak English the very best you can. You learn all the speech anomalies, all the things that make up the accent, and then you talk like a person trying to conquer the anomalies so he won't have an accent."

*Mutiny on the Bounty* proved such an enervating experience for Marlon that his residual energy was inadequate to cope with further legal infighting. Throughout the summer and fall I received only two letters and a few phone calls from him. In October he called from Japan where he had stopped en route to Thailand for preliminary location scouting for *The Ugly American*. "I was saddened to learn of Dag Hammarskjöld's death," he told me, somewhat obscurely. After several other non sequiturs, he said, "Well, I have to hang up now. I have an appointment with the Emperor. Bye." I doubted that the Emperor could distinguish Marron Brando from a French dessert.

Our next courtroom joust came at the end of the year. It featured ample outbursts to attract scores of reporters and photographers. Marlon had returned to Los Angeles in November and had immediately petitioned the court to extend his visiting privileges. Devi, now at the age of three and a half, needed, so Marlon avowed, an accelerated father-son relationship.

My new attorney, Mr. Eugene Trope, filed an Affidavit in Opposition to OSC re Modification (I stand in awe of such *lex scripta*), denying that such extended visits would be in the best interests of the child.

In court Marlon proved to be in a particularly vicious mood. He denounced me from the stand as an incompetent and irresponsible parent and painted himself as a doting father. He told the judge (Benjamin Landis) that "I tried to give Christian more companionship by playing games with the boy. I encouraged him to play with [his half brother] Miko. I made a special point to go out with him, hunting, hiking, playing Indians, or visiting the fire station down the road from our house. . . . I always stressed a sense of family unity . . . telling Christian to give his mother a kiss for me when he started home." He ended with a plea for an end to the courtroom brawls: "I dislike being in court. . . . I consider it an invasion of privacy. . . . I'll do anything reasonable to avoid it."

When my turn on the witness stand came, I was boiling with fury—so much that Judge Landis ordered parts of my testimony to be stricken from the court records. My milder comments were printed in the newspapers: "If Mr. Brando feels so strongly about his private life being private, I can't see why he spends three-quarters of his time telling the public how private he wants it to be. As things are going now, he's turning my life and our little boy's as well into public property. . . . I realize Mr. Brando has troubles of his own, but, as far as I'm concerned, Christian Devi comes first. The things my little boy has repeated to me after visitations with his father disturb me beyond words. . . . In my mind, the quality of visitation is more important than the quantity."

Judge Landis ruled mostly in favor of Marlon. A nurse need not accompany Devi into his father's home, he decreed, and he awarded Marlon additional visiting privileges of every third weekend plus two weeks during the summer months. He was in the process of adding Thanksgiving, Christmas, the

Fourth of July, and Devi's birthday when I could no longer restrain myself.

"What do you want to do—eliminate motherhood from America?" I screamed at him, standing up at the plaintiff's table.

"Five hundred dollars for contempt of court!" he answered. It was an effective answer, with no appeal.

I stormed out of the courtroom, stopping in the corridor amidst a swarm of reporters. I was talking with them when Marlon emerged. "It's surprising what money can buy," he mumbled as he passed. "That miserable son of a bitch," I rasped to the reporters, "I'll fix him." I lunged at him and swung, striking him across the cheek. He fled down the corridor, protecting his head with both arms. I turned to the photographer who had just clicked his camera. "Don't say I never gave you a good picture."

I should have felt contrite but I didn't. The following day I admitted to the press, "I'm not a bit sorry. I should have whacked him four years ago."

The matter, of course, did not rest with Judge Landis's verdict. I soon filed a Petition for Rehearing and Reconsideration, and Marlon retaliated with OSCs, Depositions, and Declarations.

One of his complaints averred that I had abused and insulted his "then present wife," Movita. This "crime" was committed when I delivered Devi to Marlon's home for a scheduled visit in January 1962. Movita and Miko had been invited so the two boys could play together. (Marlon was continually promoting what he referred to as "group therapy sessions," mixing wives, mistresses, ex-mistresses, legitimate and illegitimate children in various combinations. Devi and Miko, in particular, were thrust together by their father. "Kiss the baby, little brother, kiss the baby," he urged Devi at every opportunity. "Marlon, you can't force love on children," I insisted. Finally, a moment came when Marlon said, "Kiss your baby brother," and Devi wound up and punched Miko on the nose.) Movita objected to my presence and demanded that Marlon throw me out. In response, I threw out a few choice epithets at her and then delivered the coup de grace: "How do you like your husband wearing my wedding band three years after we've been divorced?" Such were the abuse and insults I perpetrated against Marlon's "then present wife."

I had, in the settlement of this altercation, engaged a new attorney, Mr. Albert Pearlson, who differed from his predecessors in directing his efforts primarily toward negotiating peace rather than promoting further litigation. Mr. Pearlson tempered my OSCs and other legal counterattacks to less inflammatory contents. Marlon's attorneys reacted similarly, and the outlines of a truce began to form. Marlon, I, and our respective attorneys gathered in Mr. Pearlson's Beverly Hills offices for a lengthy smoking of the peace pipe. It marked the first time in years that we managed a pleasant meeting, devoid of bitterness. As a result, I allowed Marlon to keep Devi overnight at his house, and the next morning Marlon personally returned the boy to me.

Scheduled court hearings were canceled. OSCs re Contempt and Motions for Modifications of Custody Orders were taken off calendar. Judges, bailiffs, and stenotypers in the Santa Monica Courthouse sighed with relief. More than two years were to pass before the next round was fired in legal combat.

Occasional outbreaks marred the two-year peace period but were often overlaid by redeeming elements of humor and did not seriously threaten to renew hostilities. Several times in the spring of 1962 Marlon found it jolly sport to rummage through my lingerie, searching for my diaphragm—whether or not I was at home. When he found it, he would then perforate it several times with an ice pick. The local pharmacist thought it odd indeed that I ordered six diaphragms from my prescription in less than a month.

Late one evening I was struck by the ludicrousness—and the symbolism—of Marlon's interference in my intimate affairs. I jumped into my car and drove up to his house on Tower Road to tell him I would tolerate no further attacks on my prophylactics.

A year earlier, Marlon had relinquished his lease on his Japanese-style home and removed to the fabled Tower Road estate on a six-acre site above Beverly Hills. John Barrymore had remodeled the mansion after buying it from director King Vidor. The house features Italian glass windows, six marble fireplaces, and two doors from India allegedly over two millennia in age. A saloon bar taken from a Virginia City bawdy house (complete with bullet holes) stands on a floor of redwood trunks in the rathskeller. The garden is enriched with olive trees brought from Palestine, cypresses from Italy, and dwarf cedars from Japan. An artificial waterfall overlooks a 45-by-55-foot swimming pool surrounded by fir and palm trees. Despite the splendor, Marlon never regarded himself and the sprawling house as truly espoused. The home on Mulholland Drive bore numerous resemblances to his childhood home in Illinois, and, in his continuing efforts to resolve the psychological problems of that childhood, he was drawn back to it. He purchased it outright after two years' absence and resettled permanently in its more modest but secure enclosure.

When I arrived at the Tower Road estate that evening, no one answered the doorbell. A side entrance was unlocked, and I wandered about the house calling his name. I opened the bedroom door. Marlon was lying in bed, wearing a silk robe, flipping the pages of a magazine. Next to him lay a young Filipino entertainer whom Marlon had met in a Manila hotel the previous year. She was nude.

Marlon panicked. The young lady panicked. While Marlon stuttered and drew the bedcovers up to his neck, she grabbed a lamp from the bedside table and threw it at me. I ran out of the house, back to my car. Marlon's temper veered from embarrassment to anger. He followed me out, tackled me on the front lawn, and proceeded to knock my head against the curbstone. From experience, I knew that his anger, while it can provoke him to superhuman fury, soon subsides. I didn't fight back—I couldn't, in the event, since I was still weak from laughing over the sight of them in bed together.

Marlon dropped me abruptly and stalked back to the house. My senses were reeling from the pounding; instead of driving home, I found my way back to the kitchen for a drink of water. There, Marlon pounced on me and bound my hands and feet. I was not released until the police arrived, whereupon the incident was smoothed over and I departed under a flag of truce. The police found the lady cowering in the shower, but no mention of her name entered their report.

When Marlon was asked by a *Newsweek* reporter if he were in the habit of having ladies in his home for sexual reasons, he answered, "I have ladies in my home for many purposes, including sexual. But I would not like to give the impression that people are invited to my home primarily for sexual reasons."

On February 27 of the following year (1963), the unnamed damsel gave birth to a girl (several weeks before Marlon's mistress-elect, Tarita, produced a boy). She registered her daughter as Maya Gabriella Cui Brando and in July of that year filed a paternity suit against Marlon. Her complaint averred that Marlon had sent her to his doctor for prenatal care but later refused to provide for her and the baby. Marlon denied her Declaration but admitted the possibility that he had fathered her child.

Coincidentally with the issuance of a summons for the paternity suit, Marlon entered the pediatrics ward of Saint Johns Hospital in Santa Monica. His physician, Dr. Kositchek, pronounced him to be suffering from acute pyelonephritis, an inflammation and virus infection of the kidneys. "He is a very sick man," said Dr. Kositchek. The private investigator who penetrated hospital security and served the summons expressed his medical opinion: "Mr. Brando was sitting up in bed, joking with the nurses. He looked as healthy as I am." No one explained Marlon's presence in the pediatrics ward.

Blood tests absolved Marlon of responsibility, and the paternity suit was dismissed. Some suspicion of tampering with the findings arose from those conducting the tests but the issue was not pressed. The lady was adequately if unofficially recompensed; she remains on friendly terms with Marlon. Her daughter, Maya, is frequently invited to join the Brando menagerie of juveniles in outings and family reunions. Again, Marlon's generosity, even after fighting a lawsuit as in this instance, exposed the basic decency and honesty beneath the thick layers of idiosyncrasy.

Except for scattered episodes such as "la jeune fille dans le lit," Marlon and I had little contact during these months between court appearances. Our few meetings were cordial; no disputes arose over the frequency, place, or nature of his visits with Devi. When rumors of recriminations or of further strife appeared in the press, Marlon was quick to write, denying responsibility.

One of the major newspapers carried a story that quoted Marlon and others as accusing me of mistreating his son. ("Anna Kashfi is too unstable for motherhood.") Within two days I received a letter from Marlon denouncing the article. He denied talking to the press about me at any time and threatened to attack physically and legally the "shitmongers" who were responsible. "Don't allow those dirty, sick, and twisted cruel minds to make you lose your composure," he pleaded. He went on to offer effusive and embarrassing testimonials to my qualities as a mother. Even our violent battles in and out of court were referred to as "little differences of opinion only natural with parents."

During much of this time Marlon was either out of town for motion-picture work or he was preoccupied with his newest avocation: the struggle for civil rights.

For many years Marlon had opposed racial prejudice in the entertainment industry; he was the first major actor to insert a nondiscrimination clause in his contracts banning the exhibition of his films in segregated theatres. He had also enlisted in such extraneous causes as the campaign to save Caryl Chessman, the condemned rapist, and the American Indians' movement to reverse their screen image as "cruel, uncivilized losers." In March 1961, he sponsored (along with Eleanor Roosevelt, Nat King Cole, Henry Belafonte, Sidney Poitier, and others) a *New York Times* advertisement soliciting funds for Martin Luther King, Jr. He picketed an all-white residential tract in Torrance, California. He was vocally critical of publicized prejudices—such as the Alabama police treatment of blacks. He joined protest marches in Gadsden, Alabama, and (with Burt Lancaster and Sammy Davis, Jr.) in Mississippi supporting black voter registration drives.

Sammy Davis, Jr., announced that "Marlon's a stand-up guy who has the courage of his convictions. I'm just sorry more Hollywood people aren't able to join us." "Sammy Davis?" said Marlon. "He's an applause junkie."

In mid-July 1963, Marlon addressed an ACLU meeting in Hollywood and urged an end to discrimination in the motion-picture industry. "Producers offer many excuses for not using Negro actors," he said. "'People aren't ready for it'; 'we have a moral responsibility to the bankers'; '40 percent of the market might be lost if Negro actors are used.' Those who raise such objections are not necessarily bad men but are ignorant, absolutely ignorant. Some of them will have to be forced, some demonstrated against, to make them see the light."

After Marlon joined in the civil rights march on Washington (August 1963), political columnist James Wechsler wrote, "There are few people with whom I have conversed who seem to know—and care—as much as Brando does about the quest for human dignity in which we are now engaged."

Interrupting his filming of Bedtime Story to fly East for that demonstration, Marlon justified his contribution: "I hope to accomplish a simple statement as a private citizen ... who believes these rights should be recognized." Not all Negro organizations were appreciative of his support. One published an open letter declaring, "We don't want or need Marlon Brando there. He's exploiting himself personally." "It's not a Negro cause," Marlon rebutted. "It's mine as well as every-body else's."

Marlon exchanged correspondence with Senator Everett Dirksen on proposed civil rights legislation and spent weeks in Washington cultivating other political figures. Through his friend George Englund, he was introduced to and dined with Jacqueline Kennedy at the fashionable Jockey Club in Washington. And he was accorded the ultimate governmental honor when columnist Jack Anderson accused the FBI of snooping in his affairs and tapping his telephone. It was alleged that reports of Marlon's activities and conversations constituted President Lyndon Johnson's favorite bedtime reading.

To promote his social views Marlon appeared on the Johnny Carson Show, where he traded insults with Zsa Zsa Gabor, and thence on the television show "Open End," where he traded insults with David Susskind. Mr. Susskind, the moderator, suggested that Marlon was really more interested in making money than in making pictures with social themes. Marlon responded by asking Mr. Susskind how he rationalized working for a cigarette sponsor when it was known that cigarettes cause cancer.

Social reform led Marlon to speculate more grandly on reform of mankind. "If it's true that Man is in a constant search for Good," he philosophized in a magazine interview, "then it's true that he is also searching for Evil. We have our angels of Love, but there are archangels of Evil as well. Man must find both the mask of the devil and the mask of God in everything he does."

There was never a moment I doubted Marlon's conviction and dedication to his causes. I could almost hear the old rebel inside of him nagging at him to preach the liberal faith. Unfortunately, he couldn't distinguish fad from social movement, fashion from revolution. Not one of his ideas could have won him respectable marks in a freshman philosophy course. And, as ever, he qualified his involvement: "I prefer that people think of me as an actor, not a social activist."

In mid-1963 Marlon was in Tahiti negotiating the purchase of Tetiaroa, the thirteen atolls thirty-two miles from Papeete. I had been undergoing treatment for what was described to me as an epileptic condition and had received several encouraging letters from Marlon promising his support through the ordeal. He invited me and my attorney, Mr. Pearlson, plus Mrs. Pearlson and their two children for a month's vacation in Tahiti.

Mr. Pearlson accepted the invitation and we (his family and I) flew to Tahiti together. His alacrity in so doing and his frequent communication with Marlon planted suspicions in my mind that his professional loyalties were not undivided. I discharged him two years later in April 1965. Attorneys in divorce cases are often subjected to a "Caesar's wife" standard; few can meet it.

The holiday served to restore my psychological balance more than could any therapy administered by doctors and psychiatrists. Except for a fleeting encounter with Tarita, nothing occurred to mar the tranquil existence that Tahiti offers. It is a wasteful, vacuous existence; I cannot understand its attraction to Marlon for long intervals. As a respite from the pressures of a more active life, however, it is unsurpassed.

Back in Los Angeles, I continued my treatment for epilepsy

and incipient alcoholism. Marlon continued sending encouraging notes, invariably beginning, "Stick with it and hang on tight because it's really worth the ride when you get there."

My ex-husband and my current attorney spoke often. "I talked to Al [Pearlson]," Marlon wrote typically, "he told me that you had been feeling blue and empty and depressed and if you can believe it, it's really a good sign because it means you have stopped turning your face away from your real anguish and you have been brave enough to stop running away from these feelings. Anna, I mean it with all my heart, that I'm proud of you. . . . Your going [for treatment] is the finest moment in your life."

Marlon's support and reassurances—his notes arrived regularly from New York, Tahiti, etc.—seemed oblique despite their sincerity. As ever when I was debilitated, he was magnanimous by his own coordinates. "Anna, I would cut off my arm if it would help you," he wrote, "but it wouldn't help. . . . I assure you that there are people who really really care about you and want to help and will stand by you no matter what you do feel or say. . . . You have to explore the depth of your soul by yourself no one can do it for you—you must take, as someone put it, 'the underwater journey through the night sea.' "

From the tone of these letters, an outside observer might have concluded that I was undergoing a prefrontal lobotomy. Yet the sympathy was genuine. Marlon even surrendered his visitation rights in his compulsion to cooperate: "I want to call often of course, but if there are conflicts that arise it is too upsetting for [the baby] if he hears and he is so bright and alert he hears everything and what he doesnt hear he feels. So you must realize that when I don't call it is not forgetfulness so much as remembering when he called on the phone crying and saying he didn't want to see me cry more because as he expressed it, 'the operators are listening.' I know that I am still an upsetting factor in your life and I don't want to make it any worse or be in anyway an irritation. I sincerely want to do what is right but sometimes it is hard to know."

I responded with equal courtesy, personally and publicly. A Hollywood columnist printed a modest comment as sensational news after the years of bickering: "Marlon and I have had our differences," I was quoted, "but they have been as individuals."

Improved relations turned Marlon to a playful mood. He telephoned one evening to say, "I want to tell you something before you read it in the newspapers. I don't want you to hear it from some other source." Judging by his tone, I decided the news was pleasant and personal: "You're getting married?" After a pause his voice continued, with a lugubrious note: "No, I have terminal cancer. I'm going into the hospital now for a biopsy."

I rang my doctor to seek further details. I rang my attorney. I rang Jay Kanter. I rang Universal Studios for Lew Wasserman (whom I had met at Jay Kanter's home) to enlist the studio's aid for Marlon. I fretted by the telephone for an hour. Then my doctor called back. "Marlon's in the hospital for an ulcer," he said. "He put a silk handkerchief over his head and walked in for a checkup. Don't worry about it." I should have known.

Our two-year hiatus from filing OSCs was temporarily interrupted after Devi's sixth birthday in May 1964. Marlon petitioned for longer and more flexible visitation rights during the summer months since he was engaged with a film (*Morituri*) and could not adhere to the prescribed periods. Judge Lawrence J. Rittenband granted the request, a move that in years past would have triggered fervid court battles. However, Mr. Pearlson met with Allen Susman, Marlon's attorney (O'Melvany and Meyers had been replaced by Rosenfeld, Myer and Susman), and an amicable accord was reached. Further, I agreed that "defendant may take the minor child of the parties to Tahiti on June 13, 1964, and return said minor child on July 13, 1964."

"Said minor child" later told me that his month in Tahiti with his father was "more fun than a month at Disneyland with Donald Duck." A perennial nine-year-old himself, Marlon has ever been more at ease with children than with adults; the feeling is mutual. "I love children around me," he has said often. "Their function is to enjoy themselves."

Although no additional legal documents were submitted for six months, the spring of dissension between us was again winding up. It broke on December 7—with a thunderclap that shattered the accomplishments of two years' equanimity and nearly killed me.

I had been taking Dilantin, an epilepsy-inhibiting drug prescribed by Dr. Gerald Labiner, my personal physician of the past year. Reactions to the drug had often included extreme dizziness, but I had never before lost consciousness. My memory of the sequence of events on that occasion remains hazy. Marlon's recollection is recorded in a Declaration filed the same day:

"At or about 2:00 A.M. of the morning of December 7, I received an emergency phone call from the Los Angeles Police Department. They were calling from Miss Kashfi's home. I was told that my 6½-year-old boy was unable to arouse his mother, who has been unconscious. The boy called the operator who called the police. The police came to the house and found Miss Kashfi comatose and Christian alone with his mother. I then immediately went to Miss Kashfi's house and discovered that she had been taken to the emergency ward of the UCLA medical center suffering from an overdose of barbiturates. I was further advised at UCLA medical center that the medical findings showed that she had taken 4 mgs of a short-acting barbiturate, a very dangerous dosage.

"When I arrived at her house, there were empty bottles thrown on the floor, and my son had had nothing to eat all day. He was frightened, hungry, and uncared for. I took the boy to my house. When I left for work that morning he was still highly upset, nervous, and agitated, and had been unable to sleep all night. My secretary [Alice Marchak] and my maid remained at home with Christian.

"At about 1:00 P.M. [that date], and while I was at work, Miss Kashfi insisted and obtained her release from the hospital, broke through the gate and fence around my house, broke into the house, assaulted and struck my secretary, threw a table through the plate glass window, and ran off with our son. Christian was crying and screaming with fright.

"I have discovered that [Miss Kashfi] has kept a loaded revolver at her home and she carried it around and played with it while she was under the influence of barbiturates and intoxicants. My son's safety and welfare are in extreme and immediate danger. . . . The child is in a terrible distraught state; [Miss Kashfi] is incapable of taking care of his needs and welfare."

Marlon filed a report at a North Hollywood police station accusing me of "malicious mischief." Then, at the Santa Monica Courthouse, he submitted his Declaration. Temporary custody of Devi was granted by Judge Edward Brand, thereby igniting yet more violent explosions that same day.

Armed with his court order, Marlon drove directly to my home in Brentwood, accompanied by his lawyer and two private detectives. No one answered the doorbell—I had taken Devi to a nearby hotel to thwart just such an attempted countercoup.

It was never explained to me how Marlon discovered my whereabouts. I had registered at the hotel under an alias and had acted as inconspicuously as my turbulent state of mind had permitted. Nonetheless, within an hour of leaving my Brentwood home, Marlon and his attendant policemen and detectives had tracked me down.

I was in the bedroom of the hotel suite, clothed in a nightgown and peignoir, preparing to retire. Devi was in the front room; despite the earlier confrontation at Marlon's house, he was now calm and had finished his supper. I heard scuffling noises as I left the bathroom and rushed through the doorway. Devi was gone, the front door open. I glimpsed Marlon and several police officers dragging him down the corridor.

The headline in the *Herald-Examiner* screamed, "Nightie Rampage Jails Brando's Ex." A two-column article on the front page began, "Bruised, barefoot, and belligerent, actress Anna Kashfi, 30, bailed out of jail early today after allegedly slugging two police officers in a 24-hour bout of violence with her ex-husband, actor Marlon Brando, over custody of their six-year-old son."

I had, of course, raced after Devi and his abductors with the bloody-minded vindictiveness of a mother eagle after a predator. If I fought the police, my concern for my child could not be tempered by a uniform.

"Screaming and fighting, and clad only in a sheer nightgown and light robe, Miss Kashfi ran through the lobby of the Bel Air Sands Motor Hotel when she learned that Brando had spirited the boy from her room, police said. After she slapped a police sergeant, she was handcuffed and taken to the West Los Angeles police station and booked on suspicion of battery on a policeman."

Not only a police sergeant, but two other men had also, it was alleged, been assaulted by me in the hotel lobby. The police clamped handcuffs on my wrists, towed me out to a waiting paddy wagon and to the police station. After three charges of battery and one of disturbing the peace were read, I phoned my lawyer who arranged for the $276 bail. A trial date was scheduled, and I was released.

I went back to the hotel for no explicable reason. Dr. Labiner was called to examine me. As he later testified, he found me "rational, sensible, coherent, without any trace of barbiturates or narcotics. . . . But I found her highly nervous and emotional. . . . She is a stable person, except when under mental stress, at which time she does become hysterical and emotionally upset." Beyond question, I was under mental stress on that date.

After I petitioned to regain my son, Judge Brand sent a probation officer to Marlon's house to investigate Devi's surroundings. The officer reported that toys and neighborhood children were available. Judge Brand thereupon refused to rescind his decree awarding custody to Marlon and instead ordered a psychiatric examination for Devi. "If it is found to be in the best interests of this child that he be placed in a neutral home, this court will not have the slightest hesitancy in so doing."

My nervous state caused continuances of the trial for several weeks. In mid-February 1965, three days of testimony were needed to unravel the full story of the December 7 upheavals from the numerous points of view.

I testified to my still shaky memory of the events. I admitted that I had not allowed Devi to visit his father recently on the grounds that Tarita and her child were at Marlon's home. "On December 7," I confessed, "I did something stupid. I tried to kill myself but had enough sense not to take too many pills and told my son to call the operator for help." A sense of being smothered—by the legal system, by the pervasive power that Marlon could unleash—had overwhelmed me. I had, indeed, seized Devi from Marlon's house, but without breaking in and assaulting his secretary. I also admitted that I kept a gun—a .22-caliber Biretta—which was taken by Marlon—but that I kept it because my life had been threatened, and I had been assaulted. (The gun—and a hypodermic syringe I had not previously seen—were brandished by Marlon's attorney, Allen Susman, with impressive dramatic effect.)

Marlon informed the court that he had married me because I was pregnant, that he wished only to legitimize the baby. "Soon after the baby was born," he said, "she began having fits and soon after that she began taking tranquilizers and barbiturates. . . . From the time the child was three months old, visitation rights have been denied me periodically. . . . Many times when I attempted to see the youngster, Miss Kashfi was in a drunken stupor. On one occasion she attempted to stab me; this occurred in front of the boy. On several other occasions, she threatened to kill me, the child, and herself."

Alice Marchak, ash-blonde, square-jawed, fastidious, was given her moment on the witness stand. She described the details of Rita Moreno's suicide attempt and other "not unusual" events at Marlon's home. "On December 7," she said, "Miss Kashfi broke into our home and struck me. I told her if she hit me again, I'd hit her back—and I did."

My character witness, Dr. Labiner, fashioned a defense that seemed more like an attack: "Miss Kashfi has a wide, swinging personality, episodes of deep depression to normal elations, all with hysterical overtones. . . . She was often in a moderately controlled hysterical state, sometimes appearing 'like a drunk.' Even as little a stimulus as a glass of beer could produce a reaction." Dr. Labiner discussed my history of epileptic seizures, emphasizing a grand-mal seizure that had occurred after Marlon had regained temporary custody of my son. He had prescribed Dilantin and other sedatives, he said, to decrease the frequency of the seizures.

Before ruling, Judge Rittenband interviewed Devi in his chambers and read statements from clinical psychologists and school officials regarding their assessments of the child. Dr. Dunn, a psychologist, reported that Devi had deteriorated into "a tense, fearful, terrorized youngster who is very hyperactive and is unable to maintain attention or relate well with most adults. . . . The minor stated no preference for either parent and said, 'I guess older people will have to decide where I go.' He also said 'his parents argue a great deal' and believed it was mostly about him."

Administrators at the Montessori School attended by Devi reported their view that he was emotionally disturbed, "totally incapable of facing reality," and was experiencing behavior problems. "He was working far below his intellectual potential because most of the disintelligence was being channeled off to motor activities," said one instructor in the standard convoluted jargon. Mr. Tom Laughlin, the principal, drove in the last nail: "Since Mr. Brando took custody of the boy in December, there has been a behavior change that is marvelous. He is simply a different boy." (Mr. Laughlin subsequently entered the motion-picture industry where he produced such financially successful films as *Billy Jack.*)

Under the weight of this testimony, Judge Rittenband's deliberations were brief. Defendant Marlon Brando was granted custody of Christian Devi Brando, subject to further orders of the court. Mrs. Frances Loving, Marlon's sister, was "entrusted with the physical possession and care of said minor" for a period of six months. Devi was to live with her and her husband in their home in Mundelein, Illinois. It was termed a "Solomonlike decision."

Its wisdom was lost on Devi who offered to write a letter to Judge Rittenband requesting that he be allowed to remain with his mother; the offer was refused. It was also lost on a little elderly lady who encountered Marlon in public and whacked him over the head with her umbrella. "How could you take a child from its mother?" she berated him.

Plaintiff Anna Kashfi Brando was "enjoined and restrained from annoying, molesting, harassing, threatening, interfering with, or in any way causing embarrassment to the defendant, any of the defendant's agents, representatives, or employees, any member of the defendant's family or household, or the minor child of the parties, and from being present at the home of defendant except upon express invitation."

Judge Rittenband also ordered me to undergo a six-month rehabilitation program. He appointed two neurological and psychological specialists from UCLA to supervise the program. "Miss Kashfi's reliance on drugs and alcohol both contributed to her uncontrollable temper" was the judge's verdict. "With her own problems, I feel that she will have enough trouble taking care of herself, let alone taking care of her son." His concession to my presence consisted of "Miss Kashfi is emotionally not stable, but not irreversibly so."

I raced from the courtroom, tearful, wrathful, incoherent. "I'll subpoena the judge. I'll subpoena the court," I shrieked at the flock of newsmen who convoyed me to the parking lot. "If you call this fairness, you can keep it. Is there anything wrong with a mother's wanting her own child, good Lord? He's being given away to a woman I don't even know. God! I bore him and brought him up. Where the hell was Marlon Brando when the child was being brought up?"

I may have been crazy, as Judge Rittenband proclaimed, but I could never be accused of a lack of persistence. I replaced Albert Pearlson with Merle Horowitz and, within a month, Mr. Horowitz with Ralph Marks. A barrage of OSCs re Modification, Petitions, Affidavits, and Orders to Overturn were filed. Mr. Marks charged that "Brando was using the courts of California for wrongful purposes. I believe that Anna Kashfi's so-called crime was created by other parties. I contend that forged evidence was used to take away her baby son." He then proceeded to accuse the city attorney's office of "obstructing the normal discovery procedures in connection with police records, photographs, and other material pertinent to Miss Kashfi's arrest."

Unfortunately, Mr. Marks's zeal led him to repeat his charges on the Joe Pync Show, a syndicated television program. He was replaced by Paul Magasin, one of my previous attorneys. ("It's like marrying an ex-wife," said Mr. Magasin.)

My trial for assault and battery on police sergeant John Hall at the Bel Air Sands Motor Hotel the previous December was scheduled for July. The prosecutor attempted to have Marlon called as a material witness. When the marshals arrived at his house with the process papers, Marlon ducked around the back rooms and released two large Saint Bernard dogs who chased them outside the gate. There they camped, while Alice Marchak served them coffee and cakes every few hours. Marlon, at this time, was shooting *The Chase* on the Columbia lot. For a week he was smuggled through the studio gate each day in the trunk of the producer's car—to no avail, ultimately.

Mr. Marks, still my counsel at this time, told Judge Joan Dempsey Klein and the jury that "Anna Kashfi may be guilty of stupidity but she is not guilty of battery." Marlon testified that he knew me to be suffering from "psychoneuroses, which at times caused hysterical blindness . . . barbiturate poisoning . . . occasional malnutrition . . . a psychological and physical addiction to barbiturates, alcohol, and tuberculosis."

Deputy District Attorney John B. Harris conducted the prosecution with a bandaged hand and one arm in a black kerchief sling. A battalion of police cadets sat in the audience, cheering him on. Mr. Marks's oblique defense did not impress the jury. I was convicted and fined $200 or thirty days in the Los Angeles County jail. I paid the $200.

Less than two weeks after the trial, Marlon, Sr., died. He was stricken with a heart attack, taken to Saint Vincent's Hospital, and passed away four hours later. He was seventy years old. At his request no funeral services were held. I was unable to reach Marlon to express my condolences. (He was on location for *The Chase*.) Later he declined to discuss his father's death—with me or anyone. I thought of Leo Stein's comment after his sister Gertrude's death: "I can't say it touches me. I had lost not only all regard but all respect for her." I quite believe that sentiment expressed Marlon's filial feelings. Further, the dead were to be shunned by the living in Marlon's philosophy, lest the one contaminate the other. "It's like discussing God outside of church," he once remarked.

Four years after his father's death Marlon was asked by an interviewer if he had ever tried to kill anyone. "I once tried to kill my father," he said. "Really. I always used to imagine I was killing him by pulling out his corneas."

In August I saw my son again for the first time in more than six months. Marlon's sister, Frances Loving, had reported in several letters to the court that the child was backward, fearful, and mistrustful of adults when she first received him, but that under her tutelage he had grown into a happy, obedient, secure youngster. It had been necessary, she reported, to spank him on occasion. Devi's version, when he spoke to me of his experiences with his aunt, were at variance with this view. On one instance, he told me, his aunt, Uncle Richard, and his cousins had buried me in effigy. "We made up a troll to look like you, Mommy, and then Auntie Fran said, 'Your mother is wicked. She has to be buried deep down.' "

An Affidavit of prejudice having been filed against Judge Brand—by Marlon's attorney, Allen Susman—jurisdiction over the custody question was transferred to another district where Judge A. C. Scott awarded alternate visitation rights for me and Marlon. In effect, we shared custody of our son.

Judge Scott, a courteous, dignified gentleman with a shock of white hair and metallic blue eyes, also read two rather testy letters to the court from the UCLA psychologists who had examined me. They were unable to reach any conclusion, they said, due to lack of cooperation on my part, and they resented further attempts by the court to coerce them. Their report concluded, "There is little that can be done to help her as long as she does not want help unless she reaches a point where control and reality are given up to such a degree as to make involuntary treatment a necessity."

On the first of October Judge Scott awarded me full custody of Devi with Marlon retaining reasonable rights of visitation. We were mutually enjoined from annoying, molesting, or harassing each other. Marlon appealed with more OSCs but was defeated. The judge quoted a statement of Marlon's from the February trial: "I think the best of all possible worlds is for a man and wife to be together with their child. Barring that, a child in its early formative years should be with the mother if she can be responsible, and certainly if Anna can repair herself and be rehabilitated, I think she should certainly have access to Christian and could make a great and important contribution to his life. I have every hope that she will."

Devi had been waiting in Judge Scott's chambers. I grabbed him and dashed from the courtroom as if the least hesitation would reverse the verdict.

Over the next several years our legal battles were fought at long range—without the hand-to-hand combat of a trial. Another procession of lawyers registered on the balance sheet.

Appeals, OSCs, and several poetic-sounding nunc pro tunc's were filed, all seemingly nullifying one another.

Ten years of postmarital warfare was commemorated in 1969 when my original alimony payments ceased. My attorney requested additional payments, and these were granted.

Marlon passed much of the second half of the 1960s in Europe, Africa, and Tahiti—working on motion pictures, traveling, or relaxing on his private island. (In 1966 he concluded his purchase of Tetiaroa.) At the end of 1964 he had told columnist Earl Wilson that 1968 was his target date for retirement from films. On Irv Kupcinet's late night talk show from Chicago, he declared in April 1967, that he would unquestionably quit acting within two years and devote himself to other interests. "Was he procrastinating about his retirement?" he was asked in 1971. "Not at all," he said, "merely postponing."

Social causes occupied fragments of Marlon's energies during his U.S. stays and assured him occasional headlines. He subscribed $500 to a fund for the protection and aid of South African political prisoners. He contributed to liberal causes in politics and antiwar causes throughout the world. In Washington State he engaged in a "fish-in," protesting a state law prohibiting Indians from netting fish outside their reservation. For this cause he paddled his own canoe onto the Puyallup River (Olympia, Washington) to snare a salmon. He was arrested for illegal fishing, but the charges were quickly dropped. Said the prosecutor: "I don't see any purpose of allowing Brando to sit in jail and make a martyr out of himself."

In April 1968, Marlon marched in the procession at the funeral of Martin Luther King, Jr., and in the same month attended the Oakland funeral of Bobby Hutton, the seventeen-year-old Black Panther slain by the police. From the flatbed of a truck, Marlon addressed the mourning crowd: "I have just come from the funeral of Bobby Hutton. . . . That could have been my own son lying there. . . . The preacher said that the white man can't 'cool it' because he has never 'dug it.' . . . I am trying to 'dig it.' That's why I am here."

Three weeks later, on the Joey Bishop Show, Marlon insisted that the police had shot Bobby Hutton while he was surrendering with his arms raised. Three policemen claimed that Marlon's statements had defamed their reputations. They filed a $6 million slander suit against him, a suit eventually carried to the Supreme Court. That body, after three years, refused to hear his plea that talk-show guests should be exempt from slander suits if their criticisms specified no names. The case was settled out of court.

Marlon often appeared on the Berkeley campus during the student unrest of the late sixties. Addressing Negro militants from a campus podium, he raised his voice for brotherhood: "I believe, with the late Martin Luther King, that we are either going to learn to live together as brothers in this country or die separately as fools. It is either nonviolence or non-existence."

Evidence suggested that Marlon's support of humanitarian causes hindered more than helped their furtherance. He was accused of firing peashooters at elephants—and missing. Columnist Morrie Ryskind, commenting on his demonstrations against racial discrimination in a housing tract, wrote, "[Brando] could have, had he wished, demonstrated in his own neighborhood, which has few Negroes. But that would have been too easy. He preferred integration somewhat farther away."

That barb too may have been misdirected. Marlon makes an elusive target with his fast-moving oratory. It is one of his fascinating qualities.

And although his own targets are often beyond his range, his intense emotional commitment to them immeasurably deepens his understanding of human suffering.

Women—nameless and faceless—continued to tramp in and out of Marlon's life. As one left his bed, the next was fluffing the pillows. Despite marriage to Movita and despite the patient Tarita in Tahiti, Marlon focused on the girl at hand. "Being a movie star means I can do away with the necessity of a lot of preliminaries socially," he told a friend. "There's no chick I can't have if I program it right. They all fall for the movie-star bit. Watch—" He then propositioned the next passing girl over seventeen.

Affairs beyond those of the "one night" variety were still confined to dark-skinned beauties. For extended periods

Marlon was seen with Diana Ross and with Esther Anderson, a rock singer from Jamaica. Possibly his most outlandish relationship involved a dusky Haitian girl, Giselle Fermez. A practitioner of voodoo arts, Miss Fermez had a considerable reputation for her contacts with party girls. She had been asked, on occasion, to organize get-togethers. She told me that she had once been asked to put on a party for Jack Kennedy, then President-elect. Impressed and flustered, she withdrew to her bedroom: "O Holy Virgin, on this special occasion, make me a wonderful party." "Did it work?" I inquired. "I got an extra $100," she said.

After Marlon broke their relationship, she retaliated by telephoning a Hollywood mortuary and directing the proprietor to Marlon's address. Several men in white suits rang the doorbell. Devi answered and was induced to wake his father. "Daddy," he cried, "there's six men out there who said they've come for the body!"

Not satisfied with pranks, Miss Fermez resolved upon a voodoo curse. She opened my door one evening, carrying a shoebox under one arm. It contained, I could not avoid learning, a dead beetle, a dead mouse, a candle, a thorn from a rosebush, and several items of indeterminant biology. An incantation—unintelligible—was pronounced over this ghastly farrago. We then drove to Marlon's house (at midnight) where, after further imprecations, Miss Fermez pitched the box and its contents over the gate onto Marlon's lawn. If the curse affected him, it was not apparent. Giselle Fermez faded from Marlon's life but not from mine.

Not all of Marlon's women retired silently to the bleachers. In June 1967, Movita followed my precedent and filed a divorce action charging Marlon with causing her "great mental suffering." She asked $5,000 per month for herself and $3,000 per month for her two children, Miko and Rebecca. She also sued to prevent Marlon from selling their "mutual property." Her documents declared that she and Marlon had been married in Xochimilco, Mexico, on June 4, 1960. Their separation was not unfriendly. Movita told the press, "Marlon is a nice guy, but he'll never change. He can't help being what he is. I'm just tired of sitting alone all the time. I want to go out and have a little fun in life."

Judge Edward Brand annulled the marriage in 1968—after eight years and two children—on the grounds that Movita was still legally tied to a previous husband. Alimony payments were granted nonetheless. The annulment was not entered into the public court records as per custom. Details were unavailable to reporters.

Marlon and Movita remained on cordial terms; son Miko frequented his father's house upon various occasions. Four years after the divorce, Movita again sued in Santa Monica Superior Court when Marlon stopped his alimony payments on the basis that Movita had violated one of the provisions of their settlement by living with another man. Although Movita admitted the affair, the judge ruled in her favor "because the couple had not been passing themselves off as man and wife." It was a point of law that would have pleased a Jesuit scholar.

While Marlon dallied with the ladies, both in and out of court, I embarked upon a tentative return to the acting profession. My attorney-of-the-season, George Elstein, arranged for a documentary film, *India and Women*, in which I was to interview notable women in Indian society: Indira Gandhi, Sister Teresa, member-of-parliament Mrs. Lakshmi Menon, and others. I returned to India for five weeks during the summer of 1967 for the on-camera segments of the project.

Preparing for the trip, I heard that Spencer Tracy had died. He had been seriously ill for four years and had lived in semiseclusion, not wishing to inflict on his friends the pathetic erosion of his health. We had not spoken during my marriage, but immediately upon learning of my divorce he had telephoned to renew our friendship. I remembered watching with him in his home some of his earlier films. Spencer had never attended a premiere or an opening and had never viewed his own pictures until, much later, they appeared on TV. Only three weeks before his fatal heart attack he had completed *Guess Who's Coming to Dinner*, his filmic reunion with Katharine Hepburn after ten years. (He was so ill he was refused insurance coverage during production.) Mostly, I remembered the mischievous charm of his broad Irish face ("Like a beat-up barn door," he described it) and the gruff demeanor that covered one of the warmest, most generous souls ever to swelter in the Hollywood limelight.

Thirteen years had passed since I had seen my native land. The India of Curzon and Kipling, already fractured in my youth, had sundered into fragments. The India of the memsahib and the restricted club had vanished. The infuriating, oppressive conditions of mass hunger, disease, illiteracy, and debilitating poverty remained. Calcutta was still the most appalling city in the world, its streets still filled with the destitute, the skin-and-bone starving, the leprous, and the dying. India still teetered on the edge of political, cultural, and social fragmentation. *"Plus ça change . . ."*

My talk with Mrs. Gandhi took place at her modest home, then designated as the prime minister's official residence (she had occupied the office since 1966). We conversed more on a personal than a political level. She had been a frail, introverted young girl—possibly due to frequent separations from her parents when they were jailed for protesting British rule—and had suffered tuberculosis and painful neck spasms. To me, as to many others, she spoke of her childhood as "abnormal, full of loneliness and insecurity.... I never played with other children. All my games were political games. I was Joan of Arc, perpetually being burned at the stake." She was—and I found her still—a shy person, despite her ability to stand before a half-million people and sway them with her oratory.

Even as a mature woman, Mrs. Gandhi held to her childhood perceptions. She could yet dredge up her resentment against her father for subordinating her mother to his political concerns. That she had treated her husband, Feroze Gandhi (no relation to the Mahatma), in an identical manner seemed not to penetrate her consciousness. Although her involvement with politics destroyed their marriage, she would not discuss the subject and has never admitted that her husband had separated from her long before his death in 1960.

Mrs. Gandhi's personality, like that of her nation, reflects a complex of contradictions—which carried over to her role as prime minister. Raised amidst wealth, she has pursued radical socialist policies. Denouncing the warfare of others, professing Gandhian nonviolence, she engaged in battle with Pakistan to split off Bangladesh. A pious critic of the nuclear powers, she decreed India's first atomic weapon. She is admired and respected—and denigrated and detested. A more intricate, convoluted personality I have never encountered (except, on a different plane, for that of Marlon Brando).

I found it unsurprising when, eight years later, she declared a state of emergency, suspended civil liberties, jailed her political opponents, and declared herself de facto dictator. It was equally unsurprising when she subsequently allowed herself to be deposed.

Considering India's polyglot culture of ferociously antagonistic regions, religions, and castes, the wonder is that anyone would even attempt to govern. Dedicated to the ultimate unity of her country, Mrs. Gandhi was confronted with immovable attitudes. Democracy inspires little reverence among her compatriots. In India, the only sacred cow is the cow.

Mother Teresa, the "living saint of India," shares several characteristics with Indira Gandhi. She too is dedicated—albeit in a religious sense—and her innate love of humanity shines on everyone she beholds. She and her followers collect the dying from the streets and minister to the diseased. She has founded havens for the lepers that infest India and personally tends to their maggot-bloated wounds. "In the poor, we can see the Divine Image," she intoned to me. "God made the hungry, the naked, the unwanted. We meet Him in disguise in the faces of the poor."

Mother Teresa is not without critics. Many would advocate less piety, less prayer, and more action. Other worldly and rigidly dogmatic, she exalts the poor and fulminates against birth control and abortion—thereby assuring herself and her successors a never-ending supply of souls for her mission. It is India's "Catch-22."

The Indian interlude—and other similar activities—still occupied a secondary level in the strata of my life. Disputes with Marlon—pivoted about our son's welfare—continued to monopolize the primary level. Unquestionably, I was losing my son's affections through these years. As he spent more of his time with Marlon, he was rewarded with expensive gifts—diving equipment, skiing outfits, trips abroad. I couldn't compete on that scale. To a court-appointed psychologist, Devi expressed his preference for living with his father "because there is so many more things to do at Daddy's house. At

Mommy's, it's boring—nothing but TV and the market. If I stayed with Daddy, then Mommy would be free to go back to India."

Marlon was injecting him with stories of his own childhood in Illinois—of Dodie Brando's drunkenness and irresponsible behavior. "Your mother is just the same," Devi was told. By the age of twelve Devi had absorbed his father's ambivalent feelings for me (and mine for his father) and had become skilled at his three-person game of "who wants Devi more and how to prove it." At one point he repudiated his stated wish to live with his father in favor of remaining with his mother, whereupon the psychologist noted "his continued need to satisfy and manipulate both parents . . . resulting in a continual state of anxiety and fear of losing the love of one or the other." I was pleased to read in the report, "The striking fact is that this boy has been able emotionally to weather the trauma and its consequences which have been part and parcel of his life since infancy and has survived as well as he appears to have done."

Devi had, from childhood, shown ready adaptation to his environment. At an early age he recognized himself as the son of a celebrity and managed that status to his advantage. When, at age seven, he joined me in a series of fencing lessons, he constructed a crude foil that he sold to the fencing master for fifty cents. He then fabricated a second foil, for which he asked one dollar. His explanation of the price difference showed his awareness of the Brando name: "I autographed this one," he said.

Marlon's influence on Devi became more pronounced with time. One incident, typical of Marlon's style of living, occurred in the summer of 1970, when Devi was twelve. I had driven up to the hilltop house to retrieve Devi after a Sunday outing with his father. The lights were on, and the gates were open—in contrast with Marlon's usual mania for security. I entered through a kitchen door and called out for Devi in the front rooms. Devi's bedroom was last in the far wing of the house. I opened the door and flicked on the lights. Christian Marquand was lying in Devi's bed, nude, next to a blonde woman similarly displayed. I sputtered at him: "You—the godfather of my child—in his bed—with a woman!" Marquand (and the blond) could never be accused of lacking *savoir faire.* He turned to me, unperturbed: "Anna, would you mind turning out the lights as you leave and closing the door."

Despite the questionable morality of this environment, Marlon felt that Devi needed his father's home and companionship more than the courts had granted. At the end of 1970 his attorney, Norman Garey, filed further motions alleging that I had again denied Marlon his due rights. The suit requested permanent custody and physical possession of "said minor child."

In January 1971, Judge Edward Brand ruled for joint custody and care. He further ordered that Devi be enrolled as a permanent resident student at the Ojai Valley School, seventy-five miles north of Los Angeles. Physical possession of Devi outside the school was conferred on Marlon. I was left with "reasonable visitation rights."

I moved for a new trial and a reconsideration. The motion was denied. Through the summer of 1971 I filed more OSCs re Modification, attempting to remove Devi from the Ojai Valley School where he was obviously uncomfortable. "Christian Devi has a vivid fantasy life and finds such mundane matters as attending school unimportant," the psychologist had opined, and I feared the school could not cope with that attitude. My OSCs, however, were taken off calendar. I retired temporarily to the back benches and prayed that Devi would not suffer from the last ruling.

My experiences with the American judicial system left bitter feelings. The bitterness is directed, for the most part, at the judges I encountered. That a man should be elevated six feet above the rest of us, mantled with black robes, and declared an absolute dictator seems to me a hazardous guarantee of justice. Were I writing a brief on the subject, I would submit that altogether too many rulings are left to the judge's discretion.

Judge Brand, whenever Marlon and I appeared before him, opened the conversation with "Would you like a cup of coffee, Mr. Brando?" He allowed Marlon to isolate himself in the jury room while waiting for the trial to begin—guarded by the bailiff against intruders. I noticed, while in his chambers, that he carried a gun beneath his robes, and expressed some astonishment. "I have to have this gun," he declared. "There's a lot of nuts running loose in the courtroom."

Marlon, to the extent he could command, insulated himself from court appearances, depositions, and other legalistic impositions on his time and energies. "I detest being dragged into court," he complained to me, citing not only our legal battles but lawsuits from anyone he might cross. One woman sued him for $120,000, charging "reckless and negligent driving" when he dented the rear fender of her car. Film companies sued him for millions. He was sued by cranks, by opportunists, and by the mentally unbalanced. Marlon viewed it all like a man who had eaten oysters out of season. He was preoccupied with other matters.

Primarily, Marlon was concerned with the failures of his motion pictures over the decade of the 1960s. He had, still in the 1950s, deteriorated from actor into star. As the 1970s began, it seemed he was transmuting from dying star to dim, burnt-out sun.

As a precaution against artistic failure, Marlon was ever defensive about his acting. Now he grew even more defensive. "I have no respect for acting," he told a *Life* reporter. "Acting by and large is the expression of neurotic impulse.... Acting is a bum's life.... You get paid for doing nothing and it means nothing. Acting is fundamentally a childish thing to pursue. Quitting acting—that is the mark of maturity."

He did not quit, of course. Despite his professions of contempt, he required the adulation of the crowd just as Gwendoline in *The Importance of Being Earnest* required tea. No schizophrenic compromise between his public and private selves could keep him from acting.

With successive failures Marlon turned on the medium that nourished and enriched him: "It's sheer luck if you get anything good [in films] because everything is done in dribs and drabs. Nothing is sustained. There is no imagination. Movies don't inspire you as an actor. They date you.... There is no time to improvise and try out different ideas for a characterization. If you do, the production gets behind schedule and the costs run higher.... No one has a chance to grow and mature in a part as they do when they are performing nightly on the stage. . . . If you don't keep doing stage work, you die as an actor. You can't cheat on your abilities on the stage."

It was not one of Marlon's frivolous comments. He was quoted by columnist Sidney Skolsky further defaming his industry: "Movies are not an art and probably never will be. Pictures are a craft, a business. Making movies is no different than manufacturing any other item. They are an economic investment."

Marlon's resentment of his failures was clear to those who understood him. But, of course, when someone agreed with his view of the motion-picture art, he immediately reversed his position. William Redfield, a longtime friend, included in his book *Letters from an Actor* their discussion of movies vs. stage:

"Stardom in movies has to do with chemistry and personality," he told Marlon, "not real acting." Marlon insisted that it is more difficult to act on film than on the stage. "More difficult for a good actor," said Redfield, "because a good actor concerns himself with character, text, the shape and weight of words, profound emotions, and the plastic skill of voice and body necessary for reaching the upper tiers of the balcony without splitting the ears of the groundlings below. Movies are confusing for the good actor and paradise for the bad."

Redfield subsequently summed up Marlon as "the greatest actor of our time. But what difference does it make? . . . [Brando] has become as dependable as the Brazilian cruzeiro and inscribed not a trace upon the pages of acting history since 1947, when he created Stanley Kowalski."

Marlon sulked, his rapport with Redfield fractured. Others who valued his friendship sidestepped discussions of his professional demise. Marlon continued the mummery of denouncing acting, movies, producers, critics, and audiences in general. Decreasing numbers listened to his tirades.

The critical consensus maintained that as an actor Marlon had diminished to a caricature of himself. Pauline Kael summarized this feeling. "When you're larger than life," she wrote, "you just can't be brought down to normalcy. It's easier to get acceptance by caricaturing your previous attitudes and aspirations, by doing what the hostile audience already has been doing to you."

To even the most imperceptive, Marlon had shrunk from the dimensions of a myth to those of a memory.

In 1965, to promote his film *Morituri*, Marlon consented to interviews with a succession of TV reporters. The interviews, filmed and edited, were released as a thirty-minute documentary, *Meet Marlon Brando*. In it, Marlon's irritation with his failing stature clearly penetrates the fog of words. He distracts, embarrasses, attacks, and contradicts his interviewers. He is rude, mocking, and ill at ease. He is without tact, bluntly declaring, "I'm a huckster and I'm here thumping the tub for *Morituri*."

Those who did not understand the transformation that had overtaken the reputed island of moral strength in the sea of Hollywood turpitude could readily gain enlightenment. They had only to see his pictures.

**P**auline Kael had written that after *On the Waterfront*, Marlon's work was becoming progressively more self-parody. That judgment was gaining credence with each successive picture. When he had finished the production phase of *Mutiny on the Bounty* early in 1962 (except for the re-re-revised Pitcairn Island ending), Marlon signed a multipicture contract with Universal Pictures. Five films were produced under this contract—by most assessments, the five worst of his career.

Jay Kanter, Marlon's MCA agent, converted to an executive at Universal when that studio was absorbed by the MCA octopus, arranged for release of the first film in the series, *The Ugly American*, a Pennebaker production. (One year later, Pennebaker was sold to MCA-Universal for $1 million, Marlon's dream of using the company to create "meaningful" pictures included in the price.) Taken from the Burdick and Lederer best-selling novel about the inept American aid program in Southeast Asia, the film also incorporated material from *Tiger on a Kite*, the script that Marlon had drafted years earlier. Marlon's friend, George Englund (chaperone to our first date), directed the picture—or misdirected it, if the critics were correct. In playing the lead role of silver-moustached Harrison Carter MacWhite, Marlon apparently modeled his characterization on Englund: suave, sophisticated with a subdued arrogance, secure inside a Brooks Brothers suit.

Marlon procured a supporting role for his sister Tiddy (Jocelyn), as he was also to do in *The Chase*. (She had been blacklisted by the film industry for alleged Communist sympathies.) A competent actress, she is probably known best for her television performances in *Alfred Hitchcock Presents* and her part as Glenn Ford's wife in *The Big Heat*. Her career never emerged from her brother's eclipsing shadow.

In signing for the film Marlon rationalized his participation: "For all our incredible facilities for modern communication, we have communicated very little with the world. I think we are insulated. I've seen Westerners in Thailand, in Java, in Japan, and most of them made no effort to learn the language or participate. They have their air-conditioned offices and Scotch in their iceboxes. They bring in a little society of America to the place they live in." This theme, a drooping cliché by 1962, was adopted at Marlon's insistence as the picture's principal thrust.

The concept of *The Ugly American* was denounced in the Senate by J. William Fulbright (Marlon referred to him as "Senator Halfbright") and in Hollywood by Samuel Goldwyn. Yet the film proved eerily prophetic of American involvement in Southeast Asia. (Also curiously prophetic was the casting of Kukrit Pramoj as the prime minister of [the mythical country of] Sarkhan. Kukrit later rose to become prime minister of Thailand.)

Marlon attended the premiere in Bangkok in April 1963, and was presented to the King. "Every Thai is an ambassador," he proclaimed to the press on his arrival. "I'm genuinely overwhelmed." It was a one-sided emotion; reviewers described *The Ugly American* as dull, labored, with a quaint and outmoded simplicity.

*Bedtime Story*, Marlon's sixteenth motion picture and the second of his five films released through Universal, is, by almost every judgment, the nadir of his career. It was co-produced by Pennebaker and written by Stanley Shapiro (with Paul Henning), originator of *The Beverly Hillbillies* and author of numerous Doris Day/Rock Hudson sex comedies (e.g., *Pillow Talk*), who also functioned as producer.

Shapiro voiced his reservations to Marlon before filming began: "I've heard some wild stories about you. Whether or not they're true, I'd like to disregard them and have the understanding that you'll be on the set on time and that when we shoot you'll know your lines."

"You don't have to worry," Marlon replied, "I'll be a good boy." Shapiro should have worried.

The story features a contest between two womanizers, Marlon and David Niven, over who should rate as the more efficient seducer (thereby becoming "King of the Mountain," the picture's original title). Women, chiefly Shirley Jones, the seductee, are portrayed in their male-fantasy stereotypes as gullible, yielding, and muddle-headed. Were Women Libbers organized when the picture was released (1964), they might well have picketed it. Later, it was forgotten.

Watching Marlon in the role of Corporal Freddy Benson, the unscrupulous seducer, brought on a feeling of sadness—from respect for the magnificent actor he had been and also from the obvious physical deterioration. He must have weighed over 220 pounds at the time of the filming. Once, after I had quit our home on Mulholland Drive, Marlon had sworn to reduce and had snapped a lock on the refrigerator door; when temptation grew irresistible, he cut it open with a hacksaw. I thought of that incident as I listened to his oft-repeated "seductive" line in the film: "I haven't eaten for six days—I'm saving my money for my grandmother's operation" (the line purports to arouse sympathy). It was truly unbelievable. Niven's line about his competitor's attitude toward women was, for me, the movie's redeeming moment: "The poor man is probably the victim of improper potty training."

Marlon's self-parody reached an apex in this picture. To win the affections of the heroine, he sits in a wheelchair, pretending to be a paraplegic veteran. I couldn't understand how Marlon would agree to such a desecration of *The Men*. Critic Dwight Macdonald, appalled at the sacrilege, proposed that some sadist might arrange for a double-bill showing of *The Men* and *Bedtime Story* at a hospital for paralyzed veterans. Other critics were less kind.

The following year came *Morituri*, a film with several notable aspects, mostly noncinematic. Producer Aaron Rosenberg and Trevor Howard renewed their association with Marlon despite the harrowing experience of *Mutiny on the Bounty*. Also notable was the participation of Marlon's friends, Wally Cox and William Redfield, in bit roles. *Morituri*'s story revolves about an attempted mutiny (unsuccessful in this instance) aboard ship. After the obligatory sex and violence (both perpetrated by the Nazi crew on a Jewish girl unaccountably on board), Marlon scuttles the ship as the picture ends.

A German director, Bernard Wicki (*The Bridge; The Visit*) was no more successful than Lewis Milestone had been in controlling Marlon but he remained on the set throughout the filming. Marlon's view of his director veered, as usual, from approval to condemnation. "Bernie Wicki," he later sniggered to a television interviewer, "smokes the worst cigars of anyone I ever knew. I hate his cigars.... They're made of dogshit." His view of the film was philosophical: "It's like pushing a prune pit with my nose from here to Cucamonga, and now I find myself in Azusa. Of course, if this picture is good, all the grief will be forgotten. But when a picture is bad, all you can do is stick a lampshade on your head and stand real still and hope nobody notices you."

Self-parody persisted—Robert Crain, the Brando character, is Christian Diestl of *The Young Lions* without the strength and introspection of the latter. Again, Marlon cropped his hair and adopted Germanic speech patterns with an "accent that reeked of Limburger cheese."

*Morituri* was shown in major theatres for several weeks without attracting a profitable audience. Fox executives then changed the title twice (from *Morituri* to *Code Name: Morituri* to *The Saboteur: Code Name—Morituri*) as if adding words to the marquee might add money to their coffers. It didn't.

Why did Marlon agree to such a picture? "I needed the money" was his candid explanation. "It's like a car and the oil dipstick. You look at it once in a while and find you need oil.

Well, every so often I look at my financial condition and I find I need money, so I do a good-paying picture. You see, I have three households to support and I pay alimony to two women."

Much of the film was shot off Catalina Island aboard a twenty-six-year-old freighter that Rosenberg had found in Yokohama Harbor. A Japanese submarine was also required, and a plywood replica of one was built on the Twentieth Century-Fox lot. Between takes on the freighter, Marlon sat in his dressing room and pondered the fate of his acting career. He wouldn't have been true to himself if he had faced it directly: "It may seem peculiar, but I've spent most of my career wondering what I'd really like to do. Acting has never been the dominant factor in my life. In six or seven years, who knows, I'll have to do something but I don't know if it will be acting." His future, said Marlon, would see some truly great film before he retired. "After *Morituri* I plan to do Jean Genet's *Forbidden Dreams* with Tony Richardson, probably in Europe, and then *The Deputy* for Anatole Litvak. I don't care if *The Deputy* doesn't make a penny. I'd do it for free."

Instead, Marlon was induced by producer Sam Spiegel to star in *The Chase*, Lillian Hellman's contrived drama of sex, violence, and confrontation in a small Southern town. Mr. Spiegel retained his admiration for Marlon through every pitch of the roller coaster: "I have always liked Marlon very much. He was a tortured man in the early days and he was great on the screen. When he ceased being tortured, he had to pseudotorture himself in order to function." If *The Chase* were selected by Mr. Spiegel to elicit another *On the Waterfront* achievement from Marlon, he was disappointed. "He tried but it was a different Brando. At times I thought he was sleepwalking. He gave an adequate performance, but the soul wasn't there."

Ironically, Mr. Spiegel had previously signed Peter O'Toole for the role of *The Chase*'s protagonist, Sheriff Calder. Mr. O'Toole, whose fame derived from the role in *Lawrence of Arabia* that Marlon had rejected, now maneuvered his release from the commitment to Spiegel after reading the muddled screenplay. Marlon, in turn, fancied the script and signed for the picture, thus completing the roundelay.

Bosley Crowther in the *New York Times* called the picture "a phony, tasteless movie." Pauline Kael labeled it a "liberal sadomasochistic fantasy." It was an afternoon soap opera that had escaped the television set onto the motion-picture screen. It was treated accordingly.

For Marlon, the picture's sole redeeming moment was the climactic scene where he is pummeled into bloody insensibility. Elsewhere, he mumbled and shuffled his way through the part. "Fuck 'em," he declared. "If they're going to be so stupid, I'll just take the money, do what they want, and get out. I don't give a damn about anything."

Lillian Hellman ducked the line of critical fire by claiming in a *New York Times* interview that her screenplay had been distorted by director Arthur Penn: "Decision by democratic majority vote is a fine form of government, but it's a stinking way to create. So two other writers were called in and that made four with Mr. Spiegel and Mr. Penn, and what was intended as a modest picture about some aimless people on an aimless Saturday night got hot and large." Mr. Penn claimed that injudicious editing had destroyed the force of his footage, even though the screenplay was "stilted and excessively expository." Mr. Spiegel and Columbia Studios shrugged philosophically and recouped in their subsequent projects.

*The Appaloosa*, third in the Universal package, was a pseudoart Western vaguely similar to *One-Eyed Jacks*—a loner on the trail of revenge along the Mexican border country in the latter half of the nineteenth century. This time Marlon is roped to a rampaging horse, dragged through a rocky stream and over rough ground, and then hung from a tree branch while his prized stallion (an Appaloosa) is appropriated. He sets out to avenge his lacerations and to reclaim his horse. When he espies the villain (John Saxon), a bandit leader entrenched in his Cocatlan headquarters, Marlon challenges him to personal combat. Saxon accepts—the duel takes the form of an Indian arm-wrestling contest with a scorpion on either side to sting the loser. Marlon is defeated but recovers to retrieve his horse, steal the bandit's girl friend, and dispatch the bandido himself.

British director Sidney Furie (*The Ipcress File*), on being introduced to Marlon, extended a courteous gambit: "I'm really looking forward to this picture. I consider it a real privilege to be working with you."

"Bullshit," said Marlon.

With that auspicious beginning, director and star were already dueling as production opened (at Saint George, Utah), albeit with words rather than scorpions. Marlon called Furie "a phony, a liar, and a dirty double-crosser." Mr. Furie was more incisive in his criticism of Marlon: "To me, making a picture is like waging a war. I expect trouble. I'm ready for it. It's part of the creative process. In the first session Brando asked me, 'What makes you think you know what actors are all about?' . . . He loves chaos. You simply can't get past 'B' in a conversation with Brando and you can't get him to discuss a script rationally. . . . He's disorganized, no discipline at all, a procrastinator. One little scene that should have taken us a few hours to film took ten days. Every day he had another complaint—his tummy ached, his head ached—you should have heard the moans. What a performance! Then he'd be searching for his lines. Anything to procrastinate." Furie then added the usual directorial charges: Marlon didn't know his lines, he didn't take the picture seriously, "he questioned everything, even if the full cast were there and we had only five minutes left to finish the scene."

Script problems, evidently endemic to a Brando picture, proliferated as shooting progressed. Marlon demanded the elimination of all scenes involving Indian fights, thereby vetoing twenty-five pages of the script. "I won't kill any Indians," he insisted. Producer Alan J. Miller, a longtime MCA executive, reflected on his experience with Marlon and announced his retirement from the business.

Two years later, Marlon encountered Furie in a London hotel lobby. "Let's do it again sometime," Marlon offered. Mr. Furie coughed politely. "Uh . . . I don't think it likely," he said.

Charlie Chaplin, for virtually everyone in the entertainment field, ranked as their most ingenious, most revered figure emeritus. When he appeared briefly at the 1972 Academy Awards ceremony, he received a standing ovation that surpassed by minutes the previous record of acclaim. Marlon admired him to the extent that he accepted an offer to star in *A Countess from Hong Kong* under Chaplin's direction without reading the screenplay (written by Chaplin). "Anything—absolutely anything—by Chaplin would be worth doing," Marlon assumed, and signed with producer Jerome Epstein for the film.

Afterward he described his initial meeting with Chaplin in less adulatory terms. Marlon met the great silent-screen star in London where Chaplin enacted the *Countess* script for seven hours. "He said I was the only one for the role," Marlon recalled, "but I think if I said no, he was already dialing Sean Connery. I also told him he must want someone like Jack Oakie for the part—it's comedy. But he was very flattering, said I was the only one."

Marlon arrived in London in December 1965 (the picture was scheduled at London's Pinewood Studios). He rented a sumptuous apartment off Berkeley Square and installed a motion-picture projector. Each day he and a group of friends conducted their personal Chaplin Film Festival, running some of the old silent movies (*City Lights; Modern Times; The Tramp; The Gold Rush*) several times over. As Marlon studied these classics, the prospect of working with "the maestro" on *Countess* grew ever more enticing to his sense of professionalism.

*Countess* was first conceived by Chaplin in the early thirties. It would have been dated then. As a piece of nostalgia, it offered evidence for the definition that nostalgia is the love of one's former self; only its heirs could love it. Its plot and construct were appropriate to a 1920 two-reeler. An American millionaire diplomat, Ogden Meara (Marlon), sailing from Hong Kong to America, finds an attractive and penniless Russian émigré named Natasha (Sophia Loren) in his stateroom. A stowaway, she is hiding from the authorities for lack of an entrance visa to the United States. Most of the picture takes place in Meara's cabin and consists of a series of frenzied efforts to conceal Natasha from the flow of visitors to the diplomat's quarters. Romance is inevitable under such circumstances, and Meara forsakes both his wife and his profession in favor of Natasha's charms.

On the first day of shooting Marlon's awe of Chaplin

churned his stomach into buttermilk: "I didn't know what I was doing there. . . . I started to think I had gone raving mad, Charlie had gone raving mad, and it was impossible. I can't do fades and triple takes and things like that, and I was longing to go to Charlie and say, 'I'm afraid we've both made a horrible mistake.'"

The awe and respect carried Marlon through the first week. Chaplin treated Marlon as he did all actors: he told them what to do, how to do it, and mimed for them every gesture of every scene. In essence, he invited Marlon to imitate Chaplin ("Did he see himself in Marlon?" I would like to have asked him), but the Chaplinesque quality could not be transferred to another actor—especially to one of Marlon's distinctiveness. Marlon was left no latitude for his own artistic expression. In one scene, fighting seasickness, he waves away cigarette smoke from his face. "Chaplin intervened," Marlon complained to a friend. " 'No, no, Marlon,' he said, 'let's have the four-finger waving instead of two-finger waving,' and we would rehearse the four-finger waving." In his *Playboy* interview thirteen years later, Marlon had not mellowed his opinion: "I was a puppet, a marionette. . . . I was miscast. . . . He was a mean man, Chaplin. Sadistic. I saw him torture his son."

With another director, Marlon would have walked off the set. With Chaplin, he became disenchanted by the second week. "God, he really made me mad," Marlon exclaimed to the *Playboy* reporter. "I was late one day; he started to make a big to-do about it. I told him he could take his film and stick it up his ass, frame by frame." By the end of the production schedule, he and Chaplin were barely on speaking terms.

Chaplin laughed uproariously at his own humor and praised the rushes as some of the greatest footage ever filmed. His was an opinion isolated from all except his family. Usually Oona O'Neill Chaplin and several of their eight children plus Sydney Chaplin (who played a small part in the film) clustered around their paterfamilias on the set. After a scene Chaplin turned to his wife for approval. It was always forthcoming.

Although Marlon soon realized the mediocrity of the picture, he was loath to criticize Chaplin in public. "[Chaplin] doesn't direct as much as he orchestrates or conducts," he allowed in oblique detraction of his former idol. "With Charlie, it's chess, chess at ninety miles per hour." Behind Chaplin's back, Marlon burlesqued the Chaplinesque style for his coterie of hangers-on. Chaplin, for his part, was known to perform in private unflattering imitations of the Stanley Kowalski mannerisms. To Marlon's face, he could apply the grand condescension of the maestro: "Marlon, if only you could dig down into yourself and gather the talent you possess."

Sophia Loren, Marlon's costar, joined the lengthening list of Brando antagonists. She had met Marlon several years earlier when she first arrived in Hollywood, and "he just walked into my dressing room and prowled around, staring at the group of original paintings I had hung on the walls. After a long pause, he shook his head at me and said, 'You're sick. Emotionally disturbed. You should see a psychiatrist.' I asked him why, and he told me, 'These pictures show your state of mind. You're suffering. Deep down you have a secret emotional wound.' I didn't yell at him. I only said, 'Never mind, at least I keep it secret. Too bad you don't do the same.' "

While Miss Loren's detractors emphasize her limitations on the stage, they concede her rigid professionalism. She arrives on the set promptly, knows her lines, and tolerates no pranks during working hours. A clash with Marlon was inevitable. He matched her fresh, energetic look each morning with a bleary-eyed exhaustion (after all-night revels). He slept much of the morning in his dressing room and flubbed his lines with her, necessitating countless retakes. In one intimate scene, as he embraced her, he whispered *sotto voce*, "You have black hairs in your nostrils." Behind the camera, he playfully pinched her on the fanny. She grabbed his arm: "Don't ever do that again. I am not the sort of woman who is flattered by it." When Marlon suffered an "appendicitis attack" during production, cast and crew sent him a get-well bouquet and greeting card. (To minister to Marlon's appendix, Dr. Kositchek again was flown overseas to his patient's bedside at London's University College Hospital. The pathology was diagnosed as an abdominal upset.) Everyone signed it except Sophia Loren. Upon completion of the picture, she sent me a three-word telegram: "My deepest sympathies."

"I had to keep reminding them it was a love story," Chaplin complained. "The antipathy between the two stars was evident on the screen when each clasped the other as if embracing a werewolf."

After the London premiere in January 1967, attended by most of the cast except for Sophia Loren, the occasion was celebrated at the home of Jay Kanter (then head of Universal's London productions). Those present labeled it a first-class soiree. "It's too bad we can't release the party instead of the film," an executive from Universal lamented.

Reviews of the cliché-filled farce were unanimously devastating. Bosley Crowther, in the *New York Times*, wrote, "If an old fan of Mr. Chaplin's movies could have his charitable way, he would draw the curtain fast on this embarrassment and pretend it never occurred." Only Chaplin dissented: "If they don't like it, they're bloody fools. Old-fashioned? They are old-fashioned.... I'm not worried. I still think it's a great film, and I think the audiences will agree with me rather than the critics.

As Marlon's string of film disasters stretched over the 1960s, it was broken by his next picture, *Reflections in a Golden Eye*. The film adaptation of Carson McCullers' novella of Southern grotesqueries was initially cast with Elizabeth Taylor and her close friend, Montgomery Clift. After Clift's death in July 1966, Marlon agreed to substitute even though, for the first time since *A Streetcar Named Desire* and Vivien Leigh, he was not accorded top billing. In accepting the role Marlon became the first major star to portray a homosexual on the screen.

Despite the Georgia locale of the story, the picture was shot at the Dino Di Laurentiis Studio in Rome and in the countryside nearby. Richard Burton then resided in Rome; Elizabeth Taylor did not wish to be separated from him; Miss Taylor's wish was the studio's command. In November 1966 the company assembled in Rome (where Italian craftsmen had constructed a Southern military command post).

Marlon imported Tarita and their three-year-old son Tehotu to his rented home on the island of Tiberia. There, two paparazzi, seeking a family portrait, had the temerity to pop flash-bulbs at them. Marlon dropped the child and charged across the street. A right uppercut decommissioned one photographer; he pummeled the other until the man broke free. Then Marlon stomped into his house and reemerged waving a broken bottle. The paparazzi called the polizia.

Throughout the filming, Marlon and director John Huston maintained a mutual respect, a rare accommodation that contributed to the picture's absorbing felicity. Marlon and Elizabeth Taylor maintained a distant wariness when off the set. Early in the shooting, Miss Taylor called him to her dressing room. "Young man," she said, "just remember: you're only a replacement for Montgomery Clift." With Richard Burton standing nearby, Marlon voiced no reply. Uncharacteristically, he retained a friendship—if somewhat reserved—with both Mr. and Mrs. Burton. "Liz Taylor is a great lady," he announced publicly. "She's great people." He offered her no pranks or commentary in their common scenes.

The screenplay of *Reflections* adheres closely to the original story line. Marlon fills the part of Major Weldon Penderton, a fetishist and a latent homosexual stumbling through an undemanding life on a rural military post. His relationship with his wife Leonora (Elizabeth Taylor), a lusty, luscious, and domineering vixen, is seemingly nonsexual (although she tantalizes him by stripping in front of him). Leonora's dominance permits her to taunt her husband for his lack of virility and to whip him across the face for any intemperance, such as his beating a favored horse. She pursues an adulterous affair with a neighbor, Lieutenant Colonel Langdon (Brian Keith), whose deranged wife (she has cut off her nipples with garden shears) knows of the affair. Mrs. Langdon, in the linked triangle, forms a blurred hypotenuse with her Filipino houseboy. An enlisted man, Private Williams (Robert Forster), further complicates the geometry through his lust for Mrs. Penderton and through being the homosexual object of Major Penderton's figments. Private Williams, a fetishist and an exhibitionist, sneaks into Mrs. Penderton's bedroom at night where he passes the hours till dawn staring at her sleeping body and fondling her underclothes. Meanwhile he is being stalked by Major Penderton who picks up and treasures bits of trash he drops and otherwise admires his soldierly demeanor. One night Major Penderton spies the Private entering his home. Presuming the visit for the initiation of a homosexual liaison, he primps and sits waiting in his room. But the Private again sneaks to Mrs. Penderton's bedside. Jilted and cuckolded simultaneously, Major Penderton seizes a pistol and, in a jealous rage, kills the Private. Hell hath no fury like a homosexual scorned.

I thought Marlon's performance in *Reflections* was totally committed—I was mesmerized viewing the picture. After the opening scene, I forgot Marlon and could only see Major Weldon Penderton. Director John Huston had wrung from him one of the most complex and convincing acting achievements of his career. Watching the character as he gradually realized his homosexual nature was like staring at a cobra as it tensed to strike. Producer Ray Stark described the film as a story about "the underworld of your mind."

To my surprise *Reflections* was greeted with deprecation and even hostility by most of the critics and the public. It was listed by Judith Crist among her "ten worst pictures of 1967." The box-office returns mirrored that opinion. Even with a sincere and superb effort on Marlon's part, it seemed, the fates had scowled their disfavor on his career.

After the production phase of *Reflections in a Golden Eye*, Marlon was offered the use of the Burtons' Swiss chalet. He remained there for several months, acting in two other pictures and flying to New York for an interlude during which he accepted for Miss Taylor the New York Critics' Award as Best Actress of 1966 (for *Who's Afraid of Virginia Woolf?*).

Marlon's next two European-made films were *Candy* and *The Night of the Following Day*, the latter the fifth and last of his Universal Studio package. Although *Night* was filmed first, its release was delayed fourteen months—until March 1969. Locations were in Paris and the seascapes of the northern French coast.

I never understood the theme, the concept, or the sense of *The Night of the Following Day*, nor have I ever met anyone who did. It was memorable for me only in observing Rita Moreno, long recovered from her suicidal bout, working with Marlon.

With his hair again dyed blond, his weight trimmed by fifty pounds, Marlon looked quite attractive. His name in the movie is Bud, his childhood sobriquet, although he is usually referred to as the chauffeur. He is entangled with a sadistic, psychopathic pervert named Leer (Richard Boone), a drug-addict blonde (Rita Moreno), and a doltish thug (Jess Hahn). This motley quartet kidnaps and holds for ransom the teen-age daughter (Pamela Franklin) of a rich businessman. The scheme collapses in a barrage of bullets. The blonde shoots Marlon, but he survives to kill Leer, who has just machine-gunned virtually everyone else in the picture except the kid-napped heiress whom he has treated to a brutal sexual ravaging.

Producer/director Hubert Cornfield committed the sin of accepting Marlon's suggestions for shooting the movie. Marlon thereupon reciprocated with contempt. He addressed Mr. Cornfield as "Herbert," mocked him to the other actors, and demanded, two weeks from the final shooting, that the director be dismissed. (Richard Boone directed the remaining scenes.)

If *The Night of the Following Day* was a cinematic centipede, *Candy* was a millipede. It was directed by Marlon's intimate companion, Christian Marquand, in his first such effort beyond a calamitous venture titled *Le Grand Chemin*. Marquand persuaded Marlon to do the picture, and Marlon in turn beguiled Richard Burton into a drinking bout and convinced him to lend his name.

With the magnet of Marlon, Richard Burton, and Buck Henry's script, Marquand acquired financing and such additional luminaries as James Coburn, Charles Aznavour, John Huston, Walter Matthau, Ringo Starr, and Sugar Ray Robinson. All these rich ingredients in the soufflé simply exploded in the skillet. Throughout the shooting, Burton would harangue Marlon: "To hell with this movie—let's get pissed! It's easier when you're smashed!" Of Marlon, Burton told an interviewer, "He surprises me. He's the only one who does. . . . But he talked me into this while I was drunk. I never saw the picture."

I asked Buck Henry if Marlon had interfered with or demanded revisions in his screenplay. Mr. Henry stoutly defended Marlon's contribution but admitted that even when he was retching from an attack of food poisoning, Marlon picked him up from the bathroom floor, laid him out—semiconscious—on the bed, and proceeded with their scheduled story conference.

*Candy* is based on a Terry Southern sex-spoof novel published by Olympia Press. It consists of a muddled sequence of episodes linked only in the director's mind, wherein the young girl of the title (Ewa Aulin) is seduced by a succession of weird, manic swains. Marlon plays the girl's final lover, a Jewish guru named Grindl who converses with vegetables (the most intelligent dialogue in the picture) and roams about the United States countryside in a mobile sanatorium. His Indian accent roams about the Asian subcontinent, occasionally crossing into the Pakistani lowlands. At the fadeout Marlon mystically freezes into a human stalagmite. Audiences were left equally frozen.

Back in California by March of 1968, Marlon decided that he really had no wish to star in *The Arrangement* as he had provisionally promised Elia Kazan the preceding November. Mr. Kazan had directed three of Marlon's successes (*A Streetcar Named Desire; Viva Zapata!; and On the Waterfront*); he was then the only director permitted to reenlist in a Brando film and was being heralded as Marlon's last anchorage from the critical storm. *The Arrangement* was based on his own novel, a semiautobiographical work. Because of their felicitous alliance, Kazan regarded Marlon as his filmic alter ego and was tailoring the screen role accordingly. But when Marlon came to him in tears and explained that Martin Luther King's assassination had left him emotionally devastated, Kazan released him from the commitment. (Kirk Douglas starred in the picture, the critical bottom of Kazan's roll of credits.)

Instead, after rejecting the lead in *Butch Cassidy and the Sundance Kid* as well, Marlon signed with producer Alberto Grimaldi in April for a "socially significant" film, *Burn!*—an indictment of colonialism, corporate intervention, and slavery. Director Gillo Pontecorvo (*The Battle of Algiers*) at the beginning of the project said he intended it to "join the romantic adventure and the film of ideas." The historical foundation for the picture's social theme was the 1520 razing of a Caribbean island by the Spanish to quell a native uprising. A colony of African slaves was imported to supplant the exterminated population and to operate a sugarcane industry, the proceeds from which were relinquished to Spain for the next three centuries. Marlon's role was that of a splendidly seedy agent provocateur sent to the island to protect the interests of the Royal Sugar Company. He spoke with the same accent cultivated for *Mutiny on the Bounty*.

Problems in the production began even before the cast and crew converged in Cartagena, Colombia—problems similar in style if not in scope to those of *Mutiny*. As Marlon boarded a plane in Miami en route to Cartagena, he turned to a stewardess and inquired, "Is this the plane for Cuba?" It proved an ill-considered joke. The stewardess reported to the captain. The captain reported to the airport police. Marlon was ushered from the plane into a room for questioning before he was recognized: "My God, it's Marlon Brando!" Evidently he was in his "movie star" mood; he refused apologies and the invitation to reboard the plane and telephoned his attorney in Los Angeles. Threats of lawsuits and counterlawsuits, all rhetorical, echoed around the airport. Later that evening he boarded a flight to Jamaica, and thence arrived in Cartagena by chartered plane.

For nine months—through the summer of 1968, the winter, and the spring of 1969—the film company suffered the torments of the Colombian countryside: 120-degree heat, supersaturated humidity, dense swarms of insects, poisonous snakes, marauding bandidos, tent quarters under mosquito nets, and open-air toilet facilities. "Tempers," said a crew member, "grew shorter than a flea's prick in a snowstorm."

Marlon and Pontecorvo squabbled from the first scene. The director regarded himself as an *auteur* and the actors as lightbulbs in his lamp—to be screwed into place and turned on or off when he wished. He pressured Marlon into dozens of retakes on many scenes and resented any resistance. "Brando is a little—how you say?—paranoiac," he grumbled. "He thinks when I make forty takes, it is because I want to break him. Why? Why should I want to break him?" Marlon's view was more succinct: "He [Pontecorvo] has no fucking feeling for people."

Marlon was also grieved to learn that the picture's theme of social rectitude was being controverted in its own creation. Black actors had been signed for salaries about half those of comparable white actors. Facilities and services were also dispensed with a racial bias. Marlon's complaints to Pontecorvo brought only Italian shrugs *("Che si fa?")* and a dismissal of the inequalities as outside his jurisdiction. Marlon was unable to inspire the director to mount a local civil rights campaign and never forgave him his indifference.

After nine months of troubled gestation, the film was still far from parturition. Marlon rebelled. He produced a letter from his physician attesting to his deteriorating health in the Colombian climate. "Either we move this fucking production back to civilization," he shouted at producer Grimaldi, brandishing the medical document, "or I'm fucking well finished with the whole fucking mess. You'll fucking well never see me again."

Balancing the expense of transplanting the production to a new locale against the expense of reshooting the picture with a new leading man, the producer reluctantly—and probably against his own emotional preference—removed the menagerie to the mountains near Marrakesh, Morocco, a site not incompatible with the original and one which satisfied Marlon's specifications (although I wondered if all the "M's" at the new location—the company stayed at Marrakesh's luxurious Mamounia Hotel—didn't confuse Marlon; he wrote me that the film was to be completed in Morondava, Madagascar).

Two months in North Africa and another three weeks in Rome's Cinecitta sound stages ended the production, not with a cheer but with a sigh. Pontecorvo forgave Marlon and issued gracious comments to the press: "I think Marlon Brando is the greatest actor of the contemporary cinema. With one expression he covers more than ten pages of dialogue. And he is the only one who can do it. His eyes simultaneously express sadness, irony, skepticism, and the fact that he is tired." Marlon's angle remained narrower. Speaking to a *Life* reporter about Pontecorvo, he swore, "I could have killed him."

The Italian distribution company was not as forgiving as Pontecorvo. It sued Marlon for $700,000, charging that he had shown "incomprehensible attitudes" and open hostility toward the director and was responsible for the extensive delays and excessive costs.

After the ordeal of *Burn!*, Marlon summered aboard the Burtons' 150-foot motor yacht, *Kalizma*. Cruising about the Mediterranean islands could not distract him from anxieties over his career and the restlessness of his disposition. He and Richard Burton tangled in a push-and-shove match with light fisticuffs (considering Marlon's superior physical condition, it must have been a lopsided bout). Marlon left the yacht and withdrew to his private island in Tahiti for a period of decompression.

A year passed before he ventured from his silence into another motion picture. He was persuaded to do so by Jay Kanter, who had recently formed his own independent production company, Winkast Films. The picture that Marlon contracted for under Kanter's warrant was *The Nightcomers*, adapted from Henry James's classical mystical novella, *The Turn of the Screw*.

James's tale of a fey governess convinced that her two charges, Miles, ten, and Flora, eight, are haunted by two evil spirits has been transferred to four other media since it was published in 1898. As a stage play (1950) by William Archibald, it was titled *The Innocents*. It appeared as an opera (1959) by Benjamin Britten and as a television play with Ingrid Bergman starring as the governess. In 1961 a British film company produced it from a screenplay by Truman Capote and playwright Archibald. More mysterious than the story itself is the reason another screen version was needed.

This latest adaptation, produced and directed by Michael Winner, expanded and interknit the parts of the two spirits in their corporeal days. Marlon played the role of Peter Quint, the valet to the governess's employer, and played it with a convincing low-key Irish accent. He is killed at the film's conclusion by the boy Miles who calmly punctures his head with arrows. A sadomasochistic affair between Quint and Miss Jessel, the previous governess, is also added; the children become eager voyeurs to the curious sexual couplings of their elders and initiate their own innovative gropings. A feeling of muted horror beneath a placid surface pervades the film.

Marlon's performance, I thought, was a tour de force. No other actor could be relied on to portray so eloquently both sides of Quint's perverse split-level character—kind and attentive to the children and yet ruthless and bitter to the governess. Investing a diverse range of temperament into a single characterization requires an actor of extraordinary accomplishment. The achievement went unappreciated. By its premiere in February 1972, *The Nightcomers* was already submerged in the prepublicity wave of Marlon's next picture, *The Godfather*.

Fourteen motion pictures had starred Marlon since *The Young Lions*. Some of them were passable, some were pathetic. All fourteen had either lost money or returned a nominal profit. Hollywood theologians pronounced excommunication rites. That knack of illuminating the character from within, that transcendent personal magic—so accessible to the younger Brando—now threatened to slip from his reach. Yet, however abysmal the vehicle for his talents, there was not a performance wherein Marlon's characterization did not rise above the printed page. It was his public image that obscured his shape as an actor. It was his luster as a box-office star that had tarnished into dull rust. The public swallows its heroes whole, digests them at leisure, and voids them as soft, pulpy, waste products. Marlon's picktooth demeanor and aphronic actions no longer attracted the younger generation but alienated the spectrum of ages. Brandolotry had died and was awaiting interment. Its hero had become an ormolu character whose reputation as an ill-omened signpost daunted all but the naïve and the Pollyannas in the film industry. The rise and fall of Marlon Brando was now relegated to the historical dustbin, his days of glory shrunk to a statuette on the mantel (where it had been promoted from its station as a doorstop). Lakshmi, the Hindu goddess of fortune, had shown her backside to him. It seemed to be a "mooning" with a curse.

Innumerable theses have been advanced to explain

Marlon's decade of mediocre films. Some felt the world had advanced to knee pants while Marlon still crawled about in diapers. Others suggested that he had isolated himself in almost megalomaniacal egoism and did not recognize that the spotlight had moved elsewhere. He was compared with Hemingway, who lived his myth for a generation, faced his own decay with little grace, bullied others, and eventually destroyed himself. Speculations of a Marlon Brando suicide were heard.

Many in the motion-picture industry believed that the account book of Marlon's film life was now being brought back into balance. Lewis Milestone told me, "True, he's a great actor but he's done things which from another actor would have driven him out of the business. And still he was lauded for them. Now they're catching up with him. He's got a tremendous pool of talent but he doesn't want to put it on the screen." Another of Marlon's directors was more accusatory: "No decent director would baby-sit Marlon through a picture," he said (insisting on anonymity!). "Any self-respecting person wouldn't take the crap from him, and the picture would be wrecked in twenty-four hours. Maybe a director who is a virgin could work with Brando. But if you've already learned a trick or two and can reason, you wouldn't touch him with a whale's backbone."

Elia Kazan remained one of his rare defenders: "He's been good in everything he's done but he's been a trapped giant in all those lesser films. . . . People were always ready to say 'he's had it.' It makes me furious. Talent is delicate. It can hide for a while, go underground, get discouraged. It's human but it doesn't go away." And, of course, Marlon defended himself: "I've had good years and bad years and good parts and bad parts, and most of it's just crap. Acting has absolutely nothing to do with being successful. Success is some funny American phenomenon that takes place if you can be sold like Humphrey Bogart, Shredded Wheat, or Marlon Brando wristwatches. When you don't sell, people don't want to hire you, and your stock goes up and down like it does on the stock market."

As with analyses of Marlon's personality, so analyses of his screen personae are both largely true and largely false. I think of Marlon as a polyhedron rolling down the street. The view depends on which face catches the eye. I never believed the Hemingway analogy, however; Marlon's suicidal fulminations were pure sham. Rather, like Shaw and Chesterton, Marlon invented a caricature of himself and then wore it as a disguise. Beginning with our marriage, the disguise became a part of the man; ultimately, he couldn't discard it. Or—perhaps—this view too is merely a glimpse at one of the whirling faces. Art may be infinite but artists are doomed to repetition. Marlon's acting, his antics, his entire mystique, were presenting the world with a sense of déjà vu.

Whatever Marlon may have thought about critics hammering nails into his coffin, he remained publicly unconcerned. "Don't let the critics bother you," he quoted Samuel Goldwyn. "Don't even ignore them." To an interviewer from *Oui* magazine, he left his mind ajar: "I feel fame and success are symptoms of a serious psychic disease, because so frequently they are not connected to achievement. . . . People no longer care about achieving something, so long as they can be famous. . . . It is a destructive social disease we all suffer from. . . . You have this conflict—everybody has it from time to time—and sometimes you say 'Fuck it,' and you quit."

Privately, he seemed lost in a surrealistic swamp somewhere between farce and fantasy. When I looked into his eyes, I couldn't see who was looking back.

In the *Ramayana*, a young stonemason named Balan carves the statue of a beautiful woman. It is admired by the Prince who demands to see the live model—as an alternative to executing the sculptor. Their being no model, Balan contrives to present the Prince with a local harlot, Lotus Blossom; in the dim light of his darkened apartments, the Prince cannot distinguish the differences between the girl and the statue—except that Lotus Blossom is not made of stone. For reward, Balan is declared an officially acknowledged genius and is raised to the rank of Sculptor Extraordinary with full court privileges.

From that day to his death forty years later, he scarcely touched a chisel again. He was too busy being an officially acknowledged genius.

# Nine

**M**arlon's advent in *The Godfather* was hailed as the Second Coming. Deep in the American psyche lies the need to worship the transgressor redeemed: the sinner repented, the drunkard reformed, the Communist who renounced his politics. Through witch trials, prohibition, and McCarthyism, these were the people acclaimed, held up as paragons of righteousness. By the 1970s the need had turned toward another phoenix: the faded and faulted movie star making a comeback.

In view of Marlon's erstwhile stature and influence, only an apotheosis of cinematic achievement could serve as a comeback vehicle. By a concatenation of circumstances, he found that vehicle in *The Godfather*.

Mario Puzo's best-selling novel about sex, violence, and nepotism among the Mafioso was published late in 1969. Puzo had begun the novel solely as a scrambling effort to recover from indebtedness incurred as a serious writer. Nearly 700,000 copies of it were eventually sold in hard cover and 10 million copies in paperback. Well before publication date the film rights were sold to Paramount Studios, which then hired Puzo to write the screenplay. A "modest" sum of $2½ million was allocated for the picture and Al Ruddy (whose principal prior credit was *Hogan's Heroes* on television) was signed as producer. Paramount could invest neither a high budget (having just lost $15 million with *Paint Your Wagon*) nor a high degree of confidence (a recent Mafia film, *The Brotherhood* with Kirk Douglas, had been indifferently received).

Virtually every major male actor over forty whose name ended with a vowel was advanced for the title role. Before a decision was reached by Paramount executives, Francis Ford Coppola, whose credits (*You're a Big Boy Now; The Rain People*) included no major successes, was selected to direct. He was chosen according to Paramount production chief Robert Evans because of his Italian descent: "He knew the way these men in *The Godfather* ate their food, kissed each other, talked. He knew the grit."

Coppola was dissatisfied with Puzo's first script. He appointed himself co-writer, and the two men rewrote the script to incorporate more of the book's theme of dynastic power. He persuaded studio executives to increase the budget to $6,200,000 (Paramount, with the success of *Love Story*, was again solvent) and to shoot the picture in period and on location.

To decide the actor for the title role, Coppola pursued two lines of thought. "The best way, the obvious way," he said, "is to cast a real, old Italian, a true Godfather type." He interviewed scores of Italian actors and nonactors, and even a number of Mafia Dons. "The other way to go is to get the best possible actor. In my opinion there are only two actors who can play the part: Laurence Olivier and Marlon Brando." Olivier, Coppola was informed, lay temporarily *hors de combat.*

Mario Puzo had proposed Marlon for Don Corleone when he first began the screenwriting. Now Coppola embraced the idea. Studio executives reacted as if struck by a putrefying fish: "Brando is anathema to the film industry. He's dead in this business—worse than dead, he's a vampire." Nonetheless, Coppola prevailed upon producer Ruddy to broach the idea to

Marlon. To their surprise, Marlon expressed interest and agreed to read the book and the screenplay.

At a meeting with Robert Evans, Stanley Jaffe, Frank Yablans, and other Paramount moguls, Coppola pleaded for permission to sign Marlon. Mr. Yablans, in particular, was adamantly opposed. "Let me talk for five minutes," Coppola persisted. "That's all I'm asking. Let me argue for him—give me that courtesy." After an oration worthy of Cicero, Coppola won the right to nominate Marlon conditional to a screen test. Coppola fell to his knees, stretched out his arms, and sighed "Hallelujah."

Ruddy and Coppola grabbed a video-tape camera and rushed up to Marlon's house. To their continuing surprise, Marlon consented to the test, his first in the more than two decades since his early Broadway plays, and a humiliation for any established actor. Marlon designed and applied his own makeup. "He just put some black shoe polish under his eyes, streaked his hair with gray and pulled it back, penciled a moustache, and stuffed out his cheeks with toilet paper," Ruddy described the scene. He puffed an Italian cigar, postured over a cup of coffee, and gradually, as the camera recorded the spectacle, transformed himself into an old Italian Mafioso: Don Vito Corleone.

When they viewed the tape, executives at Paramount were impressed. With some apprehension, they announced in January 1971 (after insisting that Marlon post a bond against his delaying the production, an imposition later rescinded) that months of testing lead actors had ended with Marlon Brando being awarded the part of Don Corleone. Shooting was to begin in March.

Marlon's identification with the role was immediate and integral. At his arrival in New York he was invited to a preproduction dinner at Patsy's Italian restaurant in East Harlem. Coppola had assembled there the screen children and associates of Don Vito Corleone: Michael (Al Pacino), Sonny (Jimmy Caan), Tom Hagen (Robert Duvall), et al. As the dinner progressed each actor adjusted to the characterization of his screen counterpart. Pacino became soft-spoken and pensive, Jimmy Caan displayed the hotheaded temperament of

Sonny. If anyone could be designated godfather to the entire acting profession, it was Marlon. All the actors held him in awe and played up to him accordingly. He was The Godfather.

During production Marlon continued as surrogate father to the cast. On the set he abandoned his famed belligerence and irascibility for an attitude of cooperation. He was rarely tardy and offset his few absences with unpaid overtime. Afterward Coppola declared, "[Marlon] was a delight to be involved with. I'd like to work with him again."

His zeal for pranks, childish and psychological, remained undiminished. In a scene where he was to be carried on a stretcher, he slipped weights from a crab dolly into the canvas; four extras strained futilely to lift the frail Don Corleone, an old man who apparently weighed in excess of a thousand pounds. The four extras were replaced by four husky grips dressed in tuxedos. Muscles bulging, the grips hoisted the stretcher poles while the canvas bearing the Godfather sagged to the tearing point. Marlon climbed off the stretcher, weak with laughter.

Marlon and James Caan engaged in a "mooning" contest throughout the shooting. "My best 'moon,' " Caan boasted, "was on Second Avenue. I was in one car and Brando was in another. As my car drove up beside him, I pulled my pants down and stuck my ass out the window. Brando fell down in the car with laughter." Marlon, of course, could not accept second-place honors. According to one crew member, he competed with a "double-moon." In a scene where James Caan is filmed entering a room, he opens the door—to find Marlon bending over, his buttocks aimed at the doorway. Marlon then swung his bare behind into the camera lens. A concluding group "moon" was achieved during the wedding scene when Marlon, James Caan, Al Pacino, and Robert Duvall jointly dropped their pants and shorts before five hundred little old Italian ladies who had been hired as extras. Caan and Duvall presented Marlon with a silver belt buckle with the inscription: "Mighty Moon Champion."

Most of the dissension and postponements of the production arose from arguments between Paramount executives and Coppola, who was several times threatened with dismissal.

Marlon supported his director and declared he would also quit if Coppola were forced out. Coppola, in turn, defended not only Marlon but all the principals he had personally assembled. Except for his sister, Talia Shire, whose participation he regarded with tepid enthusiasm, he would suffer no criticism of the cast.

Marlon's failing memory hindered his otherwise strict adherence to the schedule. In addition to "idiot cards" held near the camera, he wrote notes on shirt cuffs, watermelons, on a desk blotter, and on bits of paper tacked onto props and other actors on the set. A bit actor, Lenny Montana, confronting Don Corleone in one scene, stuck out his tongue—on which was pasted a tape with the words, "Fuck you, Marlon." Marlon convulsed with laughter and in the retake retaliated with a note affixed to his own tongue. It read, "Fuck you too."

Marlon's portrayal of Don Vito Corleone as a corporate tyrant rather than as an Italian hoodlum lifted the characterization to a level transcending the basic story. "I don't think the film is about the Mafia at all," he said. "I think it's about the corporate mind. In a way the Mafia is the best example of capitalists we have. Don Corleone is just any ordinary American business magnate who is trying to do the best he can for the group he represents and for his family. I think the tactics the Don used aren't much different from those General Motors used against Ralph Nader. . . . Big business kills us all the time—with cars and cigarettes and pollution—and they do it knowingly. . . . The film shows that a man with a briefcase can steal more money than a man with a pistol."

Director Coppola joined his star: "It is not about the Mafia. The Mafia is nothing more than the ultimate capitalistic phenomenon . . . . What if the United States took care of its people the way Don Corleone took care of his own? To me, *The Godfather* is total fiction and metaphor." In the film neither the Mafia nor the Cosa Nostra are mentioned. Producer Ruddy had agreed to delete any such reference in response to the Italian-American Civil Rights League and in return for cooperation from wealthy Italians in the Staten Island location where much of the picture was filmed. It was not a deletion that impaired anyone's understanding of the story.

After Marlon viewed the final cut, he was pleased to announce, "I consider this one of the most powerful statements ever made about America." He then backed up his opinion by agreeing, for the first time since *Morituri*, to submit to interviews and public appearances to promote the film. (One interview took place in an exorbitantly expensive, elegant New York restaurant. Marlon, proving he had not lost his flair for the antic gesture, ordered a peanut-butter sandwich.)

Within nine months of its release, *The Godfather* had surpassed the record box-office gross of $81,500,000 established by *Gone With the Wind*. In little over a year it garnered more than $100 million. Marlon's contract gave him $100,000 plus 2½ percent of the first $10 million, 5 percent thereafter up to $25 million, and then 20 percent of the remaining gross. To date he has received about $20 million for his role.

Marlon's performance won plaudits from all but the most captious critics and clinched the Academy Award for Best Actor, reportedly without close competition. (*The Godfather* received ten nominations, winning three: Best Picture, Best Actor, and Best Screenplay based on material from another medium.) His handling of the Don's death scene was particularly noted. He slices an orange peel into a zigzag pattern and fits it over his gums, frightening his grandson with his mock ferociousness. It was a trick he had enjoyed with Devi and his other children in previous years.

Even the naysayers were frivolous. One elderly lady leaving the theatre after viewing *The Godfather* remarked, "I couldn't understand a word he said but I loved every syllable of it."

Brando, the public decided, had been prematurely embalmed. The corpse rose again to dance before a reinvigorated audience. The requiems faded as voices of the Hallelujah chorus overpowered the mourners. Once again, a celluloid Messiah ruled the screen.

The world premiere of *The Godfather* took place in New York on March 11, 1972. Marlon was required to attend the opening (a benefit for the Boys Club of New York) by his Paramount contract. He invited many of his New York friends—Edith Van Cleve, Stella Adler—to a post-theatre celebration. He did not appear. He was diverted to Los Angeles, engaged with me in the climactic battle over our son, Devi.

I had, at this time, been costarring with Marlon in the

California courts for fourteen years. The run had witnessed some of his most dramatic performances—and some of my best tantrums—and had left me exhausted. I was becoming increasingly depressed with the course of my life and found myself drinking more heavily than ever. The inevitable consequence of depression was rendered the more obvious by the parallels of two close friends, Pier Angeli and Gia Scala.

Anna Pierangeli's divorce from Vic Damone in 1957 was followed by seven years of bitter court battles over the custody of their son, Perry. Dissension over visitation rights, verbal abuse, and physical intimidations also embroidered her litigation. She testified that Vic Damone had broken into her Bel-Air home, kicked her, and snarled, "I'm going to kill you." Judges Lawrence Rittenband and Merwyn Aggeler heard her custody case, and—further coincidence—attorney Paul Magasin represented her. On the morning of September 10, 1971, she was found in her Beverly Hills apartment, dead of a barbiturate overdose.

Her spindly figure, wistful face, and delicate, winning smile haunted my thoughts, much as I feared dwelling on the similarities of our lives.

Gia Scala, an intimate friend since she replaced me in *Don't Go Near the Water*, had also experienced a ruptured marriage and had obtained a divorce in 1970. One year later she was confined to Camarillo State Hospital for psychiatric treatment. She had attempted suicide several times, most spectacularly in 1958 when a passing taxi driver prevented her from hurling herself off Waterloo Bridge into the Thames. I visited her at Camarillo Hospital where she was left unattended to wander the grounds in a mental fog. I persuaded the authorities that I could better minister to her needs. She was released in my custody and stayed with me for two months. Still in a depressed state, she then moved into a home in Universal City where, on April 30, 1972, she died from an overdose of drugs. She and I had been born within a few weeks of each other. Her death, at thirty-six, brought to me, with a shock, the realization of my mortality.

Early in 1972 I was distressed—in addition to my deepening depression—with Devi's environment and lack of progress in the Ojai Valley School to which he had been assigned by the court. I visited the premises and found them in a disorganized, dirty condition. My letters to the school inquiring about my son's condition went unanswered. I telephoned the school several times but those in authority were always in conference or unavailable. The first of February 1972 I received a letter from the headmaster (also addressed to Marlon) reporting that Devi was finding it quite difficult "to make attitudinal and academic adjustments to the resident situation." He had, so the headmaster wrote, set a fire in the dormitory and activated a fire alarm sensor, "actions which endangered the safety of all who live in the dormitory."

There was an obvious similarity between these acts and Marlon's pranks during his late teens at the Shattuck Military Academy in Minnesota. I remember Devi recounting some of the tales his father had told him of his school days: "Dad said the school was very useful. He used to take paper clips and break them off in the locks. They spent the time fixing them — instead of in classes. Dad said he never got caught but got kicked out anyway." Devi, it was evident, was being drawn under by his father's twisted wake. I resolved to extricate him from that vortex.

At the end of February, while Marlon was occupied in Paris shooting *Last Tango*, I drove to the Ojai Valley School to collect Devi for the weekend, promising to return him by Monday. However, he shortly developed bronchitis, and my physician, Dr. Gerald Mark, recommended that he forgo his schooling for several days. Dr. Mark also advised that Devi would recover more quickly in a warm, dry climate and suggested that a sojourn in Mexico could prove beneficial. Giselle Fermez, one of Marlon's former romances, was helping me to change residences that weekend. She offered her friend, Mr. James Barry Wooster, as one who might drive us to Mexico.

Mr. Wooster accompanied Devi and me to Marlon's house to pack Devi's clothes for the trip. Before we were prepared, Marlon's attorney, Mr. Norman Garey, arrived with several other men. They attempted to detain us, and an altercation ensued (subsequently I sued them for assault and battery; I dropped the suit when Mr. Garey apologized with a new Pinto automobile).

242

Mr. Garey's version of the events to this moment—the episode later became known as "the Devi kidnapping caper"—was stated in his Declaration: "On March 1, my office was informed that Christian Devi had left his school and was proceeding with his mother, Anna Kashfi. I was also informed that [Miss Kashfi] telephoned the school to say that Christian had bronchitis and had seen a doctor. The school telephoned Mr. Brando's home and spoke to his housekeeper, Reiko Sato, who said that Christian had [recently] visited the defendant's residence and had not complained of ill health.

"On March 2, I requested that Mr. James Briscoe, a private investigator, go to [Mr. Brando's] residence to ascertain whether [Miss Kashfi] and Christian were there. Mr. Briscoe was informed by Miss Sato that Christian appeared at [Mr. Brando's] home that day to obtain some clothes and that Christian was in the company of a young man with blond hair driving a blue pick-up truck with an out-of-state license plate. . . . Further, Miss Lynn Lawrence, who was living with [Miss Kashfi], called Miss Sato to inform her that [Miss Kashfi] was creating disturbances at their home. Lynn Lawrence put Christian in a cab and sent him to [Mr. Brando's] residence. At about 1:30 A.M. on March 4, the boy did arrive. [Miss Kashfi] went to [Mr. Brando's] home that morning and had a heated argument with the boy. Miss Sato called me. The boy was still at the residence when I arrived, and [Miss Kashfi] was outside in the car, at which time I asked Christian what he wanted to do. He answered that he wished to stay at [Mr. Brando's] house for a few days, that he didn't want to go back with his mother.

"He then went to the kitchen. I followed him and saw [Miss Kashfi] standing outside the back door. I opened it and asked what she wanted. [Miss Kashfi] began yelling at me. A few minutes later, I saw the glass shattered and [Miss Kashfi] coming through to pick up the boy.

"The police were called. They arrived as [Miss Kashfi] was pulling Christian away with her. Christian now indicated that he was willing to go with his mother to appease her and stop the commotion, and that he would return to his father's home later in the evening.

"Mr. Brando was called in Paris; . . . He said that he wanted to bring the boy to Paris [to be tutored there. Meanwhile], it was learned . . . that [Miss Kashfi] and Christian had not returned to their home, and that [Miss Kashfi] had made some remarks about taking Christian to Mexico. The boy, in the company of the blond-haired gentleman in the blue pick-up truck, went back to Mr. Brando's house to pick up some clothes and other belongings.

"Mr. Briscoe, the detective hired by me, approached the man in the truck and found out that he had been hired by [Miss Kashfi] to help [her] move her residence. Mr. Briscoe reported that the pick-up truck left with Christian in it [and with] no indication of its destination."

Mr. Garey's account neglected several details. In court, I testified that when I entered Marlon's home for Devi, he [Garey] began screaming "bitch" and "whore" at me and battered me about the kitchen. I produced photographs and a doctor's corroboration that I had sustained bruises and a deep gash on my hand during the beating.

The blue pickup truck drove off with Devi and me, Mr. Wooster, and a friend of his. We headed south into Baja California—to the fishing village of San Felipe. Devi seemed pleased and relaxed with the relief from parental and tutelary pressures. For the first time in many months he was moved to smile. (Although his features are mine, his smile is Marlon's; were my genes removed from his makeup, he would be no more substantial than the Cheshire cat.) I left him with Mr. Wooster and his friend and returned to Los Angeles after agreeing on a rendezvous several days later in Calexico, a small border town.

On March 9 Giselle Fermez and I traveled back to Calexico to meet Devi and the two men. They did not appear. I called my attorney, Mr. Barry Rose, who advised that we board the next bus for Los Angeles—which we did. Meanwhile, a Mexico City newspaper, *Excelsior*, had uncovered some of the details and printed a front-page story reporting that Christian Devi Brando had been kidnapped. Other papers followed that lead, and within hours the news had reached Paris.

Marlon struck like a cornered cobra. He phoned Norman Garey. He phoned the newspapers. And he phoned another private investigator, Mr. Jay J. Armes, with the assignment of locating Devi.

Giselle and I had carried a few cans of beer onto the bus at Calexico and, drinking, we must have become a bit unruly. The driver stopped the bus and summoned police who deposited us in the nearest jail. As the journalists described it,

"Anna Kashfi faces trial in Westmoreland Justice Court on charges of being drunk and disorderly and of disturbing the peace. She pleaded innocent and was freed on $750 bond after spending the night in the Imperial County Jail in California. She and a companion, Shirley Giselle Hauptman [Fermez], were taken off a Los Angeles-bound bus after the driver said they were acting belligerent and intimidating the other passengers."

I alerted my attorney, and he dispatched his secretary, Juana, to the Imperial County Jail. The three of us drove to San Diego (Juana had rented a car) to board a plane for Los Angeles. I was wearing blue jeans, a white T-shirt, sneakers, and no makeup. We huddled in a remote corner of the airport lounge and ordered dinner. After one drink, Giselle began regaling us with her tales of Marlon's sexual proclivities. We missed three flights to Los Angeles.

Meanwhile Mr. Armes, the super-sleuth with no hands (he had lost them in an accident at the age of twelve; hooks protrude from his coat sleeves) and one of the three American members of Interpol, had tracked Devi and Mr. Wooster to Baja California. Working with the Mexican Federal Police, he searched across the peninsula and, piloting a helicopter himself, spotted the blue pickup truck at a campsite outside San Felipe. He returned with four Mexican officers who approached the campsite with drawn guns. Devi, according to Mr. Armes, lay in a tent, barely breathing and suffering from a serious bronchitis condition. In the camp were eight "hippie-type" adults, including Mr. Wooster, five other bearded, long-haired men, one fifty-two-year-old woman, and a nude twenty-one-year-old girl in a sleeping bag who refused to give her name. The group claimed that "Miss Kashfi had promised them $10,000 each to hide Christian Devi."

By 7:00 P.M. on March 10 Marlon and Devi were reunited at

Los Angeles airport. I was unaware that Devi was safe until I phoned Marlon's house the next day.

Again, legal weaponry was unsheathed. I filed an assault and battery suit against Marlon, Norman Garey, and ten John Does, accusing Mr. Garey and the John Does of beating and injuring me while they were in Marlon's employ on March 5. I added punitive damages of $100,000 apiece and general damages of $100,000 apiece.

Marlon's countersuit brought us together before Judge Rittenband in Santa Monica Court on March 13. Mr. Armes and the other participants in "the great kidnapping case" testified. Marlon appeared, dressed in black suit, black shirt, and black tie. ("When Daddy's dressed like that," Devi remarked to me, "he must be in a bad mood.") Judge Rittenband arranged for Marlon to be escorted in and out the back door by marshals acting as bodyguards. I was tempted to ask if he thought a public courthouse were a private club. Windows in the courtroom doors were sealed with tinfoil. Photographers were barred.

Judge Rittenband awarded Marlon sole custody of Devi and, with my consent, allowed him to take our son back to Paris. April 21 was set for further proceedings. (Subsequently, I regretted acceding to the Paris trip when I learned that Marlon was involved in nude scenes in his production of *Last Tango*.) As Marlon left the courthouse, a photographer raised his camera. Marlon grabbed the man's arm and, pushing stomach to stomach, backed him into the street. This ludicrous ballet continued for fifty yards around the sidewalk and the courthouse green. Norman Garey finally pulled Marlon away and into his car. They drove off with Marlon hiding his head from other photographers. It was understandable that many reporters hinted the court appearance was a sham—a publicity stunt for *The Godfather*.

A continuance from the April 21 hearing sent the custody case into May. At that time Judge Rittenband interviewed Devi in his chambers and then confirmed Marlon's sole custody rights. I was left with nothing.

Devi remained in Paris with Marlon for six weeks, and subsequently vacationed with him in Tahiti, Sun Valley, and elsewhere. Unquestionably, father and son regained a measure of compatibility. I feared that compatibility would smother Devi even more with his father's characteristics. I feared his surrogate mother, Alice Marchak, would prove unable to provide a maternal counterbalance. For two years following Devi's return to his father's custody, I spoke with my son rarely and only on the telephone. Our conversations inevitably ended in mutual recriminations. "You sound pretty funny to me," he would say, typically. "Have you been drinking? Are you drunk?" "I'm your mother. How can you talk like this?" I would ask him, only to hear: "Alice told me the judge said you were an unfit mother." I learned that he deliberately provoked my wrath, taping my voice with a recorder to replay for his neighborhood cronies.

Pranks of this nature seem to be encouraged by Marlon, who has ever been a permissive parent. In one instance during this period of Marlon's exclusive custody, Devi filched a "Yield" sign from a crossroad near the Mulholland Drive residence. When the police arrived at the house to investigate, Marlon answered their inquiries by pleading ignorance and astonishment that his boy should be accused of vandalism. Devi listened behind the door, giggling and clutching the sign.

I believe Devi has seen every one of his father's pictures. He glorifies Marlon as the world's greatest actor and extols each film uncritically. Yet he has never applied for membership in the acting fraternity—to the contrary, he preaches Marlon's dogma that actors are phonies, spongers on society, or—at best—unfeeling businessmen. He has also adopted Marlon's aversion to personal publicity. I have seen him rudely turn away from anyone soliciting his knowledge of his father.

Although in accord on these matters, Devi and Marlon rarely remain consonant for long on a personal level. Much of their dissension is provoked through Marlon's propensity to act more juvenile than his own son. During a skiing trip to Sun Valley, where the two shared a hotel room, Marlon shoved Devi, fresh from a shower and clad only with a towel, onto a terrace and closed the sliding glass door behind him. The outside temperature was 15 degrees. Devi pounded on the door and screamed obscenities and demands to be let into the room. Marlon dropped his pants, pressed his buttocks to the glass, and yelled, "Here, climb into this!"

I was further vexed to learn that Marlon had acquired another pet raccoon (the first, Russell, had been disposed of twenty years earlier). I was fearful that it might bite Devi. In the event, the raccoon's last acknowledged scene was played out in a two-shot with its master. Marlon was at home sitting in bed, conversing on the telephone and holding the raccoon on his lap while scratching its ear. The raccoon evidently took offense at this familiarity and nipped Marlon on the arm. "Excuse me for a moment," Marlon said softly into the phone. He gently picked up the raccoon by its scruff, cocked his fist, and swung with a looping right to the snout, knocking the animal insensible. He then returned calmly to his telephone conversation. Devi was unable to revive the raccoon for some moments. When it did regain consciousness, it decamped the Brando homestead without further ceremony for the more friendly environs of the adjoining coyote-inhabited canyon.

When *Last Tango in Paris* was released, I filed yet another OSC (in April 1973) in a futile attempt to regain custody. My Petition asserted that Marlon performed the role of a "sexually maladjusted and perverted person, wherein he exhibits himself in various stages of nudity and simulated sex acts. Throughout the film he utters obscene, foul, shocking, and distasteful profanities. [His conduct] has further caused my child additional humiliation and embarrassment and held him up to ridicule by his contemporaries." In January 1974, I resigned myself to the knowledge that the Petition could not succeed. Through my attorney, Marvin Mitchelson, I announced, "I am very happy Marlon is taking the interest in Devi a father should. I am pleased that in spite of past misunderstandings, Marlon and I are working toward the same objective—Devi's [welfare]."

Mr. Mitchelson had garnered widespread publicity by representing Michelle Triola Marvin in her suit against Lee Marvin. The case, concerned with community property division for unmarried couples, established an oft-cited principle (the implied marital contract) known as "the Marvin decision." In my case Mr. Mitchelson further distinguished himself by his adroitness in serving Marlon with the necessary legal papers. Frustrated through the usual channels, he arranged for a helicopter pilot to hover above the Mulholland Drive house and then land on the lawn. Marlon emerged to inspect the intruder. He was handed the subpoena.

Marlon's motivation in accepting his role in *Last Tango* has always puzzled me. Even before *The Godfather*'s stupefying success, he was searching for an "offbeat" film project as the only "logical" sequel. He signed with David Merrick and director Sidney Lumet (who had worked with Marlon on *The Fugitive Kind*) for the film version of Robert Marasco's drama, *Child's Play*. Early in the rehearsal stages it became evident that the dominant role belonged to James Mason. Marlon reneged on his contract and left the production. (He was replaced by Robert Preston.) Producer Merrick explained, "What really happened with Marlon was that he picked the film and . . . then decided it was going to be a flop. He's a very smart fellow. So he started thinking of ways to get out of it. He wanted to change the location . . . and all sorts of wild things. When I said it was too late to make radical changes in a finished screenplay ready to shoot in ten days, he said, 'Well, then I'll just mumble my way through this.' I had visions of a thoroughly useless actor on a very low budget picture running the cost up about a million dollars. . . . We let Brando go just to save money, which is what he wanted anyway. The picture wouldn't have been any better with him."

Late in 1971 producer Alberto Grimaldi (who had sued Marlon over production expenses on *Burn!*) telephoned Marlon from Paris where he and director Bernardo Bertolucci were encountering casting difficulties for their film, *Last Tango in Paris*. Bertolucci had offered the lead roles to Dominique Sanda and Jean-Louis Trintignant, the costars of his previous picture, *The Conformist*. Mlle. Sanda accepted, but M. Trintignant expressed his embarrassment at the script's explicit sex scenes and rejected the offer.

Marlon flew to Paris where he was introduced to Bertolucci by Grimaldi. "For the first fifteen minutes he didn't say a word; he only looked at me," Bertolucci recalled their meeting. "Then he asked me to talk about *him*. I was very embarrassed but I got around it by talking about the character I had in mind for the film. He listened carefully and then said yes right away, without asking to read the script. . . . We had

249

communicated through the instincts. Since we had to speak in an alien tongue for both of us [French], we had to look at each other more intently. That gave us deeper understanding." Bertolucci followed Marlon back to Hollywood for two weeks of mutual psychotherapy—discussing their sexual experiences and philosophical outlook. Summarizing the sessions, Bertolucci said, "[Marlon] is an angel as a man and a monster as an actor. He is all instinct but at the same time he is a complex man; on one side he needs to be loved by all; on another he is a machine incessantly producing charm; on still another he has the wisdom of an Indian sage."

Shooting began in February 1972. Marlon had rented a Left Bank apartment the month before and participated in the preproduction work. His evenings were spent in the company of his friend, Christian Marquand, who, it developed, was coupled romantically to Dominique Sanda. In a *sexe à trois*—or *á quatre* or *á cinq*—Mlle. Sanda became pregnant with Christian Marquand's baby. She was replaced by Catherine Deneuve, who thereupon discovered that she too was pregnant. Finally, the female lead was conferred on Maria Schneider, a twenty-year-old redheaded actress of modest achievements whose willingness to perform her screen test in the nude impressed Bertolucci.

As with *The Godfather,* Marlon's behavior on the *Tango* set was exemplary (by his standards, at least). He again found it necessary to paste scraps with written dialogue on props around the set and on parts of Mlle. Schneider's anatomy. ("Is it all right if I write my lines on her ass?" Marlon suggested.) It was apparent that his short-term memory was not functioning properly, perhaps impaired by the residual effects of an earlier disease. The picture had become autobiographical to him, as he admitted to his friends and co-workers. Christian Marquand explained to an interviewer that "forty years of Brando's life experiences went into the film. It is Brando talking about himself, being himself. His relations with his mother, father, children, lovers, friends—all come out in his performances as Paul." Many lines spoken in the picture by the American expatriate Paul (Marlon) support this thesis. In one scene Paul reminisces with his girl friend,

Jeanne: "My father was a drunk, a screwed-up bar fighter. My mother was also a drunk. My memories as a kid are of her being arrested. I can't remember very many good things." Bertolucci conceded that Marlon was responsible for much of his own dialogue. "The only reality is before the camera," he said. "The movie is only born when the camera has a kind of sexual relation with the reality it sees.... I told Maria [Schneider] she is to be the interviewer and I told Marlon he must tell the truth. It is a documentary." Such lines as "Let's just say we're taking a flying fuck on a rolling doughnut" and "I went to Melbourne U. and studied whale-fucking" were immediately recognizable as typical of Marlon's speech. I half-expected him to swear on screen, "Up your cloaca."

In another scene Marlon stands at the bier of his dead wife and rages obscenities at her body. Then he breaks down and weeps. More than one reviewer suggested that "he drew on his feelings against Anna" to play the scene.

Marlon admitted to Bertolucci as the shooting ended, "Never again will I make a film like this one. For the first time a picture made me feel that I violated my innermost self. It should be the last time."

Because most of its footage was improvised, the picture required a lengthy editing period. Then producer Grimaldi was plagued by Italian censors. Obscenity charges were filed in a Bologna court against Grimaldi, Bertolucci, and Marlon. The indictment stated: "Obscene content offensive to public decency, characterized by an exasperating pansexualism for its own end; ... dominated by the idea of stirring unchecked appetites for sexual pleasure, permeated ... with crude, repulsive, ... unnatural representations of carnal union with ... exhibitions of masturbation, libidinous acts and lewd nudity—accompanied offscreen by sounds, sighs, and shrieks of climax pleasure." With such stupefying damnation, box-office success was assured.

Legal contentions continued for a year. Bertolucci appeared before the court. Marlon did not. The defense attorney spoke on Marlon's behalf: "Marlon Brando personifies the fall of man. It is he himself who falls into the bottomless pit. And this is the message: 'Every man risks the same end.' The beast which we find inside Marlon may be in us too, but we are cowards, and we try desperately to suffocate it." The three judges hearing the case granted an acquittal.

When it was released, the picture split its audiences into sharply divergent groups: those who hailed it as "the most brilliant work in cinematic history" and those who panned it as "a piece of pornographic filth" (I was inclined toward the latter group). Pauline Kael, previously a Brando detractor (she had called him a "self-parodying comedian"), printed the most incredible gush. "[The date of *Tango*'s opening]," she wrote in *The New Yorker*, "should become a landmark in movie history comparable to May 29, 1913—the night "Le Sacre du Printemps" was first performed—in music history. . . . This must be the most powerfully erotic movie ever made, and it may turn out to be the most liberating movie ever made. . . . Bertolucci and Brando have altered the face of an art form." A contrary view to Miss Kael's was expressed by Norman Mailer: "If this is 'the most powerfully erotic film ever made,' then sex is an Ex-Lax to the lady. . . . [*Tango*] is like a Western without horses." Also at the negative end of the spectrum, the Harvard University *Lampoon* named it "Worst Movie of the Year."

Bernardo Bertolucci could scarcely contain his admiration of Marlon: "My camera isn't worthy of his acting." Later, he declared, "I made *Last Tango* to prove I could make a film in English."

In retrospect, Marlon couldn't define his feelings about the picture: "I think it's all about Bernardo Bertolucci's psychoanalysis. . . . I'm being facetious . . . *he* didn't know what it was about either."

Most of Marlon's peers were disparaging. "If we actors make movies like this," said one major star, "it's the best solution to the writers' strike. There's no need for scenarists anymore. No need for the word. Just act out perversions and throw four-letter words at the camera."

For me, *Last Tango in Paris* is a dance to a broken rhythm. A tasteless mélange of pornographies dressed up as art, the picture's disjointed portrayal of sexual perversion as superior to our conventional rituals (tangoing) was, ultimately, merely embarrassing.

I was embarrassed for Bertolucci who tried, but failed, to present a coherent tale with consistent characterization. His attempts at "pornographic modernism" remains filth, as Robert Graves insisted it would. The "cop-out" ending was only the final lump in the story line. Perhaps he was intimidated by Marlon.

I was embarrassed for Maria Schneider. Had she consulted a vocational counselor earlier in life, she might have found a truer calling. Unencumbered by a shred of talent, Miss Schneider's was a disastrous nonperformance. Later cast as Drusilla in *Gore Vidal's Caligula,* she was dismissed after one rehearsal. She appeared at a psychiatric hospital in Rome and asked to be admitted. Subsequently, her mother had her committed to a psychiatric clinic in Paris after she was found wandering the streets.

Most of all, I was embarrassed for Marlon. As an actor, he was superb. But acting with Miss Schneider is like playing tennis against a wall. It doesn't make for much of a match. And it is about as dramatically exciting as masturbation—as *Last Tango* proved.

Perhaps the final word was spoken by Ingmar Bergman, who suggested that Marlon and Bertolucci had planned to make a movie about homosexuals. "Marlon Brando and Maria Schneider were both intended to be male," he said. "The meaning of the film becomes clear when the viewer understands this. Then it becomes very interesting. Except for her breasts, that girl Maria Schneider is just like a young boy. There is much hatred of women in this film. But if you see it as being about a man who loves a boy, you can understand it." A friend suggested to me once that "Ingmar Bergman would label as a phallic symbol anything longer than it is wide. If it isn't, he'll turn it 90° and make it into one."

"Why," I asked myself, "did Marlon accept this project? Why did he bare his buttocks—the ultimate moon—to the entire world? (At least in *The Godfather,* "mooning" was left in the out-takes.) Why did he lend himself to a vulgar, obscene, misguided spectacle? Was it a *fin de carrière* gesture, a sign of what T. S. Eliot called 'the still sad music of infirmity'? Or did he regard the role as launching a new mode in living, in acting, or in exposure?" I have explored the phrenology of Marlon's mind for many years. I still can't locate his driving force. I don't believe Marlon can either.

Shortly after the premiere of *Last Tango*, Marlon reclaimed the headlines with his rejection of the Oscar for his acting in *The Godfather*. To explain the reasons for his rejection, he sent to the Award ceremonies a young woman dressed in Western costume. She gave her name as Sacheen Littlefeather but was later identified as Maria Cruz, a would-be actress who had been proclaimed "Miss Vampire, 1970" for a motion-picture promotional campaign (she was introduced to Marlon by a neighbor, Francis Ford Coppola). "Marlon Brando regretfully cannot accept this award because of the treatment of American Indians in the motion-picture industry, on TV, in the movie reruns, and the recent happenings at Wounded Knee," she announced before being ushered from the stage.

Miss Littlefeather then handed to the press a 650-word statement from Marlon. It excoriated the United States for its dealings with the American Indians: "For two hundred years ... we have lied to them, cheated them out of their lands, starved them into signing fraudulent agreements that we call treaties that we never kept. We turned them into beggars. . . . We were not lawful. . . . It would seem that the respect for principle and the love of one's neighbors has become disfunctional in this country of ours. . . . I do not [therefore] feel that I can as a citizen of the United States accept [this] award."

He had gone to Wounded Knee, Marlon indicated, where his services were needed more than at the Academy Award ceremonies. In reality, he and Christian Marquand, who was visiting from Paris, drove to Trona, California, on the edge of Death Valley. They registered at a Trona motel under the names of Mr. Marquara and Mr. Christian.

He also essayed a retroactive rejection of his *On the Waterfront* Oscar: "I've done a lot of silly things in my day. [Accepting it] was one of them. At the time I was confused about it and I made an error in judgment."

The furor over Marlon's surrogate spurning of his Oscar bubbled behind him. Daniel Taradash, president of the Motion Picture Academy, felt that Marlon had demeaned himself: "[Brando] has no guts. If he had any class, he would have come down there and said it himself." MC Charlton Heston also reproved Marlon: "It was childish. The American Indian needs better friends than that." Other comments from leaders in the film industry and from the public were mostly critical. Sentiment centered on "insulting," "embarrassing," and "typical Brando crudity."

I know that Marlon acted from sincerity—but, as usual, without mature consideration of the consequences of his act. Again, he listened to the siren of self-deception that rings in his ears. Academy Awards are conferred by one's fellow actors, not by the public. To interpose an irrelevant issue, however worthy, without the courtesy of appearing himself before his peers, is inexcusable. The gesture itself was so theatrical it could not fulfill his intention, however idealistic. I fantasized that next year an Indian actor would win and then reject the Oscar on the basis that the country was being beastly to Marlon Brando.

My favorite remark was that tendered to him by his two longtime business associates, George Glass and Walter Seltzer. "Marlon," they said, "stop worrying about a hundred million starving Indians, and worry about two Jews who are your partners."

With *Last Tango in Paris,* Marlon ceased to be the ruler of his fantasy life. Now it ruled him. *"Das Mensch ist was er ist,"* wrote Goethe ("Man is what he is"). Ultimately, if indulged, an actor acts what he is. To avoid repetition, he can only retire, die, or reduce himself to caricature.

Marlon was not oblivious to the mental and professional moat that encircled him. "I've got to break out of this fucking chicken coop I'm in," he told me at the time.

In fleeting pursuit of his "breakout," and provoked by a feud with Frank Yablans (who was angered over Marlon's snubbing of the Oscar Awards), he declined an offer to star in *The Godfather* sequel. "The problem with Marlon," Francis Ford Coppola opined, "is that he just doesn't want to work. I know because this project really excited him. We met a couple times about the sequel, and he came up with some terrific ideas. Then he and Paramount had a big falling-out—over money, probably. He was no longer available to us." Instead, Marlon announced he was preparing—with Abby Mann—a film exposing the plight of the American Indians.

*Wounded Knee,* a story of the Amerindian siege of that historic site for seventy-one days in 1973, was initiated by Marlon as his "conclusive salute," his "retirement film." He enlisted Abby Mann, ex-neighbor and Academy Award winner (*Judgment at Nuremberg*), as screenwriter. Mann became enthusiastic over the subject and credited Marlon with "marvelous contributions—he can sit down and improvise a story better than I can probably write it." (Marlon credited Mann with "three really bad scripts" in attempts to write the story.) Principal photography was scheduled for October 1974. Director Martin Scorsese *(Mean Streets)* signed on and signed off—after disagreements with Mann, producer-elect John Foreman, and a clan of kibitzing Indians. Marlon then nominated Gillo Pontecorvo as director—despite their near-violence on the set of *Burn!* However, the first (and only) powwow between Pontecorvo and the Indians sparked a greater cultural clash than that between their respective countrymen in 1492. "I thought they were going to scalp me," said Pontecorvo. "They scared the shit out of him," Marlon confirmed. "Indians are very strange folks until you understand them." The "socially conscious" film project sputtered along for another two years in posse, then apparently faded away without a formal death certificate.

Robert Evans offered Marlon the role of Jay Gatsby but was confronted by outrageous salary demands. "[He] wanted the moon and the stars," Evans complained, "because he was angry about not having a bigger percentage of *The Godfather.* I told him we did not have that kind of a budget, and he said, 'Well, take a slice of *Godfather.'* " Subsequently, Marlon dismissed his agent, Robin French, telling him acting was no longer his profession.

In the summer of 1975 Marlon signed for an $8 million horse opera titled *The Missouri Breaks.* It seemed that experience left no trace on him. Rats scurrying through a maze have displayed superior learning processes. "What can you say about a cowboy film?" Marlon rationalized. "It's a picture everybody's doing for the money. . . . I just want to get back to

Tahiti and do some environmental experiments." Both Marlon and his costar, Jack Nicholson, received $1.5 million for a few weeks' posturing before the cameras. Nicholson also issued deprecatory comments: "The contract took longer to write than the script." Marlon played an effeminate psychotic assassin dressed in frontier drag. His surplus poundage in addition to the ponderous Irish brogue he laid onto the character proved too heavy for his horse to bear.

Director Arthur Penn (who had previously directed him in *The Chase*) tried but failed to accommodate Marlon's desire to inject a lo!-the-poor-Indian theme into the picture. He ultimately turned against his star's interference: "I personally don't like actors who write or rewrite scenes and I'm very respectful of [writer] McGuane's work."

Through filming of *The Missouri Breaks*, Marlon was quartered in a mobile home near the set (fifteen miles from Billings, Montana). Evenings, isolated from the cast and crew, he rode a Honda trail bike for hours over the nearby mountain paths. At age fifty-one, he had not yet abandoned the motorcycle with its suggestion of mental wanderlust.

Two years later, in a step that obliterated his goal of "breaking out," Marlon accepted the role of Superman's father, Jor-El, in producers Alexander and Ilya Salkind's $25 million comic-book film version of the comic-book fantasy. For this act of self-betrayal, for permitting his image to age a full generation, for mouthing some of the most dreadful expository lines since Flash Gordon's dialogues with Dr. Zarkhov, Marlon was paid $2.5 million for a twelve-day stint—the most expensive salary recorded to that time. His contribution is peripheral—Jor-El dies on Krypton when the planet explodes (albeit death does not deter him from reappearing on earth as a sort of crystalline Banquo's ghost to counsel his son Kal-El, the junior Clark Kent, who is consequently motivated to don blue leotards with red jockey shorts on the outside and rush about saving the world in general and Lois Lane in particular).

As for the celluloid Superman, he should be convicted of material violations of the laws of physics, and his dramatic license revoked for all time.

Marlon evidently regretted even his minimal participation.

He filed a $50 million lawsuit against the Salkinds, Warner Bros., the film's distributors, and a dozen other corporations.

Francis Ford Coppola's antiwar film, *Apocalypse Now,* was more consonant with Marlon's beliefs. A powerful, obscene polemic against American intervention in Vietnam, its script antagonized Defense Department officials who consequently refused government cooperation. Marlon's character, Colonel Walter Kurtz, a Green Beret officer, rebels against the slaughter and sets up an independent military base of operations where, supported by hordes of worshiping natives, he combats both the Americans and the Viet Cong. A C.I.A. agent, Captain Willard (Martin Sheen), is dispatched to "terminate" Colonel Kurtz "with extreme prejudice." The theme obviously carried great appeal to Marlon.

The picture contains some of the most graphic and strikingly effective scenes ever shot. Fifty pounds overweight, his head shaved for the role, Marlon appeared only at story's end. He seemed unable or unwilling to provide the crashing climax demanded by the gathering drama of the preceding scenes. His portrayal of Colonel Kurtz as a posturing looney deflected the film's dynamic thrust.

I could detect Marlon's influence at scattered points throughout the picture. In one vignette, for example, an American soldier breaks an arrow (shot at him by a Vietnamese native) and affixes the segments on either side of his head. It was Marlon's old trick while riding his motorcycle back and forth along Sunset Boulevard.

*Apocalypse Now* was filmed in the Philippines in 1976. Coppola belabored the editing process over the next three years until many in the industry referred to the picture as *Apocalypse When?* Marlon's $3.5 million contract specified three weeks' work in Pagsanjan, a sylvan region north of Manila. At the conclusion of his shooting schedule, Marlon hosted a party for cast and crew at the Lake Calairaya Country Club, a water-skiing resort for wealthy Filipinos. A tribe of Stone Age villagers had been recruited as extras, and Marlon invited the entire tribe to his party (replete with magicians, jugglers, and fireworks). Advised against the invitation—on the premise that the aborigines would desecrate the immaculate facilities of the country club—Marlon's great pleasure during the production was watching the barefoot, loinclothed natives enjoying his soiree among the gentry.

*Apocalypse Now* marked a settling of Marlon's view of his career. Years before he had shrugged that "if producers are so reckless as to give me the absurd fees I ask for, then all I can do is carry on the game and give them the rope to hang themselves." He had repeated so often the charge that film makers were flinthearted businessmen without compassion— like all other businessmen—that he finally circumnavigated himself and sailed into the ranks of the accused. Asked by Coppola to cooperate for a retake of a one-line closeup shot beyond the allocated schedule, Marlon demanded the $65,000 called for by his overtime clause. "One line, Marlon—one line, as a favor. We'll do something for you," Coppola pleaded with him. "I don't do $65,000 favors," said Marlon, "just as the president of General Motors doesn't do $65,000 favors. You pay the money, I'll do the line."

The shot was never filmed.

# Ten

It was said of Chagall that his paintings are his autobiography, his life. So it is with Marlon Brando: he is as much a creation as his pictures. More: his work—like his life—ranges from infrared to ultraviolet. He is all the characters of his films: the boor, the rebel, the motorcycle-mad delinquent, the tyrant, the expatriate, the lover of men and women, and, ultimately, the Godfather. In unison, these characters assure him that he may still lay claim to the Superman legacy—and no traveler has arrived from another planet to tell him otherwise. To strap on a mask with the fervor that Marlon is capable of can trigger a Pirandellian effect; it becomes easy to confuse oneself with the role one is playing. To separate fact from fiction is to deny that life often follows art—and a merger of Marlon's offscreen portrayals of his on-screen characters, his contradictions, and his inconsistencies is more interesting than any idealization he affects.

He continues to decry the acting profession. "[Actors] are like household pets," he said in a recent *Oui* interview. "People think of us much like they think of a favorite cat or dog. When you have a pet you talk about it as if it were something special. You become emotionally involved with the animal and you endow it with qualities and characteristics it might not have. It is the same with an actor. You have one or two emotional experiences with him and you begin to trust him — he becomes your favorite fantasy-maker."

"So, you are like the beloved household pet?" the interviewer asked.

"Well," said Marlon, "not always beloved."

He continues — in acting — to reverse his field, eluding (or straight-arming) would-be tacklers. After years of scorning TV offers, he solicited a cameo role in "Roots: The Next Generation." Playing Nazi leader George Lincoln Rockwell constituted another reversal — against portraying unrelieved villains (his performance was an exemplar of overblown Method acting).

He also continues to issue sporadic announcements of his imminent retirement from acting in favor of (1) writing; (2) promoting civil rights; (3) international diplomacy; (4) environmental studies; (5) none of the above.

He continues his guilt complex over his success, protesting the nuisance of his fame while devouring its fruits. "Navel-picking" is his stock term for interviews with famous people. To *Life* reporter Shana Alexander he bawled, "Because of this nutty thing they call the American success story, I'm willing to be a product. I have my peaked cap on and my pushcart and I'm out hawking my tomatoes ... aauuggh.... It's navel-picking and it's odious."

The motion-picture industry still receives an annual brickbat from Marlon's hand. Typical was a letter addressed to the Conference on Western Movies at Sun Valley, Idaho (1976): "Hollywood ... has served to perpetuate the most gross and revolting stereotypes of non-whites.... We after all share with minorities a sense of intellectual deprivation of the historical facts. We have been spoon fed through literature, the myth of motion pictures and now, through television, with the preposterous perspectives of ourselves culminating in this schizoid, bifurcated bicentennial."

In his social causes Marlon pursues his gadfly approach to civil liberties and political freedom. He is simply not convincing as a social crusader; there is the smell of greasepaint around him. He attends benefits (most notable: the $125-a-plate dinner with Ethel Kennedy at the Waldorf-Astoria), grants television interviews (Mike Douglas, Dick Cavett, Edwin Newman), has deeded property (after some contention over liens and rightful ownership), and even tried to donate the family farm in Illinois ("Over my dead body," said sister Fran Loving), all on behalf of the Amerindians and other minorities. But the effect is muted since Marlon himself is the drawing card (attendant Indians are usually ignored). "The Indians have no access to the media so they have to speak through my mouth," said Marlon. "Many bad spirits here," muttered one observant brave.

At Marlon's invitation, tepees have been set up on the lawn of his home on Mulholland Drive. When the Indians encamped there ran afoul of the law and were booked on marijuana and drinking charges, it was Marlon who bailed them out. In 1975 he joined a group of Menominee Indians occupying—and demanding the deed to—a monk's abbey in Gresham, Wisconsin. Shots were fired before the confrontation was resolved—by treachery, according to Marlon, on the part of "those goddamn Alexian Brothers," the priests who owned and ultimately retained the property ("they took it back after everything died down, after giving their word the Indians could have it"). When the Indian activist Dennis Banks fled sentencing in South Dakota (on riot and assault convictions), it was in a vehicle owned by Marlon; the car was shot up by the highway patrol. Marlon sheltered Banks in Tahiti, praising him as an inspiration for young Indians. A lesser man might have been charged with aiding and abetting a fugitive.

Marlon has corralled celebrities to support his causes and expends efforts to persuade others to his view (without notable success—as one example, he failed to enlist Elizabeth Taylor despite an evening of declaiming on the "white man's responsibility to the red man"). His accusations of genocide against the Indians ("murders, massacres, enforced starvation unprecedented in history.... This country was built on the blood and bones of the Indian race"), his deprecation of

263

American motives ("The Hitler side in Vietnam"), and his general distortions of history have repelled many who might otherwise rally to his side.

Marlon's messianic urge to reform the world has failed to move mountains or even to shake molehills. He remains challenged by the world, and his skin is sensitive to the winds of change that gust across its face. I believe he suffers from a Christlike atonement for becoming a famous movie star and possibly from a deeper Christ complex that compels him – at times – to take unto himself the sins of mankind. I doubt that he is capable of exerting a significant influence on the existing social structure – for he lacks completely the thinker's ability to build up consecutively, to construct, to synthesize more exacting standards than those of popular esteem. Yet he will persist in his "unreasonable," spurious, and frivolous striving to provoke change. A German proverb purports to explain this aspect of human nature: "It is always a cripple who wants to lead the dance."

Those who work with or are close to Marlon occasionally resort to a private piece of doggerel to lament their feelings of his do-gooding nature:

Brando bleeds for the masses,
But the people he works with get kicked in their asses.

Part of Marlon's Tetiaroa island complex was intended to hold an environmental studies program (to tap solar energy, wind energy, and the nutrients in seawater) as well as to provide for an "artistic-intellectual" colony of researchers and resident engineers. An eighteenth-century "working village" of Tahitians was planned—a South Seas Walden Pond—insulated and isolated from the remainder of the planet. But even as the concept evolved, Marlon could foresee disillusionment with his brave new world. "This is a snowflake civilization," he told a visitor to Tahiti. "As soon as it hits the ground it will melt. . . . The Tahitians are being sold on an acquisitive society. They buy refrigerators and TV sets, not because they need them, but because such things give them status. . . . Within a few years Tahiti will be covered with gas stations and smog."

It seems that the island's bluebird of happiness may turn out to be a raven in disguise.

Marlon passes several months each year in his frangipani-scented universe (dubbed "Brando's Hideaway"). His home is a thatch-roofed hut at the edge of a white-sand beach. "I love to walk the beach naked at night," he confessed to a reporter, "with just the wind caressing my body. It's an awesome sense of freedom and very sensual. Sometimes I sleep all night on the beach."

His solitary stance is diluted somewhat by the presence of two young ladies—Eddy, a Polynesian, and Eriko, a Japanese—who tend to the needs of the island's lord and savior. Marlon does not live on breadfruit alone.

A recent advertisement in the English language Polynesian bulletin of Tahiti read, "Visit Marlon Brando's island. For information, call—." Several people dialed the number. No one answered—another of Marlon's peculiar practical jokes.

Most of Marlon's ambitions for his island paradise have foundered in impotence. Perhaps ashamed of the lack of achievement, Marlon reacts defensively. When a reporter waded ashore on the private atoll to investigate the project's progress and, if possible, to obtain an interview, he was greeted with Marlon's fury: "I'm going to give you to the count of three to get out, and then I'm going to punch you right in the face."

Others who trespass on his cherished privacy also receive his wrath. At the gateway to Marlon's Beverly Hills home, the sign warning "Beware of Raccoon" now bears a more threatening message: "Trespassers Will Be Destroyed." Nonetheless, the occasional tourist will blunder onto Marlon's driveway. Two elderly women once mistakenly drove into the courtyard. Marlon first hid behind a bush and then emerged to shout obscenities at them. Recently, he has hired armed guards to patrol his house around the clock. "Mulholland Drive is full of crazy people," he declared to a *Playboy* interviewer. "We have nuts coming up and down all the time. . . . I didn't want somebody coming in my house and committing mayhem. . . . My next-door neighbor was murdered, strangled in the bathroom. . . . Three or four times I've pulled a gun on somebody."

His passion for privacy persists—"I'm not going to lay myself at the feet of the American public and invite them into my soul; my soul is a private place"—and can extend beyond the boundaries of his home. He broke the jaw of photographer Ron Galella (famed for his pursuit of Jacqueline Kennedy) when Mr. Galella attempted to photograph him while he and Dick Cavett were walking along a New York street (after a listless interview on the latter's TV talk show). Marlon asserted, "The guy *wanted* to get hit. He was looking for some kind of incident like that." Marlon's hand was cut and infected from the blow. Mr. Galella required nine stitches and a brace; he sued for $250,000 but settled, according to Marlon, for $40,000.

A successful rebel should not only be articulate about what he is against but about what he is for. Marlon tilts too far to the negative. Typical was his rejection of the 1973 Golden Globe, an award as "World Film Favorite (Male)," conferred by foreign writers covering Hollywood for their newspapers. "There is a singular lack of honor in this country today," Marlon cabled the sponsors, "what with the government's change of its citizens into objects of use. Its imperialism and warlike intrusion into foreign countries and the killings of not only their inhabitants but also indirectly our own people. Its treatment of the Indians and the blacks and the assault on the press and the rape of the ideals which were the foundations of this country. I respectfully ask you to understand that to accept an honor however well intended is to subtract from the meager amount left." Undeterred, the writers again voted Marlon the Golden Globe in 1974. Equally unenlightened by experience, the NAACP conferred on him their 1975 Humanitarian Award. It was spurned—"I don't think there is a white man who can know what the black experience is." Fortunately for Marlon, it seems he will be judged more by his pictures and by his personal idiosyncrasies.

In his sexual relations no "breakout" is possible since Marlon's spectrum of sexual practices probably exceeds that known to Kinsey. He continues to emphasize variety. In November 1973, an Italian starlet, Krista Niel, named Marlon as the father of her baby. "I'm proud to be having Marlon's baby," she said, "and I want absolutely nothing from him."

Only Tarita, of all his mistresses, remains available whenever Marlon returns to her. In the Tahitian culture, two persons are considered "married" when they set up housekeeping together. Tarita has expressed no need for a formal ceremony. Nor has Marlon, for reasons of a different character. Tarita produced a second child, a daughter, Tarita Cheyenne, in 1970. She is apparently content to remain in Tahiti, although Marlon imports her to California for an occasional visit. (He escorted her to the Hollywood premiere of *Mutiny on the Bounty* in November 1963; dressed in a bare midriff sarong-type evening gown, a frangipani in her hair, she looked like a small girl masquerading in her mother's clothes.) Asked her views on her famous consort, Tarita's response revealed the toll that Marlon exacts for a relationship: "Marlon is Marlon. He does what he wants. My opinion of his work doesn't count. . . . I just see Marlon when he comes to visit me and the children. That's enough." With this permissiveness, Marlon and Tarita have avoided the perpetual conflict that plagued his relations with me and the lesser conflicts with Movita and others.

The question of Marlon's homosexuality—or bisexuality—is of concern to me only to the extent that trait might exert an influence on our son in his emulation of his father. Marlon has portrayed homosexuals in his films, most notably in *Reflections in a Golden Eye*. In her review of that picture, Shana Alexander commented, "Either he [Marlon] is a great actor or he really is a homosexual." Other reviewers have pointed out the homosexual overtones in *The Missouri Breaks*. (In his "rebuttal," Marlon declared, "If there is someone who is convinced that Jack Nicholson and I are lovers in this film, may they continue to do so. I find it amusing.") Marlon's portrayals, of course, are not admissible evidence to the judgment of his actual life. But parallels have been strong, particularly with respect to the Stanley Kowalski characterization. Jean Renoir insisted that "all actors should be homosexual." Marlon has several times intimated to me that his relations with friends such as Christian Marquand were of a peculiarly close nature; however, I was never certain of the adverse interpretation of his remarks.

With Wally Cox, Marlon's emotional investment was deep,

multifarious, and enduring. Rumors of a homosexual liaison were pumped around the Hollywood cocktail circuit, and more than once reporters vowed to divulge detailed accounts of the relationship. Whether withheld by respect for Marlon and Wally Cox or suppressed by threats of lawsuits, the story never reached the printed page. When Cox lay ill, Marlon brought his current ladylove to his friend's bedside and snuggled with her unabashedly. Wally Cox died February 10, 1973. Marlon flew from Tahiti to Los Angeles for the wake. He was granted possession of his friend's ashes and reportedly scattered them over a mountain stream in northern California.

In mid-1976, Marlon—for the first time, to my knowledge—discussed his homosexuality in public. To the reporter from a French film magazine, he confessed, "Like a large number of men, I too have had homosexual experiences and I am not ashamed. I'd never paid much attention to what people think about me. Deep down I feel a bit ambiguous and I'm not saying that to spite the seven out of ten women who consider me—perhaps wrongly—a sex symbol. According to me, sex is something that lacks precision. Let's say that sex is sexless. . . . Homosexuality is so much in fashion, it no longer makes news."

Of course, even Marlon's "confessions" must be viewed through a skeptical lens. "I might have said anything," he remarked after one interview. "I can't remember where I left my car yesterday." But then again, who can believe *that?*

Mistresses, male lovers, illegitimate children, lawsuits, paternity suits, child custody battles, psychoanalysis, social reform—all these elements have contributed to Marlon's character. Yet he remains more than their sum. The reality behind the Brando myth is, by definition, inaccessible. He is like a conjuror who makes objects disappear and reappear. Since he can do nothing more with them, the significance of his trick eventually loses its interest.

He remains a tortured man, searching for an elusive, if nonexistent, grail. Anthony Quinn expressed this quality of Marlon's to me with an actor's insight: "I often liken [Marlon] to the oyster who has to carry around the irritation of the grain of sand in order to create a pearl. Though I envy [him] his talent, I do not envy the pain he must carry around with him constantly." I have heard other actors express similar sentiments. They excuse or overlook Marlon's erratic behavior as inconsequential in view of his acting genius.

Mr. Quinn remembered fondly his association with Marlon on *Viva Zapata!* (even his "pissing for distance" contest from the bank of the Rio Grande). "When I last saw [Marlon]," he wrote to me recently, "he spoke to me of how he loved to look into the pools of water in Tahiti. God only knows what he was looking for but I do hope he finds it. He has given the world so much wonder I hope he finds some of that wonder to keep for himself."

Other admirers and detractors as well have elevated Marlon into a polemical figure—not because of his acting prowess so much as because of his offscreen eccentricities. They too are misdirected. Nothing should detract from Marlon's effectiveness on the screen. He has carved a special and unique niche for himself in the cinema. He is yet the most respected actor in America. But because he is tied up in his own Gordian knots of mannerisms, because he has become encrusted with the debris of past idiosyncrasies, neither he nor others can always distinguish the patina from the corpus. With sleight of hand Marlon has persuaded the world—and himself—that he is not constrained by the ordinary considerations that constrain others. Thus he is often judged apart from others—and his solid accomplishments overlooked.

He retains his interest in people—at a distance. "Human behavior has always fascinated me," he said in a *Life* interview. "Actors have to observe and I enjoy that part of it. They have to know how much spit you've got in your mouth and where the weight of your elbows is. I could sit all day in the Optimo Cigar Store telephone booth on 42nd Street and just watch the people pass by." It is evident that he will continue to act out his fantasies in and out of films. As long as his fantasies appeal to others, he will stay the course.

If the "Life of Marlon Brando" were made into a motion picture—possibly an old-fashioned musical—it would not be impaired by the inclusion of a Greek chorus. At appropriate moments the chorus would be heard chanting Marlon's secret thoughts: "Love me, love me, I hate you all."

Truman Capote has accused Marlon of being dumb. "You

can't get any dumber than Marlon Brando," he has declared. "He has sensibility but no sense." (A close friend said, "He's like a string of beads held upside down—you can only count one at a time. Marlon can only grasp one subject. If you want to confuse him, talk about two things at once.") I can agree with Mr. Capote, although I think the axis of his judgment does not intersect Marlon's special genius. We all march to the sound of a different drummer, but Marlon's drummer has an ultrasonic rhythm not within our hearing range.

Our personal relationship is now in its terminal stages, worsened, oddly, by my second marriage. Early in 1974 I was married to James Hannaford, a Los Angeles businessman. Marlon telephoned on wedding's eve to extend his congratulations to us both. The following day he told a friend, "Damn! Now I'll never get her committed." My legal tie to another man seemed to drain the relationship of its feral energy, of its power to subvert the routine of existence. Those qualities were replaced by an unrelieved tone of viciousness.

While my life has ever been too untidy to be diced into neat, twelve-month matrices, when I take the measure of it I can clearly identify the moment the Brando era began to fade. That moment came when I nearly died—from a drug overdose compounded by an infelicitous medical prescription. I had been ill—not seriously, but in passing the illness left a burden of depression. It was Valentine's Day. Marlon had telephoned: "Now I've got you down where you deserve to be. All I have to do is kick dirt into your grave." I had sworn at him in return, but the exchange still rankled.

To relieve the feeling of torment, I took a few pills, neither more nor less than on other occasions when pressures from Marlon became overwhelming. In this instance I became dizzy; the walls began spinning in my head like a crazy carrousel out of control.

My husband (I had been married the previous month to James Hannaford, a Los Angeles businessman) telephoned my personal physician. "Give her enough salt solution to make her vomit," he was instructed. The doctor was drunk, almost incoherent with alcohol.

The salt doses provoked extreme diarrhea, not vomiting. I collapsed, unconscious.

A Rescue Squad ambulance rushed me to the hospital where a medical attendant consoled my husband: "I'm sorry to have to tell you this but she arrived here too late. Body dehydration has occurred beyond the point of recovery. Your wife has one hour—two at the most—to live."

A priest was summoned to administer last rites—I was first baptized since my Catholicism had been heavily laced with Buddhist philosophy. "It was like a scene from a Mabel Normand silent movie," my husband recalled the scene. "I was kneeling at Anna's bedside. She was gasping in short, rasping strokes. The priest was dully intoning Latin phrases: 'Domini patri . . .' Nurses, doctors, and orderlies were in attendance nearby. Tears were falling from every face. Streaks of mascara on the nurses' faces turned the scene into a Japanese No drama."

I lay in a coma for four days. Another three days of semiconsciousness were passed in the Intensive Care Unit, followed by a week in the isolation ward (required by California law, for psychiatric examination) and a further month of confinement for testing and observation.

My first recollection was of imagining myself in a luxurious hotel room. "How odd," I thought, "for the hotel to supply a heart-lung machine and an EEG recorder in every room." A speaker in the oscilloscope connected to the heart monitor announced in Marlon's voice, "Screep, there goes your left ventrical; squeep, there goes your right auricle; scroop, there goes your aorta . . . heh, heh, heh, heh, now I've got you. I've got your heart, your lungs, your liver." I heard a knock at the door. "I'm a reporter for the *Times*," the voice said (it sounded suspiciously like Marlon's in disguise). "Let me in. I want an interview on your condition." I rose from my bed and moved the furniture and medical apparatus against the door. Then I heard the reporter trying to climb down the chimney. I lit the fireplace and drove him back up the flue. Finally, he tried to gain entrance through the television set, which was showing "A Streetcar Named Sayonara." I switched off the set. And I survived.

Marlon was informed of my condition shortly after I was carried into the hospital. "To hell with her," he said, and hung up.

One redeeming element in the near-fatal experience was Dr. Lawrence Sensman, head of the hospital's department of psychiatry. I was singularly fortunate in acquiring his services—not only did he direct my recovery, he was instrumental in tracing the roots of my medical history and in excising their cancerous effect on my mind. His tests disclosed that I was not and had never been subject to epilepsy, as had been diagnosed and attested to in court. He substantiated the fact that such drugs as Librium, Tylenol, phenobarbital, and the like had been prescribed for me needlessly and perhaps incompetently. With this knowledge I was readily weaned from further reliance on any nostrum, whether narcotic or alcoholic.

Since leaving the hospital I have not seen Marlon nor, for many months, did I see our son. Such was Marlon's influence that Devi too displayed a callous indifference to my illness—during my recuperative period he had telephoned my hospital room to ask, "What are you doing there with all the other nuts?" At the age of eighteen he lived the better part of a year in Tahiti, employed as a "pearl diver" in a restaurant owned by his father. ("Pearl diver? That sounds exciting," I said. "For chrissake, Mom," he puffed at me in exasperation, "it means dishwasher.") Marlon conceded to him neither money nor special attention; to return to the U.S. he was made to earn his passage. He has consequently acquired a wide vein of independence and by his twentieth birthday gained the maturity to break from the stride of his father's muddy footsteps. After months in Alaska (working on fishing boats) he removed to a farm in Oregon, apart from the two parents who had all too often held his scalp as the trophy in their internecine warfare. As does his father, he demands affection at times and places of his own choosing—and only then and there. Despite the physical distance between us, we have grown closer in spirit. He is all that remains to me of a receding marriage.

The dimension of lunacy that formed one axis of that marriage has also receded. The years of turmoil have given way to a time of relative tranquillity. The excitement, the extravagance, and the flavor of celebrity are missing, but so are the loneliness, the insecurity, and the madness. It was a fine madness, and those who suffer from it, like Don Quixote, enjoy lucid intervals (which begin and end without warning). Like Don Quixote, Marlon too can claim a vision—in both cases an Arthurian vision. It is fascinating to observe; it is impossible to live with.

Today, my ex-husband and ex-Superman is succumbing to the inevitable onslaughts of middle age. At the milestone of fifty years, an introspective man will come to terms with himself, assess achievements and ambitions. distinguish practicalities and dreams. I think that in his mind Marlon will never reach fifty, will remain perpetually nine years old. He still publicly counts the hairs on his chest. He still postures as a Graustarkian figure, a God Priapus. But that is not the Marlon Brando I would wish to remember. The Brando who matters is not the dilettante of social justice nor the jaded but still sophomoric recluse from Tahiti. The Brando who matters is the transcendent star of *Waterfront*, the rebel of *The Wild One*, the compassionate man who suffers himself in the face of true suffering.

I hope it is that Brando who survives all the others and finds his destination before the last stop of the Streetcar.